Bong Joon Ho

PHILOSOPHICAL FILMMAKERS

Series editor: Costica Bradatan is a Professor of Humanities at Texas Tech University, USA, and an Honorary Research Professor of Philosophy at the University of Queensland, Australia. He is the author of *Dying for Ideas: The Dangerous Lives of the Philosophers* (Bloomsbury, 2015), among other books.

Films can ask big questions about human existence: what it means to be alive, to be afraid, to be moral, to be loved. The *Philosophical Filmmakers* series examines the work of influential directors, through the writing of thinkers wanting to grapple with the rocky territory where film and philosophy touch borders.

Each book involves a philosopher engaging with an individual filmmaker's work, revealing how it has inspired the author's own philosophical perspectives and how critical engagement with those films can expand our intellectual horizons.

Other titles in the series:
Eric Rohmer, Vittorio Hösle
Werner Herzog, Richard Eldridge
Terrence Malick, Robert Sinnerbrink
Kenneth Lonergan, Todd May
Shyam Benegal, Samir Chopra
Douglas Sirk, Robert B. Pippin
Lucasfilm, Cyrus R. K. Patell
Christopher Nolan, Robbie B. H. Goh
Alfred Hitchcock, Mark William Roche
Luchino Visconti, Joan Ramon Resina
Theo Angelopoulos, Vrasidas Karalis
Alejandro Jodorowsky, William Egginton
István Szabó, Susan Rubin Suleiman
Jane Campion, Bernadette Wegenstein
David Lean, Lydia Goehr
Chantal Akerman, Andreja Novakovic

Bong Joon Ho

Philosopher and Filmmaker

Anthony Curtis Adler

BLOOMSBURY ACADEMIC
LONDON · NEW YORK · OXFORD · NEW DELHI · SYDNEY

BLOOMSBURY ACADEMIC
Bloomsbury Publishing Plc, 50 Bedford Square, London, WC1B 3DP, UK
Bloomsbury Publishing Inc, 1385 Broadway, New York, NY 10018, USA
Bloomsbury Publishing Ireland, 29 Earlsfort Terrace, Dublin 2, D02 AY28, Ireland

BLOOMSBURY, BLOOMSBURY ACADEMIC and the Diana logo are trademarks
of Bloomsbury Publishing Plc

First published in Great Britain 2025

A catalogue record for this book is available from the British Library.

ISBN: HB: 978-1-3504-1465-5
PB: 978-1-3504-1466-2
ePDF: 978-1-3504-1467-9
ePub: 978-1-3504-1468-6

Series: Philosophical Filmmakers

Typeset by Deanta Global Publishing Services, Chennai, India
Printed and bound in Great Britain

For product safety related questions contact productsafety@bloomsbury.com.

To find out more about our authors and books visit www.bloomsbury.com and
sign up for our newsletters.

In memory of my mother, Judith Curtis Adler (1939–2024)

Contents

Figures

Acknowledgments

This book would have remained unconceived and unwritten were it not for Costică Brădățan, who encouraged me to venture a proposal for the *Philosophical Filmmakers* series and has supported this project throughout. Many thanks are also due to Liza Thompson, Katrina Calsado, Miraya McCoy, and the editorial team at Bloomsbury Publishing for shepherding this book to publication, as well as to my family and friends and my colleagues at Yonsei University. I was able, through the support of the Shinhan Short-term Faculty Exchange Program, to present two chapters from this book before the Department of Film and Media Studies at the University of California Irvine, and am grateful for the feedback that I received during my lectures. My wife, Hwa Young Seo, who introduced me to Korean film, is not only my deepest source of insight into Korea but also my rock, her spirit carved beautifully by life's floods.

Early work on this book was completed during research leave in the academic year 2021, supported by Yonsei University.

Note on Romanization

I follow the McCune-Reischauer system for Romanizing Korean, except with words or names commonly appearing in English with a different spelling—familiar toponyms, the names of authors, actors, directors, and film characters—where I defer to the prevailing usage reflected in such resources as KMDb (Korean Movie Database) and the IMDb (Internet Movie Database). When mentioning Chinese philosophical terms for the first time, I typically include both the common English name and the Romanized Korean pronunciation, separated by a slash, as well as the *hanja* character, usually in parentheses. An exception is made when the Korean equivalent is introduced separately.

Non-Anglicized Korean, Chinese, and Japanese names, unless cited bibliographically, are written family name first. Unless otherwise clear from context, "America" means the United States of America. When referring to the period following the division between North and South, "Korea" refers exclusively to South Korea, the Republic of Korea. However, what "Korean" means, and refers to, is harder to say.

Introduction

Cinema and Philosophy, East and West

The Yips

A small dog yips—piercing, staccato—as words against the black screen promise that no animals were harmed. Twenty seconds pass, the black turns green: dense, sun-bleached foliage swaying in a gentle wind. One last tinny bark, then the voice of a man: "Ah, what a nice day! I'd like to go hiking and take a nap on the mountain." The camera pans down to a human head, overcast into a dark blob, with a clumsy wireless telephone. The focus narrows in on him, leaves blurring out, as another voice rebukes him: "Wake up, man!"

"I don't think I'm cut out to be a professor," the head continues.

"Shut up!"

"Maybe it's God's will."

"God my ass! It's the dean's will."

The camera shifts to his right, revealing a blotch obstructing the view outside—his breath marked the window—and, drawing back further, shows him standing at the edge of the large balcony window typical of Korean apartments. The rest of his apartment, now in view, remains darkened, overcast by light. "You can hear it, too?" "Sure." The yipping resumes.

Sound and Vision

Watching the beginning of Bong Joon Ho's *Barking Dogs Never Bite*, an eerie familiarity, a sort of déjà vu, overcomes me. Like most units in the grey-on-grey complexes dotting Seoul's skyline, lapping the mountains' edges, my apartment also has a closed balcony with a sliding metal-framed window. Mine too overlooks the forest, darkening cave-like against the light. But as uncanny as this scene was for *me*, as familiar as it might be for a typical middle-class Korean, it's also rather bland. It's no surprise that Bong's feature-length directorial and screenwriting debut flopped at the box office while garnering mixed reviews; he'd later call it a "very stupid black comedy movie."[1] Yet, hinging on the relation between *sound* and *image*—the yip is not yet localized, tied to *this* specific dog, coming from everywhere and nowhere, from the "out-of-field"—this scene already shows Bong's remarkable ability to translate probing insights regarding cinema's formal properties into a visceral and immediate cinematic language.[2]

The synchronization of sound and image is an unremarkable quality of everyday sense perception. We hear a tweet, a woof, a yip in our vicinity—we *see* a mouth and body moving. We perceive—through a precognitive judgment—*this* dog as source of *this* sound. The yipping-sight and yipping-sound constitute one single unitary phenomenon. Breaking this synchronicity—no mere illusion of the mind but the very way the world appears to us—requires a special act of reflection. For as Martin Heidegger reminds us, we don't hear sound sensations or even sounds. We hear the door shut in the house, the dog bark, the car engine rev.[3]

While mechanical sound reproduction already existed when Auguste and Louis Lumière debuted their *Cinématographe*, synchronizing sound and image posed technical challenges taking several decades to overcome.[4] The phenomenological naturalness of audiovisual synchronization suggests the importance of this capacity to dissociate the visual and auditory. Silent film indeed separates three orders of experience—vision, sound, and the rational meaning of words. No mere aesthetic limitation, this separation constitutes the positive horizon of cinema as art form. While the full realization of its power of illusion demands fusing sound and vision, this unification demands prior division. The true power of cinema lies in this originary separation. Hence the resistance that the "talkie" encountered.[5] The pantomimic silent film presented a world that was already fully accomplished, abundantly real. Indeed, as Bela Balazs would argue, it possessed a utopian potential, bringing forth an "international human type," a universal humanity.[6] When speech was "added" to cinema, it did not fill out a conspicuous lack but developed a new dimension of signification.[7] As Christian Metz puts it: "Speech is always something of a spokesman. It is never altogether *in* the film, but always a little *ahead* of it."[8] Preempting pantomimic legibility, it imposes an interpretation on the visual image. Yet with time, this proleptic quality of speech becomes less and less apparent to the audience; the "talkie" appears as the privileged, natural form of cinema, corresponding to a reality naturally presented through the synchronization of image and sound.

By desynchronizing these three orders of cinematic experience—image-event, sound-event, meaning-event—the opening scene of *Barking Dogs Never Bite* repeats cinema's primal scene. Reading that no animals have been harmed, we expect to see and hear otherwise: the yipping distracts us, blurring boundaries between the film and the official messages framing it. We see trees, the apartment, again we hear yipping. But this hasn't been localized, tied to a specific source, and indeed the film's apparent protagonist, still only seen from behind, confronts this noisome decoupling of sound and image as a mystery to be solved. He must solve it because the *delocalized* yipping, echoing through the apartment complex, distracts him, driving him, a struggling academic, to the brink of madness. He cannot read, think, write; the yip keeps him from his scholarly vocation.

Cinematic Desynchronization

Seeing something, we also see the space where it belongs, starting from the place it occupies. Only rarely—say, when dazzled by a light—does visual experience detach from spatial articulation. Then we say we are *blinded*. Not only is visual experience always immediately oriented, but vision involves an incessant, active process of self-orientation within a field of experience always threatening to overwhelm. Focusing on a mere fragment of the visual field, the eyes, even when staring at one thing, constantly jump about with unconscious saccadic movements.[9] Auditory experience also involves a spatial field, constituted largely through subtle subconscious inferences derived from small differences in the timing of sounds received in each ear. Even lacking visual or tactile sensation, one still experiences an orienting spatial field. Nevertheless, for those experiencing the world both visually and acoustically, acoustic space becomes dependent upon, and refers to, visual spatialization. It's not just that sound localization, especially for the lower registers, is considerably less precise. Because visual experience cannot but be given spatially, visual spatiality takes precedence. While a sound can appear problematically unlocalized within an orienting spatial field, one cannot ordinarily imagine an unlocalized visual experience within an orienting acoustic field. Whereas the visual field is inherently orientating, disclosing a space wherein orientation is possible, the auditory signal, as soon as a visual field opens, demands orientation within it.

Precisely because visual experience is intrinsically orienting, cinema achieves extraordinary effects of disorientation within the domain of images. The mechanical camera-eye receives the world in fragments—a rhythmic succession of still images. These are then montaged together at the editing table, creating a semblance of continuity. While the soundtrack is also the result of montage, as well as—following the introduction of multitrack recording—mixing, not only is there no primitive *perceptible* discontinuous element, but due to the fundamental phenomenological distinction between visual and auditory experience, visual and auditory montage lead to very different effects.[10] Because visual experience is inherently oriented, visual montage is radically disorienting; with each new image, the eye must orient itself in a new space. In contrast, since auditory experience, when combined with the visual, is oriented in the first instance only relative to the visual field, auditory montage, should it ever uncouple from the visual, suggests a series of sound events falling within a single weakly spatialized field. On the mercurial camera's command, the eye flits from perspective to perspective. Whereas the ear encounters one vaguely continuous world, the eye, detached from the human body as center of abiding orientation, becomes utterly disoriented in its constant search for orientation.

Pure Movement

Countering the naturalistic synchronization of image and sound, the opening scene of *Barking Dogs Never Bite* thus reveals cinema's ability to occupy the field of tensions formed at the meeting point between the unoriented and disorienting, between a quasi-absolute space and a space thoroughly fragmented by the subject. At once disembodied and embodied, disoriented yet demanding orientation, the yipping intrudes as *pure movement.*

Pure movement is the extreme object of cinematic representation, which has a special relation to it, approaching it as no other medium can.[11] A stage actor acts out movements but only as gesture; the dancer's movement is the movement of the dancing body, whose limitations it cannot escape. Poetry and prose certainly give penetrating descriptions of movement, but only through the mediation of language with its implicit grammatical prejudices. Consider the difference between Eadweard Muybridge's *The Horse in Motion* (1878), a sequence of still images recorded over time, and Leo Tolstoy's description of horses racing over obstacles in *Anna Karenina*, published the same year. Whereas Tolstoy reveals the synesthetic experience of racing, the intimate moral union between horse and rider, Muybridge shows the movement, beggaring description, of the horse itself as it walks, trots, canters, runs—a subtle exchange of positions too rapid for the human eye to catch.[12]

Nor does cinema stop at the motions of animate beings; no movement, translatable into visible light, is off-limits. Sergei Eisenstein's *Battleship Potemkin* (1925) begins with waves crashing against embankments, montaging footage shot at two different locations. Waves are quite an ordinary, prosaic part of our world; whoever has spent time near a breakwater, port, or pier during stormy weather will have seen waves no less remarkable than those Eisenstein brings to the screen. Yet ordinarily we see the individual wave as part of a general rhythmic order. Eisenstein's montage, however, interrupts the waves' ordinary rhythms and substitutes another—artificial—rhythm; the technique of montage, elemental to the cinematic apparatus, amplifies the effect of the artificial barrier, which creates the visibly cresting wave through the very disruption of the natural harmonic oscillations of the water. No longer appearing as a natural rhythm compliantly mastered through the rhythm of perception and habit, the wave becomes eruption, disruption.

Bong Joon Ho as Philosophical Filmmaker

Bong's reputation as an *auteur* is beyond dispute. Yet despite the high level of creative control he exerts over his films, despite his obvious intelligence and thoughtfulness, there is a tendency, reflecting his own undergraduate training, to stress the sociological dimension of his films, which—as in *Parasite*—is rather on the surface.[13] By understanding Bong, in contrast, as a philosophical filmmaker, I neither wish to disregard the obvious sociological dimension of his films, nor to claim that he treats traditional philosophical problems— truth, knowledge, personal identity, justice, evil, consciousness, the mind-body relation—cinematically. Rather, he is a philosophical filmmaker because he brings a "cinematic" light to bear on the very nature of cinema as a medium, exemplifying the tendency toward self-reflexivity, emphasizing the specifically material elements of filmmaking, the *apparatus*, that, as Joseph Jonghyun Jeon argues, is characteristic of Korean cinema produced in the wake of the 1997 IMF-crisis.[14] His films are themselves, immediately and viscerally, a philosophy of cinema; again and again we find the cinematic apparatus turned against itself.

This philosophical tendency of Bong's films, however, must also be distinguished from a more familiar sort of cinematic meta-referentiality that, shattering the illusion of the real—blurring the lines between actor and character—problematizes the ontological relation between fiction and reality. Such meta-cinema, exemplified by Federico Fellini's *8 ½*, has firm roots in European theater, from Luigi Pirandello to Ludwig Tieck to Shakespeare and Calderón. Consequently, the specific difference between theater and cinema is obscured: the cinematic props—movie cameras, lights, clapboards—brought before the camera merely signify the theatrical, the artificial, the illusory. Bong, in contrast, shows little interest in breaking the cinematic illusion. When audiovisual media appear, they are so naturally integrated into the depicted reality that they can scarcely challenge the naturalistic illusion. Something quite different is going on: the cinematic apparatus, while rarely appearing in an ostentatious but superficial way, determines the very content, structure, even the meaning of his films; it is not merely represented as one object among others depicted on screen, but fills out the scene, is the scene.

In his *Erläuterungen zu Hölderlins Dichtung* (Elucidations of Hölderlin's Poetry), Heidegger characterizes the famously recondite German poet as "in a special sense the poet of the poet," tasked with bringing the essence of poetry to poetic expression. I propose understanding Bong as *cineaste of cinema, filmmaker of film*.[15] And, just as Hölderlin, for Heidegger, invites a dialogue between poetry and thinking, so Bong occasions a dialogue between filmmaking and philosophy.[16] This suggests that filmmaking is in certain respects more philosophically radical—more philosophical—than philosophy itself. Such an approach, however, will not be "Heideggerian."

Poetry is arguably the most archaic cultural form, old as language itself, existing independent of any technical mediation save articulate language, which is no mere human invention, since the human comes into existence through language. Cinema, whose technologies are still evolving, remains at the avant-garde. Hence, a dialogue of film and thinking cannot satisfy the desire of thinking to return to the origin, to banish the specters of modernity and overcome the danger of modern technology. It must move in a different direction—oriented toward the question of pure movement. The cinematic apparatus becomes the site of a decision: *either pure movement can be returned to an orienting frame, or the orienting frame will be rent asunder through pure movement.* This is the decision between the *philosophical apparatus of cinema* and the *cinematic apparatus of philosophy.*

Discussing the storybook for *Mother*, Bong invokes "movement amidst calmness": "It's sort of an Asian concept, which means on the surface something may seem calm and still, but actually it's moving inside."[17] This seemingly off-the-cuff remark suggests a deeper tendency in his oeuvre, which, in a certain way, is the perfect counterpart to Eisenstein's wave: rather than exposing anarchic movement so as to submit it ultimately to a dialectical logic subordinating difference to identity, he allows movement to appear amid, or through, its seeming negation. It would not be too much to connect this radical, elemental movement, defiant of conceptualization, with *qi /ki* (氣), the vital living force; "a dynamic all-present, all-penetrating, and all-transforming force animating every existence in the universe";[18] a "limitless source of all creation forming an omnipresent cosmic creative flow . . . visible in both cosmic and human breath."[19]

The Cinematic Apparatus of Philosophy

The cinematic apparatus of philosophy names the various attempts by which philosophy—for now we restrict ourselves to the Western philosophical tradition in its divagations—sought to comprehend pure movement by reducing it to sense and reason. Glimpsed in Heraclitus's river, Parmenides sought to deny it all being and truth. Yet to exclude absolutely is to preserve the excluded in its exclusion, if through a *via negativa.* More insidious are the attempts, laying the foundation for Western metaphysics, to "reconcile" movement and stasis, subordinating movement to the eternal and unchanging (Plato) or to a physics of telic change and a metaphysics of substantial identity (Aristotle). This provides the basis for the mathematical natural sciences, which, starting from Galileo, subsequently empowered by the invention of differential and integral calculus, capture nature's dynamic processes through a precise mathematical language. Even the statistical model of nature, from Maxwell, Boltzmann, and Gibbs to Heisenberg and beyond, may be seen as a further permutation of this tendency.[20]

But how is philosophy itself cinematic? Philosophy certainly concerns movement (*kinēsis*). The paradoxes of movement, which have often provoked philosophical research, emerge when movement is glimpsed beyond any of the orienting frames of "naïve," "archaic," pre-ontological thought. And furthermore, philosophy itself comes to create its own cinema *avant la lettre*: a theater within which movement comes to appear and is in turn arrested, neutralized.[21] The primal scene of metaphysics is Plato's cave, which appears in the seventh book of the *Republic*. To illustrate the justice of the soul, Socrates undertakes the construction of an ideal city. This leads him to claim that the ideal city's kings must be philosophers.[22] Whereas nonphilosophers wander among what is many and manifold, philosophers apprehend— literally fastening on to (*ephaptesthai*)—that which is always the same with respect to itself (*aie kata tauta hōsautōs*).[23] Compared with the philosophers, who have a vivid pattern in the soul, fixing their eyes on the "most true," the nonphilosophical multitude are as if blind.[24] Philosophers are "always in love with that learning which discloses to them something of the being that *is* always and does not wander about, driven by generation and decay."[25]

This distinction between philosopher and nonphilosopher has everything to do with movement. Motion's spectacle captivates nonphilosophers; philosophers fixate on eternal stillness. Poetic as it is, such a static, painterly depiction of the difference between philosopher and nonphilosopher can hardly convince those who are not yet philosophers. To make philosophy comprehensible to the nonphilosopher, Socrates will depict the philosopher in the process of becoming by offering a moving image of philosophical "education." And so, Socrates conjures the image of human beings shackled from childhood in a cave, whose entrance opens to light across its entire width. Their heads are fixed forward, as others, walking behind them while making sounds, carry strange artifacts and human- and animal-shaped statues before a fire, projecting shadows above the wall. With the strange image of these strange prisoners, Socrates describes cinema. Or indeed, he offers a cinematic representation of cinema, since Plato's Socrates, with all the deftness of a director, guides his listener's vision, starting out with a wide-angle shot, taking in the entire scene of the cave, and then drawing the focus first to the captives, then to the projective apparatus itself.

But Plato only leads us into this cinematic theater to lead us out of it. The next passage describes the forced liberation of a prisoner "compelled to stand up, to turn his neck around, to walk and look up toward the light," his entire field of vision becoming saturated with dizzying, dazzling, blinding light.[26] A new world reveals itself to him. At first, he sees it only as shadows and reflections, but in time he sees the things of the world themselves and even raises his eyes to the sun, the ultimate source of light.

Plato deploys his cinematic apparatus to negate the play of movement and stillness for the sake of absolute self-same stillness; the flickering play of light and dark cedes to absolute light. Plato's cave, as the first cinematic apparatus of philosophy, literally a "motion picture," is movement deployed against movement, contrast employed against contrast. The philosophical apparatus of cinema involves a countervailing project: the liberation, the disclosure of pure movement, in all its subversive potency, over and against the various frames wherein it's been captured and arrested.

Daoism

Many readers, I suspect, will be put off by such a notion of pure movement. Pure movement is not the purity gained by theoretical abstraction, as when pure form is set against pure matter. Nor is it a new transcendental principle—an arch-transcendental dis-originating origin. Pure movement is simply what's manifest without having been captured in a conceptual schema. If it can be conceptualized, it is only through concepts that recognize their own limits, that speak to the phenomena by countering their own coherence as concepts. Still, such movement is not found just at the world's margins. It is the world—*way-making* and *making-way*, the course of things.

Those familiar with East Asian philosophy will immediately think of the *dao/to* (道), and of the *Daodejing*'s enigmatic opening: "The way-making (*dao*) that can be put into words is not really way-making."[27] Bong's films develop a global and comparative perspective engaging both East Asian and Western philosophical traditions in a subtle dialogue. Within the Western philosophical tradition, the notion of a "pure"—originary, absolute—movement is found among pre-Socratic philosophers such as Heraclitus. We may recall his well-known apothegm: *phusis kruptesthai philei*, "nature loves to hide."[28] But in the wake of Plato's dualistic metaphysics, movement becomes comprehensible only in the light of an organizing rationality—be it Plato's eternal forms, the Aristotelian *telos*, the mind of a creator-God, *a priori* spatiotemporal intuitions, or mathematical formalism.

There are many points of convergence between East Asian and Western philosophy; philosophy does not emerge in a vacuum, and, cultural differences notwithstanding, the fundamental human predicament remains the same. But we may still distinguish the leading tendency of Western metaphysics from that of East Asian philosophy. The latter appears in the clearest light when we consider the most basic conceptual frame underwriting all the indigenous tendencies in East Asian philosophy, the *yinyang* schema, "the most ultimate principles of which the ancient Chinese could conceive."[29] *Yinyang* thought, Robin Wang argues, "is neither dualistic in positing two absolutely independent entities, nor even simply dialectical in projecting one single pattern for change."[30] Rather, *yin* and *yang* "contest each other in a temporal framework and in multiple ways" such as contradiction and opposition, interdependence, mutual inclusion, interaction/resonance, complementarity/mutual support, and change and transformation.[31] It doesn't offer a reductive explanatory framework, but a supple language for thinking about the multitude of movements comprising the totality of things. Nor, however, is it merely a naïve and "poetic" phenomenology of life's surface: the stillness of the depths is no less movement than a raging storm; not only are dying and birthing both modes of movement but death is no less a movement than life.

An especially important concept in this regard, playing a large role in Daoism, is *ziran* (自然). Roger T. Ames and David L. Hall translate this as "spontaneously so," "self-so-ing," "self-deriving," involving a "self-creativity" and "co-creativity" that applies not only to the "natural" but also to the social and political order. The Sino-Korean equivalent *chayŏn* is used in the sense of nature, and one could likewise discover parallels between *ziran* and the Greek *physis*, which originally means, as Heidegger puts it, that which "surges upward, growing of its own accord," and "the arising of something from out of itself."[32] But while Aristotle continues to think of nature in terms of spontaneity, he understands this natural spontaneity as telos-oriented, opposing it to *to automaton* and *tuchē*. While *to automaton* is semantically similar to *ziran*, it involves random, chaotic movement. Thus, while Aristotle, guided by a deep phenomenological instinct, is certainly more sensitive to the problem of movement than Plato, he nevertheless perpetuates the subordination of wayward, way-making movement to reason. Hence, in the *Nicomachean Ethics*, the entire sphere of human praxis becomes legible as a system of goals.[33] Daoist ethics and politics, in contrast, have everything to do with conforming to the spontaneous ordering of things, privileging the spontaneously natural over the artificial, overwrought, willful. As Harold D. Roth explains, spontaneity, a "quality of both the Way and the cultivated sage," involves "natural, instantaneous and non-reflective responses to the phenomenal world."[34] This is of the essence of *de/tŏk* (德)—"inner power," "virtue," "virtuosity." And as A. Charles Muller puts it: "As one becomes attuned to the Way, s/he, as in the disfigured characters of the *Zhuangzi*, becomes filled with charismatic power [. . .] whereby one's thoughts and actions become harmonious and natural [. . .]."[35]

Bong's films, as I shall argue throughout this book, not only play with various Daoist themes but develop a kind of Daoist *askēsis*, cultivating an openness toward pure movement. Yet this *askēsis* follows a crooked path; indeed, it proceeds by way of a *deconstruction* of the cinematic apparatus of philosophy, developing it to the point of collapse, exposing the limits where a different kind of experience becomes possible. Cinema as an art form, due to the technical complexity of the medium and the capital outlays needed, militates against spontaneity, and Bong is furthest from being a spontaneous, improvisational filmmaker. His films are carefully planned and executed with obsessive attention to detail. Nor, on the surface at least, does an East Asian philosophical sensibility pervade his films—whether overtly, as in Kim Ki-duk's deeply spiritual *Spring, Summer, Fall, Winter . . . and Spring* (2003) or, more subtly, as with Lee Chang-dong's *Burning* (2018), Ozu Yasujirō *Tokyo Story* (1953), or Hou Hsiao-hsien's *A City of Sadness* (1989). The *dao* is only glimpsed at tragic or tragic-comic limits. An analogy might be drawn with the path-breaking Korean composer Yun Isang. Trained in Western music, Yun composed in the tonal idiom of European high modernism, producing scores in which, in contrast to John Cage—a Western composer deeply intrigued by East Asian thought—little room was left for interpretation, yielding neither to chance nor the musician's discretion. Yet Yun was profoundly aware of fundamental differences between Eastern and Western music, drawing an analogy with Western and Eastern calligraphy. If the Western note is like a straight line from a pencil, and must be connected both horizontally and vertically to create form, the Eastern note resembles brush strokes, flowing and variant, carrying in themselves flexible possibilities of interpretation; changing and evolving, resonating in diverse ways, and already a complete universe.[36] It is as if he brought a "dictatorial" Western compositional practice to its conceptual breaking point.

This does not mean, however, that Bong's films merely play "East" against "West." Rather, he develops the tensions within both traditions. For the indigenous Chinese philosophical tradition, the deepest tension is between Daoism and Confucianism. These are to be understood, in the first instance, as tendencies—at once antagonistic *and* complementary—that, together, determine the outermost possibilities of a form of life (a cultural form in the broadest sense) characterized by an affirmative this-worldliness. This is clearest when the fundamental concepts of Chinese thought are approached free from the distortions introduced through seemingly innocuous translations. The risk of such distortion runs deep. As Ames and Henry Rosemont, Jr. observe in the introduction to their translation of the *Analects*, whereas English and other Indo-European languages are grammatically predisposed toward substance and essence-centered ontologies, Classical Chinese is eventful.[37] If Heidegger's "Das Nichts nichtet [The nothing nothings]" seemed nonsensical to Rudolf Carnap, it is because German, like other Indo-European languages, enforces the grammatical distinction between noun and verb, forcing Heidegger to take the extraordinary measure of verbalizing the substantive to express an "evental" nothing, even while still attributing this as the action of *the* Nothing. Classical Chinese lacks all inflectional morphology; there aren't even morphological markers distinguishing different parts of speech. Whereas analytically minded philosophers are wont to smell bullshit when *das Nichts*, safely sequestered in essentializing abstraction, appears as verb, the flexibility of literary Chinese goes so far that, as Holmes Welch notes, he's even seen "manure" used adverbially!

The transcendentalizing tendency of Western thought, issuing from the collision of Greek and Hebrew culture, might seem an artifact of language; events—however immeasurable, impalpable, incomprehensible—are concrete and immanent if only because an event is always what can somehow touch, trouble, discombobulate, resonate with . . . *us* or *someone* or *something*. The substantializing of the event, turning it into a self-contained thing, enables its banishment beyond immanence. Only as *substance* can God take flight to the other world. To get a first sense of this evental character, one need only consider that concept which most closely approaches the Christian understanding of God as transcendent creator of the world and of human beings: *tian/ch'ŏn* (天), translated by "heaven," "sky," "the heavens," "celestial," and other such words. As Brook Ziporyn explains in the glossary to his translation of Zhuangzi, "no one in the history of Chinese thought ever doubts its existence," and in this way it is far closer to the Western concept of "nature" than "God."[38]

Tian is not this-worldly, to be sure, but it is *this-lifely*. The same applies, a fortiori, to the other fundamental concepts of indigenous Chinese thought such as *qi, dao, yinyang/ŭmyang* (陰陽), *ziran,* all of which are even more explicitly eventful than *tian*. Not that Chinese thought fixates on that which is immediately palpable, perceptible, submitting unproblematically to the order of names and concepts. A Chinese theory of experience, as Michael Nylan argues, is neither passive nor automatic, but depends not only on the physical organ being properly trained to bring out connections between things but on material conditions conducive to calm reflection and on the will to think hard.[39] This theory of experience, moreover, depends on *qi,* the "spirit" or "vital energy," as the "medium facilitating these forms of resonance interaction and sensitive exchange[.]"[40] Experience is a kind of discipline, and perhaps the most radical, paradoxical discipline of experience, but certainly not the only one, is sketched out in the core texts of Daoism: the *Daodejing* and the writings of Zhuangzi. At the core of the Chinese discipline and practice of experience, Nylan suggests, is an extraordinarily rich and subtle understanding of *le* (樂), which she translates as "pleasure." In early Chinese thought, pleasure was not regarded as a luxury, let alone as a seductive temptation to evil, but as a necessity invested with the greatest cultural significance; for "the capacity to experience complex pleasures defines the highest achievement, that of being fully human, whole, and at ease."[41] Experience is not the foundation of positivistic rigor, scientific system building, technical conquest; pleasure is not the starting point of utilitarian calculus. Rather, it is the subtle element within which the problem of this life—its challenges, its possibilities, its impossibilities—first begins to unfold.

The common point is an affirmation of this life; the deepest rift emerges between the *humanism* of the Confucian tradition and the *otherwise-than-humanism* of Daoism. The guiding project of the *Analects* is *ren/in* (仁), which Ames and Rosemont translate as "authoritative conduct," but which, more typically translated as "humanness," refers not to a given human nature but an ideal of human conduct that develops vis-à-vis other human beings. It is formed from two root elements: *ren/in* (人), meaning "man," and *er/i* (二), "two." Daoism certainly doesn't deny all ethical significance to human beings, but it refuses to think of them as the measure of all things, as the heart of all meaning and truth. The jarring opening to the first chapter of the *Zhuangzi*, titled "Wandering Far and Unfettered"—it speaks of an enormous fish turning into an enormous bird with "clouds draped across the heavens"—is shock therapy to all such pretensions.[42]

Daoism is a vastly complex phenomenon, encompassing not only a body of philosophical writings such as the *Daodejing* and the writings of Zhuangzi, along with an intertwined tradition of commentary and exegesis, but also esoteric hygienic and alchemic practices accompanied by a sprawling scriptural canon, and a Daoist church, with its own pantheon and rites, that developed to a large extent under the pressure of Buddhism.[43] It might seem that in contrast to Neo-Confucianism, which was established as the state ideology during the Chosŏn dynasty and continues to leave a powerful mark on Korean society, Daoism had little impact. During the Three Kingdoms period (391–676), Daoism competed alongside Buddhism and Confucianism, complementing indigenous shamanistic practices, and it also flourished during the early Koryŏ (918–1146), developing as a folk religion combining Buddhist religion and prophecy. But during the early Chosŏn (1392–1567), Daoism and shamanism both lost ground, even though their influence remained pervasive, and by the middle-Chosŏn period (1567–1724), amid Neo-Confucian ideological hegemony, it had been forced out of the intellectual mainstream.[44] But even then, Daoist and shamanist elements, together with Buddhism, persisted within popular cultural practices.[45] Moreover, Korean Buddhism itself, dominated by the Sŏn lineage represented by the Chogye and T'aego orders, stands in a close relation to the Chan/Zen teachings, which stress "sudden enlightenment" and which themselves emerged from the confluence of Buddhism and Daoism, involving a Sinicization and Daoization of Buddhist doctrines imported from India.[46] Even so, there are also significant differences between Chan/Sŏn/Zen and Daoism, drawing attention, once more, to the this-worldliness of indigenous Chinese thought: the Daoist mind remains an "embodied mind" rather than a separable, encapsulated consciousness; Daoist "emptiness and nonpresence do not diminish but rather confirm the authenticity of the present."[47]

What matters most of all, for the purposes of this book, is that Daoism and Confucianism are polar tendencies of Chinese thought, deeply entwined in a complementary, often fecund and generative antagonism. Following a logic that, by calling attention to the efficacy of the hidden, is itself Daoist, we could say that the further Daoism is shunted from the mainstream, marginalized by the hegemonic ideology, the more it gains in a mysterious, unwieldy, awkward potency. This can be felt in the fiction of Han Kang, where a housewife, abstaining from meat, becomes vegetal, arboreal, reminding us of Zhuangzi's useless, swollen, gnarled tree. Or in Yi Mun-yol's *Son of Man*, where a seminarian explodes the premises of Abrahamic religion in the name of a Great Being beyond even the duality of chaos and orderly creation. Or when the preternaturally gifted but illegitimate Hong Gildong, excluded from all official avenues to advancement, bearing a sorrow within him that keeps him "from looking up at Heaven with pride," leaves home, declaring to his father: "I will become like a cloud and float about the world with no destination."[48] Endowed with uncanny powers over the elements, he

 Bong Joon Ho

becomes the leader of a band of brigands, eventually challenging the rule of the very king whom he had wished, above all else, to serve.

Moreover, the philosophical originality of Neo-Confucianism involved integrating a theory of emotions, ethics, and metaphysics into a single unifying picture. In this regard, it drew on the idea of the *dao* as a "structuring, guiding, and normative pattern, [running] through all things just as a single pattern governs and informs all the interacting and interdependent parts of a single living body."[49] Yet with the versions of Neo-Confucianism that became dominant in Chosŏn through the Ch'eng brothers, Daoist monism yielded to a dualistic relation between *li/i* (理) and *qi/ki*, where *ki*, while still complementary and intertwined with *i*, nevertheless assumed, somewhat akin to *hylē* (matter) in Aristotle, an "ambiguous limiting/distorting function associated with its varying degrees of purity and turbidity, fineness and coarseness."[50] It is in the context of this innovation that the Four-Seven Debate, the most famous intellectual controversy of pre-modern Korea, assumed such significance. Arguing against the famous and distinguished scholar T'oegye, twenty-six years his senior, Kobong pushed back against the *i-ki* dualism. While dualism and monism both present themselves as positions within a Neo-Confucian frame, their dispute also reproduces the deeper rift between Daoist and Confucian tendencies; Kobong seems to return to the Daoist monism that underlies and enables the dominant Neo-Confucian position but that will be sacrificed for the sake of the superficial conceptual clarity demanded by perspicacious praxis.[51] And indeed, while the concept of *li* is most often associated with Neo-Confucianism—the word is absent from the *Analects*—it also appears in texts associated with Daoism, including the *Zhuangzi*, though in such a way as forbids a dualistic interpretation. Drawing attention to the root meaning of *li/i*, which derives from the naturally occurring fractures in jade,

Roth writes: "Jade patterning is an excellent metaphor for the basic inherent patterns of the cosmos to which we must adapt and comply; both are not only structured; they also represent *natural* tendencies, unlike the more prosaic uses of *li* in classical non-Daoist works."[52] *Li*, this suggests, is not an ordering framework imposed on a restive *qi*. Arising immanently from the congealed flow of *qi*, it suggests the deepest dynamic—the *way*—of its flowing.

The Daoism whose traces and tracks we shall pursue in Bong's films is not a comprehensive, manifest philosophical program. It is a tendency: strange, subversive, hidden and hiding, gnarled, immense; an undercurrent that is always lurking beneath the dominant discourse and the main currents—be this Neo-Confucianism, or, now, neoliberalism, the careerism and social conformity of SKY-colleges and *chaebŏl* jobs, soft power and K-pop, plastic surgery and cosmetics. It manifests in the simplest acts of resistance, quiet and unassuming pleasures, but also in Korea's vibrant, chaotic political culture.

But as esoteric as this cinematic discipline may seem, the ultimate intention of Bong's cinema remains political, or indeed political-philosophical.[53] In more exoteric terms, it continues the conceptual struggles of the Korean democracy movement: the struggle to represent the people, the political subject, in the absence of whom democracy degrades into procedural formalism and technocracy. The thought of a democratic Daoism, however, is a strange thought, since even if, following Moeller, we understand the *Daodejing* as in the first instance a political philosophy, it is manifestly undemocratic: a theory of kingship, "advice to rulers for governing and ordering a state."[54] But perhaps the very awkwardness of this thought suggests, in Daoist fashion, its potency.

Trajectory

Cinema is perhaps the most controlling, totalizing artistic medium that has ever been produced, and Bong is a perfectionist, a "control freak," like few others—his nickname in the Korean film industry is "Bongtail."[55] Yet all this control is ingeniously deployed for the sake of the radical, deep, world-encompassing spontaneity of pure, anarchic movement. While it will often seem as if I am constructing a strange philosophical scaffold around Bong's films, this scaffold is meant to be tossed away in the end, once, like the bamboo frames enfolding Hong Kong buildings, it has played out its function; it is only there, in other words, to let the reader reach a vantage point where what is happening can be understood, in all the paradoxical intensity that such understanding, dancing on the abyss, demands. It leads to where one can say, with Jean-Luc Godard: *Au cinéma, on ne pense pas, on est pensé*—at the cinema, we do not think, we are thought.[56]

My trajectory is divided into three parts, three movements. I will cover all seven of the feature-length films directed by Bong to date— all of which are also based on screenplays that he co-wrote—treating these in a not-quite-chronological order. Each movement may be best understood through its dominant theme. The first movement (Chapter 1), returning to *Barking Dogs Never Bite*, focuses primarily on the dimension of spatiality. The second movement treats Bong's two explorations of crime in provincial Korea: *Memories of Murder* (Chapter 2) and *Mother* (Chapter 3). Here the focus turns from the more static to the more dynamic: temporality, memory, genre. An orienting concept is the *mythic*, used in a special sense. The third movement turns to the trinity of films treating globalization: *The Host* (Chapter 4), *Snowpiercer* (Chapter 5), and *Okja* (Chapter 6). Here the guiding concept is *monstrosity*—the monstrous sign—suggesting a move from the dynamic to the order of signification while exploring both Bong's powerful and ever more prophetic critique of the new global order of visionary capitalism as well as his attempt, above all through the theme of adoption, to envision an alternative vision of planetary community.

Although *Parasite* is widely regarded as Bong's masterpiece, I will treat it only in the epilogue. This is partly because so much has already been written and partly because it might be taken as the summation of his *oeuvre* up to that point. The elements for its legibility will already have been established. This epilogue, in turn, will continue the first movement—since *Parasite* marks a return to *Barking Dogs Never Bite*—but will also repeat all three. It will draw into focus the esoteric Daoism that underlies Bong's filmmaking.

*

Godard's formula could also be reversed: *thinking, we are cinema*. Thinking is different from argumentation, defending one philosophical position against others, but also different from the apodictic certainty of mathematical proof or the scientific method's patient inductions. *Thinking is unveiling, discovering what, for the most part, is already somewhat familiar—but in a deepening sense.* Because life itself is suspended between the unfathomable juxtaposition of life and death, the deepest thoughts cannot really be *thought through*, as if reaching some unifying element, but appear in juxtapositions. Thinking, as Friedrich Schlegel recognized, must be witty. Wit is "absolute social feeling, or fragmentary genius," "logical sociability," an "explosion of confined spirit," "a prophetic faculty," and indeed "the principle and organ of universal philosophy."[57] Montage is the cinematic correlate of wit. Just as the controvertible relation between *thinking* and *cinema* stands at the crux of the theoretical wager of this book, the method of exposition will be equally cinematic and analytic. What is sought is not so much a scholarly analysis of a cinematic oeuvre, maintaining an equitable distance throughout, as a new kind of text—a hybrid of montaged images and critical wit.

1

Barking Dogs Never Bite

Junk

Franz Kafka died at the close of the silent era, and his writings, with their strange and wondrous gestures, testify to the mostly unrealized aesthetic possibilities of silent film.[1] Nowhere is this clearer than in "Der Bau" (The Burrow), a short story written in the last year of his life and left unfinished. It begins as the narrator, an unnamed burrower, declares that the construction of its burrow is complete.[2] Soon it starts hearing a high-pitched whistling noise whose location and source, for all the creature's efforts, elude it.[3] The thematic affinity with *Barking Dogs Never Bite* (2000) is striking. Tenuous as it might seem—it's hardly a question of influence—this offers a clue for interpreting Bong's first feature-length film. This too is about a built environment, a human "burrow," that, through dividing and compartmentalizing space, promises localization even while scuttling it at the same time.

While architecture alone shapes the spaces of human dwelling and burrowing, nearly all art forms, even music, are connected and concerned with lived space. But cinema's relation is especially profound. By allowing a mode of experience that is not aesthetic but *distracted*, involving "reception in a state of distraction," film allows us to encounter built and natural environments in the very relation of inattentive, mostly unconscious awareness that we have to them in ordinary life.[4] In contrast, when literature "realistically" represents a lived space, it must do so explicitly and schematically. Explicitly, because it describes a place through a string of words commanding the reader's attention enough to be read, passing the threshold of consciousness. Schematically, because interpreting words depends on the reader's knowledge, imagination, and memory. Consider the following passage from Gustave Flaubert's *Madame Bovary*:

> In the rear, opening directly into the yard (which contained the stables), was a big ramshackle room with an oven, now serving as a woodshed, wine bin, and store room; it was filled with old junk, empty barrels, broken tools, and a quantity of other objects all dusty and nondescript.[5]

More conceptual than perceptual—we are being told what is there, not how it looks—this description subtly evokes the feelings of a viewer seeing this chaotic jumble for the first time, bewildered by it and struck by the melancholy of historical time, which condemns things not only to dilapidation and desuetude but to an even bitterer fate: obsolescence.

In contrast, cinema *shows* the place itself through a series of moving images, presenting a surplus of visual information—far more than we can consciously attend to. Mimicking the eye's exploratory movements, the camera-eye prevents us from tarrying with the scene, contemplating it as a theater audience, in moments of boredom, might do. Overwhelming with detail but depriving us of the wherewithal to process it into conscious awareness, it forces us into its own rhythms. Consequently, a significant part of cinematic detail is experienced only latently: *we perceive it without it passing the threshold of consciousness—it affects the mood of the scene, it may even trigger unconscious thought processes, but we are not exactly aware of it.*

In *Barking Dogs Never Bite*, junk plays no less a role than in this passage from Flaubert. Indeed, the lived spaces appearing throughout the film are organized around waste disposal, and if the basement figures so crucially in the action, it is not least because this is where junk accumulates. Following the opening scene, set in Ko Yun-ju (Lee Sung-jae)'s small apartment, the camera traverses the exterior common spaces of the apartment complex—familiarizing us with these for the first time—finally bringing us to the roof overlooking Seoul's southern edge, rolling mountains juxtaposed with the sprawl of mid-rise apartments jutting through the haze. Yun-ju now holds a Shih Tzu over the edge; he tries to throw—as if throwing away. He can't. Maybe he senses the old woman laying out radishes in the sun. Maybe the rooftop, with its panopticon view—individual units resembling so many prison cells—reminds him of the omnipresent social surveillance that is part and parcel of the Korean apartment complex, itself a compromise formation, characteristic for postwar Korea, between atomized individualism and community, financial speculation and egalitarianism.[6] The old woman herself—a *halmŏni*, a "grandma"—represents a threat not so much real as symbolic: the claim of the moral order. Not surprisingly, Yun-ju, unable to commit his crime in the light of day—as if evading the *halmŏni* gaze—retreats to the basement.

The third scene commences. An exquisitely composed shot shows the corner of the basement, with the visual field divided into left, right, and a slightly larger middle both by the edge where the two walls meet and by the pipes and circuit box running down the wall. A detached wooden door in the middle of the leftmost space, resting against the sidewall, appears as a parallelogram, and, together with a chromium stick shining in the dim light, forms a second, larger parallelogram, slightly askew from the vertical line framing the middle of the visual field. Whereas the right-hand region is lost in darkness, the middle of the screen is dominated by junk: several moving boxes filled with old clothing or rags, and behind these, some pieces of cardboard and what seems to be a round low table. The camera pans slowly to the right, creating a slight sense of movement, and from the dark region screen-right, Yun-ju enters. Hidden in the ill-fitting plaid shirt's long sleeve, his hand clutches the bag which, swinging around as he turns toward the junk, reveals his cute victim's face. He slowly walks across the room and then turns into the corridor, partitioned by structural walls, with pipes running above. The camera had been following him from behind, showing only the back of his head, but now a half-body shot reveals his pained face as he turns around and, glancing at the ceiling, loops the leash over the pipes.

Suddenly, his whole body comes into view. He's standing at the edge of a structural wall, looking down at the dog. Dominating screen-right is a disordered pile of junk, no longer contained in boxes, lacking the merest semblance of order: random coils of rope, odd pieces of piping, a folded stroller, a sheet of heavy cloth draped over what might be the edge of a speaker, a shiny metallic thingamajig. Holding the leash taut, he walks back toward the junk, and then—the camera closing in on his body—the hanging dog falls from view. We see only Yun-ju's upper body on the left and the junk on the right as he clenches the leash with both hands, then turns his head to the right. The camera is now behind him: the back of his head and shoulder blurred out through shallow focus, he sees himself clearly in a mirror—another piece of detritus leaning against the wall. He drops the dog down to the floor, unable to finish what he started.

A new pile of junk now consumes the entire screen, anchored by a wooden wardrobe. To the right: a fake antique bureau, topped with a record player, a small cherub, and other things beggaring description. To the left: the door, slightly ajar, of an Asian-style console, hidden behind some sort of table. Everything dusty and desolate. Yun-ju's shadow flitters across as he enters from screen left, clutching the dog. He shuts it in the wardrobe, then walks out—the basement door closing behind him—into darkness.

In the second volume of his treatise on cinema, Deleuze distinguishes between *hodological spaces*, which are organized around *praxis*, and pre-hodological spaces—a "space before action," haunted by a child or a clown or both, pointing toward the indecision of a body bereft of sensory-motorial coherence.[7] The profusion of junk— haunted by past uses but not yet trash, junk still awaits a return to utility—suggests a cinematic space that is ambiguously hodological and pre-hodological. For Deleuze, moreover, the hodological space corresponds to the "classical form" of cinema, the *action-image*; the pre-hodological space will come to dominate as, following the Second World War, cinematic classicism breaks down. In *Barking Dogs Never Bite*, however, we find ourselves before the latent ambiguity of a space that is both and neither. Action is still possible, perhaps, but it will be immediately haunted by its absurdity.

"Hodological" comes from the Greek *hodos* which, like *dao*, means a "path," a "way." Praxis, however, is telos-oriented, whereas the *dao* of Daoism is a way-making *before* praxis. The pre-hodological space—the way before the way of *praxis*—is thus the space of the *dao*.

Lived Spaces

Dominating the visual field ever more as the scene progresses, junk establishes the significance of the basement within the apartment complex as a system of lived spaces. Preceding the opening credits, the first three scenes introduce the audience to the film's primary setting by analyzing it into three distinct localities with their characteristic spatial forms, corresponding to the different aspects of life within the complex:

(1)   The rooftop (along with the other common exterior areas of the apartment complex) represents communal existence: the panoptic surveillance of each by all, but also the connectedness binding the individual units together into a greater quasi-political whole, a city within a city. Here, traditional communal activities, such as preparing the fermented side dishes, are still performed, if only by isolated individuals, but it also connects the apartment complex to its environs, visible only from this vantage point.

(2)   The apartment unit itself represents the space of privacy: the autonomy of the individual and the family unity. It is the space of mental life, of reading and thinking and spectating (watching TV), and of physical intimacy, while also looking out to the forest's edge. This suggests the dyadic relation between the interiority of the atomic individual and a still-wild nature.

(3)   The common exterior spaces are *public* and *open*, the apartment *private* and *closed*, but the basement is *public* (open to all) yet closed off and hidden from view, belonging neither to everyone nor someone but to no one.

The basement thus undermines the very idea of private property underwriting the apartment complex with its division into *private* and *common spaces*. The junk in the basement is so many abandoned objects, once-private property abandoned to where the principle of ownership breaks down, since it is these very piles of junk that make the basement the place that it is.

The beginning of the second scene reaffirms this ingeniously: it begins with a low-angle shot from behind Yun-ju's back as he looks up to the balconies running across two towers of the apartment complex that, meeting at a right angle, box him in. He rotates while the camera circles around him. This dizzying low-angle shot powerfully evokes his search for the disorienting bark. But it also reveals his submission to the architectural space of the complex. The camera coming to a rest, he's now in front of the bins in the middle of the parking lot, sorting his trash into various categories for recycling. Submitting to the apartment complex means submitting to the principle of order, whether by distinguishing between individual and common spaces, minding the difference between private and communal property, or properly disposing of your waste. Waste must be brought to the right place and sorted: plastic, Styrofoam, plastic bags, paper and cardboard, glass bottles, aluminum cans, batteries, food waste, general waste. A miracle of sanitation engineering, the Korean apartment complex preserves order and cleanliness amid a constant flood of commodities. And yet the basement—at the foundation of the complex—scuttles the order otherwise so carefully maintained: it underlies and upholds the order without submitting to it.

We can now begin to make sense of the action in these first three scenes. Within the ordering environment of the apartment complex, the dog's bark is something very troubling. It violates the very principle of order that the quasi-utopian space of the apartment complex maintains and depends on—an ordering involving the rational adjudication of the rights of the individual and the community. We later learn that, while dogs are forbidden within the apartment complex, residents routinely ignore this rule. The bark, indeed, doubly violates order: not only is the existence of dogs proscribed, but their noise, passing through the walls, mocks the segregation of spaces—of individual private spaces from each other, and of the private as such from the communal—upon which its order depends.

The bark is noise pollution and must be dealt with. How? By getting to the root of the problem. The source of the bark, its root and origin, is the dog; so the dog must be eliminated. But with no car, Yun-ju must dispose of the dog within the apartment complex itself. Throwing the dog off the roof seems like the cleanest, easiest option. Yet the roof is the space of surveillance, exposing him to the actual risk of being discovered, while also representing the symbolic threat of the ethical order and its judgments. And what is more, the exterior common space of the apartment complex is precisely where the principle of order prevails. Here, everything must have its place; all trash must be sorted away. Yet there is no recycling bin labeled "dog"! Nor could he take the dog into his apartment, killing it there and then disposing of its corpse. The individual apartment represents his own private sphere: the last thing he would want to do—he's not a budding serial killer after all, just a budding professor—is receive the dog, dead or alive, into his own space. The basement is his only option.

But now we face a mystery: Why does he stop midway while hanging the dog? Perhaps, seeing himself in the mirror, he feels a pang of conscience. Yet being left to starve is an even crueler death. While it suggests Antigone's living entombment, a Korean audience might also think of Lady Hyegyŏng's celebrated memoirs, where she recounts the death of her husband, the Crown Prince Sado, locked in a rice chest by his own father, King Chŏngjo.[8] Such a death, however, has a moral advantage for the executioner: he cannot be accused of shedding blood. He is not taking a life, but letting die, leaving to die. This moral advantage, incomprehensible from a modern juridical perspective where causal responsibility is conceived abstractly and where custodial care for the condemned extends to the moment of death, makes perfect sense within a pre-modern logic, where bloodshed against a member of the community introduces a moral pollution that must be expunged, lest it set off an escalating spiral of violence. Perhaps what Yun-ju sees in the mirror is not just his guilty face but the trash; the rice box and the wardrobe that stands in for it. Or indeed, what he sees—offering a way out of his predicament— is the basement itself: a no one's place where things can just be left about. No need to kill the dog and force it into the apartment complex's overarching order. He can simply leave it to die, abandon it. The solution to the dog's order-violating bark is to put it in the very place that at once belongs to the order, indeed originates the order, but also falls outside of it.

The Silent Bark

Watching the second and third scene, an attentive viewer may notice an odd quirk. The dog never barks. Yun-ju later learns that an operation on its vocal cords left it mute; he got the wrong dog. Bong thus exploits cinema's capacity for negative latent perception, showing a lack without explicitly drawing attention to it, and it is quite likely that the viewer won't even notice the silence of the dog until it is pointed out. Because cinema tends to privilege the visual over the auditory—a privilege that remains in effect even after the synchronization of sound and image—the acoustic plays a smaller role in signifying the real. There are, of course, cinematic conventions through which the *reality* of what appears on the screen is called into question, suggesting a flashback, dream, or hallucination, but, in general, we assume that, relative to the ultimately fictional context of narrative film, "what we see is what we get"; that the camera is objective and objectifying—an abstract impersonal eye. This assumption, however, does not and cannot carry over to the acoustic. Film scholars distinguish between diegetic and non-diegetic or extradiegetic components of the soundtrack, and yet the very need to distinguish between sounds that are audible to the characters and sounds that aren't suggests the extent to which the soundtrack undermines the assumption of objectivity.

While visual experience is inherently orienting and auditory experience disorienting, the soundtrack, seemingly joining sound to image, presents a new kind of disorientation: ontological rather than phenomenological. Of itself, the soundtrack is unitary: even with multitrack sound, what reaches the audience's ears is a single continuous acoustic wave. Yet this single wave represents two realms that are only brought together in the viewer's experience. However blurry the line between the diegetic and extradiegetic, the interpretation of the sound-event triages it into one of these two realms, hearing it *as* one or the other. It can only remain undifferentiated at the price of a certain incomprehension. Within the diegetic sound, moreover, a further ambiguity arises: is it a real sound, *heard* by the characters, or an imagined sound, an inner voice—say, the narrator thinking to herself, replaying a melody in her head? Headphones and "personal" stereos, even the humble radio, present a further possibility: a sound can be both *objective* (real rather than imagined) and *subjective* (heard only by one). The cinematic musical soundtrack itself can take up residence in real life, becoming a feature of the reality that cinema in turn represents, as with the radios playing in Peter Bogdanovich's *The Last Picture Show*.

Perhaps only one sound event fully escapes this ambiguity: articulated speech synchronized with the movements of a face. Hearing a voice *and* seeing the corresponding mouth, the voice is immediately located. Hearing a voice without a mouth, one wonders: where is it coming from? And if human lips move as if speaking but no sound comes out, one immediately notices and seeks an explanation. Is it a whisper, an attempt at silent communication? Damaged vocal cords? A deaf listener? A dream? Yet the ambiguity of cinematic sound—its deficiency as signifier of reality—is most evident from the insignificance of the *absence* of context- or event-appropriate sounds. Such sounds may contribute to a sense of the real, but their absence signifies little unless attention is explicitly drawn to this lack. Were we not to hear the softly crashing waves at the end of François Truffaut's *The 400 Blows* (1959), before they are overwhelmed by cloyingly melancholic music, we would not suppose that Antoine, having suffered one blow too many, had become deaf.

Humans rarely bite other humans. This is because we are rational animals, living beings possessing *logos* (language, speech, the word), our mouths and tongues sublimated into tools for articulate communication. Saying "barking dogs never bite" is to grant dogs a place within the human world by insisting that their bark, the effect of domestication, is also a sublimated orality. Yet dogs' place in our human world, even when their exceptional status is legally consecrated, remains shaky.[9] The dog face appears obscure and inexpressive next to the human face; species-being still dominates. We don't attend to its movements as we do to the endlessly subtle permutations of the human face, whose mastery belongs to the actor's art.[10] Dogs can be trained and handled and put on screen, but they will never be actors; even the best-trained dog lacks the fine motor control of facial expressions and bodily gestures. Yun-ju's obliviousness to his first victim's yip-less-ness casts shade at his bookishness, but it also makes an important point about the place of the dog, and its bark, within the cinematic world. While the bark is language-like, language-adjacent, it does not bring the expectation of absolute synchronicity between sound and image; it does not have the same status as human speech. This allows a deepened interpretation of the irritation inflicted by the bark: it is the irritation of that which scuttles and frustrates cinema as an apparatus seeking to *orient* movements, to place them—or in other words, as a cinematic apparatus of philosophy, a spectacular regime of orienting visuality.

Returning to the basement, we could now say that it represents the soundtrack in its essential phenomenological and ontological disorientation. Significantly, the barking, introduced with an intertitle, starts out as non-diegetic—the story has not yet begun— but becomes diegetic the moment we see Yun-ju listening to it and hear him referring to it. Yet Yun-ju never tries to *sort out* the dog's bark. He just abandons it to the basement—a basement already haunted with mysterious noises, attributed by the janitor (Byun Hee-Bong), in his long monologue, to the ghost of the entombed "Boiler Kim," murdered as the lone voice of justice in a corrupt age.[11] The disorienting bark is thus dealt with by returning it to the soundtrack in its original, yet undifferentiated, disorienting ambiguity. But this can only fail. Barking, the dog crosses into the visual cinematic field—it must be located. The soundtrack is always the soundtrack of the film. It is not the bark of the dog but its lamblike sacrificial silence that can be so dispatched.

The Cameral Apartment

All this suggests that the apartment complex, where so much of the film transpires, is not merely a lived environment represented cinematically but an emphatically cinematic space: a space wherein cinema represents itself.[12] The history of cinema abounds with such cinematic spaces. Whenever cinema wants to say something truly cinematic, something no other media can communicate, it must turn its lens upon itself. Some of these spaces—one thinks of *The Truman Show* (1998)—are obvious. Others are more subtle. If *The Wizard of Oz* (1939), a showcase for Technicolor, offers a rather clear allegory for the cinematic imagination machine, Andrei Tarkovsky's strange and somber *Stalker* (1979), shot four decades later in sepia and high-contrast brown monochrome, presents cinema not as a morally ambiguous wizardry but as the unearthly magic of a room in which, upon entering, one's deepest wishes, even without having been announced, come true. The decrepit mansion in Billy Wilder's *Sunset Boulevard* (1950) contains a theater in its living room, where the delusional former star of the silent era endlessly replays her glory. In all these cases, however, the cinematic is conceived primarily in terms of either the projection apparatus or the stage. In *Barking Dogs Never Bite*, in contrast, the cinematic space emphasizes the technical apparatus of cinema and in the first instance the camera itself.

Consider again the first scene: Yun-ju stands against the window, which only becomes visible when, steamed up by his breath, it obstructs the view to the outside. The camera retreats, revealing an apartment room that, contrasted against the natural light from outside, appears almost black. The shot seems to have been filmed with little or no artificial lighting, yet the result is not heightened "realism." While the eye's pupil, like a camera aperture, expands or contracts to control the amount of light hitting the retina, the human eye and visual cortex are more forgiving than analog film. Rather, the exaggerated "washing out" calls attention to the shot's artificiality, turning the room itself into a camera. The word "camera," of course, traces back to the *camera obscura*: the "dark room" employed by

Renaissance painters to facilitate linear perspective. Moreover, the tripartite distinction between the regions of the apartment complex allows a further characterization in terms of the presence of light. Whereas the exterior spaces—rooftop, parking lot—are saturated with sunlight, the basement, especially inside the wardrobe, is cut off from natural light. Hence, the individual apartment unit, where light and darkness meet, unites the extremes represented by the other two regions into a photographic event.

Following Deleuze, we can certainly recognize in this shadow-and-light play the traces of the cosmic struggle, that, prefigured in Goethe's *Zur Farbenlehre* (Theory of Colors) and German Romanticism, would play out, again, in German expressionist cinema.[13] Even more fundamentally, it suggests the interdependent and complementary relation of *yin* and *yang* as the conceptual matrix organizing the East Asian worldview. In one of the earliest recorded usages, *yin* and *yang* conveyed the effect of the sun reflecting off a hill; the sunny side was *yang*, the shady side *yin*.[14] From this basic complementarity of light and darkness emerges a system of rhythmically alternating differences encompassing all beings. But it also suggests the movie camera's fundamental ambiguity. While providing a tool for liberating movement, allowing it to appear as an event, the camera also signifies the privatization, "cameralization," and bureaucratization of political life: the transformation of the fundamental representational space of the *polis* from the *agora* and *amphitheater*—"open" spaces of mutual visibility—to the private chamber, office, bureau, or individual apartment. Just as the cropping of a photograph *cuts out* the rest of the world—and every photo is a cropping of reality—the cameralized spaces of modernity *fragment* a shared world into discrete private components.[15] Even the integrity of the body—for Ancient political philosophy a microcosmic representation of an ideal political order that organizes the harmoniously ordered *cosmos* as a whole—

succumbs. As Jean Epstein, describing the cinematic "upheaval in the hierarchy of things," writes: "The image of an eye, a hand, or a mouth filling up the entire screen—not only because it is magnified three hundred fold, but also because we see it severed from its organic community—acquires the autonomous character of an animal"; "this eye, these fingers, these lips are beings, each possessing its own frontiers, its movement, its life, and its own ends."[16] The Ancient Greeks could only conceive of politics in terms of a radical publicness; hence even the antidemocratic Plato must demand the king be philosopher and the philosopher be king.[17] Monarchy is justifiable only if the king has privileged access to the most radically public form of truth; democracy troubles Plato precisely because the *agora*'s openness is the pseudo-openness of the cave. Beginning with Hobbes, modern thinkers will understand the radically public sphere as the state of nature: *homo homini lupus* is not only a statement about action but appearances. Man is a wolf to man because, in nature's perfectly open space—the originary political space—the human being, no longer a political animal but exposed in his original asociality, cannot but *appear* as a wolf. Consequently, a political order can no longer exist through an order of *nomos* (customary laws) more or less continuous with *physis* (nature): rather, a private and protected sphere must be carved out from within an open, originary political space of nature. Private, protected—but not closed: not a perfect monad, but a monad with a window or even just a little hole. Through this window, the common political space is projected against an individual wall of autonomy, freedom, and spiritual independence and gets translated into its terms. This flattens the political into individual cares. It is no longer the wild, savage, errant movement that must be oriented within a public space, but the mass movement of history, penetrating through windows and walls, that gets comprehended within, and fit into, the cameral order of private life. The "masses" are the paradoxical form in which the originally political appears in the *camera obscura* of atomized privacy.

If man is a wolf to man in the state of nature, within the chambered, partitioned units of the Korean apartment complex—the perfect realization of the "cameralized" political space of modernity—all that remains of the wolf-man is a dog; the howl, separated from the bite, has become a bark. Yet the bite-less bark, at once a symptom of domestication and "non-violent" protest against domestication, is also a voice of revolutionary unrest. A would-be, will-be humanities professor, Yun-ju hears the bark as a disturbance penetrating his private space, keeping him from his studies, blocking the path to professional success. He does not yet comprehend that the profession to which he aspires consists in nothing else than orienting, managing, quelling just such revolutionary yips.

The Absent City

The city of Seoul only ever appears as a hazy backdrop, its sprawl merely intimated. We are never once granted a panoramic view; we never see the streams of cars, buses, motorcycles, and scooters coursing through the city, never feel the ceaseless, intoxicating urban metabolism. The Seoul of *Barking Dogs Never Bite* is unmistakably Seoul, but stripped of all iconic symbols, landmarks, and even the picturesque relics of its less prosperous past. It is city as an ensemble of *any-space-whatevers* (*l'espace quelconque*), to use the term Deleuze borrows from the French anthropologist Marc Augé.[18]

By excluding every synoptic or comprehensive perspective, allowing the city to appear only as a collection of anonymous fragments, Bong confirms the claustrophobic purity of the apartment complex as a cinematic space, focusing on its cameral internal configuration (the *camera obscura*) rather than its ultimate product, the projected image. Were Bong to show the city in a semblance of totality, he would have situated his film within the "rationalized" representational space that the camera imposes on the world, with local places appearing as parts of a totality: *the* modern city, and indeed, *this* city—Seoul. We'd see the city as the camera sees it: a wondrous-monstrous totality of interconnected human and physical parts. As it is, however, almost all the other settings, with a few important exceptions, appear not as locations within the city's vast sprawl but as repetitions of the spaces within the apartment complex, or indeed of one space above all: the individual camera-like apartment unit. There is no real escape from within the "cameral" political space of modernity, which tries again and again to work out a resolution between the private and public, exterior and interior.

This allows for a more concrete sociological and historical interpretation. The individual apartment unit is principally the home of the nuclear family: Yun-ju and his pregnant wife Bae Eun-sil (Kim Ho-jung). Just as the camera, as a paradigmatic modern space and political form, joins political and private, external and internal, the apartment becomes the site of a complex mediation between intimate family life and public life.

In Chosŏn Korea, the affluent dwelled in walled-in complexes with well-defined women's quarters. An outsider would have been forbidden passage through the inner gate into the space reserved for women and children.[19] Modernity brings the education of women and their incorporation into the workplace, and, consequently, the domestic sphere, while relatively segregated, becomes riven by those tensions that arise whenever conflicting hierarchical codes come into conflict. Financially dependent on his slightly older wife as he struggles to find an academic position, Yun-ju's actual situation mocks his legally enshrined status as "head of family." She barks orders at him, buys a dog without asking, and has him crack open walnuts for her with a hammer.

In one particularly telling scene, Yun-ju and his wife walk back to the apartment at night, with him trailing behind dog-like as she affectionately clutches her poodle. When he complains about the new family member, she suddenly stops and, sticking money in his face, demands that he return to the convenience store and buy some strawberry milk—for the dog. Arguing over how far away the store is, they agree to settle it through a bet: if he wins, they'll send the dog off to the country; if she wins, he'll have to call her *nuna*. Accepting the bet, he begins marking off the distance with his steps, while she mocks him: he's walking back to the store just as she wanted him to. Then he seizes one of the toilet paper rolls—exactly 100 meters in length—and sends it rolling down the street.

Nuna, translated as "older sister," literally means the older sister of a male, though its use often extends to cousins and other members within an intimate circle. *Oppa*, the correlative word of address, is used for a female's older male sibling. As Lee Kyounghoon argues, the term *oppa* plays an important role in the changing social landscape of Korea at the turn of the twentieth century: originating in traditional family life, its extension from consanguine relations to male-female friendships and even erotic relationships allows for the emergence of a "connection among youth that is relatively more equal and horizontal."[20] Relatively more: since a trace of the hierarchical still imposes itself on horizontal relations, and, consequently, the more the traditional Neo-Confucian order breaks down—the more that public horizontal spaces come into play—the more forcefully they remain organized by a vertical logic, so much so that, by the end of the twentieth century, it could seem like *oppa* was the Trojan horse through which Neo-Confucian patriarchy survived into modernity. A sign of this residual hierarchy is the asymmetry in the usage between *nuna* and *oppa*: *oppa* is frequently and easily extended beyond family relations, and it is not unusual for a wife to refer to her slightly older husband as *oppa*. But for a slightly younger husband to refer to his wife as *nuna* is far less common. Age and gender are different, potentially conflicting, hierarchical codes: it is only when they align—when the husband is slightly older—that the sibling-expression carries over to the non-consanguine relationship between spouses. Yun-ju cannot be an *oppa* since he is younger than his wife, but he still considers it degrading to call his wife *nuna*.

Moreover, their argument, and accompanying bet, hinges on the measurement of the familiar spaces of everyday life. The rationalization of space and time is, of course, a characteristic feature of modernity, and Korea, with its compressed modernity, experienced this transformation in an especially traumatizing way. Hence trains and clocks, "measuring and segmenting time and space according to a new criterion," figure so prominently in colonial-era Korean literature.[21] And by having Yun-ju roll out toilet paper to measure the distance, suggesting cinema's strips of celluloid film, Bong identifies the movie camera itself with the rationalized time and space of modernity. Since film ordinarily passes through the camera at a constant speed—though in *Barking Dogs Never Bite* variable speeds are used to cartoonish effect—a simple arithmetic relation exists between length and duration. Hence the camera functions as a system of ordering, at once causing and resolving the conflict between private and public, interior and exterior.

Many of the film's other settings are also intimate public spaces where this conflict continues to play out and which thus reduplicate the original camera space. These are semipublic, extrafamilial spaces, and yet far from giving room to horizontal, nonhierarchical relations, they remain determined by hierarchy. One could hardly expect otherwise in the bank and apartment office—formal work environments—but hierarchy appears in the most exaggerated and preposterous form in precisely those new public spaces that should allow horizontal, "collegial" relations. At a departmental dinner in a dingy restaurant, a collegial event of fellow unemployed or underemployed scholars bemoaning their common plight, we find a female colleague, sandwiched between men, speaking with the inflectional pattern of *aegyo* (cuteness). But she is also wearing a golden necklace, and when Yun-ju cannot pay for his ugly red shirt and drinks, she offers to cover him, addressing him as *hyŏng*—just as a younger brother would address an older—thus acknowledging a difference of age but not of gender. When he runs into her afterward at the apartment complex, we learn that she is tutoring students there—something he could just as well do, gaining some measure of financial independence, were he to swallow his pride. Even the public restroom, modernity's most egalitarian space, becomes the site for a hierarchical relation. After demanding that toilet paper be brought to his stall in a moment of intimate urgency, Joon-pyo (Im Sang-soo), as if rewarding Yun-ju for his subservience, tells the story of Min Namgoong's rise and fall: how he bribed the dean while studying in Germany and how he fell into the subway tracks.[22] "Even a Ph.D.'s head is no match for a train."

With both standing against bathroom walls, Joon-pyo's face stares directly at the camera, laughing with cynical confidence, while Yun-ju, visible only in profile, his chin bent down, sinks into the shadows. As Joon-pyo narrates, we see a flashback of Min's fateful evening, beginning at the room salon, where, sitting with "hostesses," the dean forces him to drink.

The room salon's table takes up the bottom of the screen and then narrows with dramatically visible lines of sight, producing a parallax effect resembling the jury table in *12 Angry Men* (1957). This itself is striking: the jury table (a paradigmatic instance of a cameralized public space) becomes a showcase for hierarchical relations. Reaching across the table with another shot of whiskey for Min, the dean, who "drinks like a madman," compels his new junior colleague, no drinker himself, to drink more and more. The dean's head appears in almost the same place as Joon-pyo's; even in telling the story to his friend and peer—they address each other by first name—he reproduces, or indeed aspires to, the toxic hierarchical relations he describes. In subsequent cutbacks to the bathroom, Yun-ju's head appears as a shrunken blurry reflection in the mirror behind Joon-pyo. As the narration progresses, Yun-ju eventually comes into sharp focus, whereas Joon-pyo is blurred and shadowed out (Figures 1 and 2). Yet we are still only seeing Yun-ju's mirror image, though this is clear solely from the syntagmatic relationship between frames.

In this ingenuous manner, Bong not only provides the reaction shot demanded by the narrative while emphasizing Yun-ju's almost ontological degradation but indeed turns the bathroom—like the apartment room—into a camera. Cinematic realism demands a back-and-forth between two expressive faces with the words registering as visible affect; expressionism distorts the real to expose a deeper truth. By simultaneously fulfilling the contradictory demands of both stylistic codes, Bong reveals the tension between them, a tension

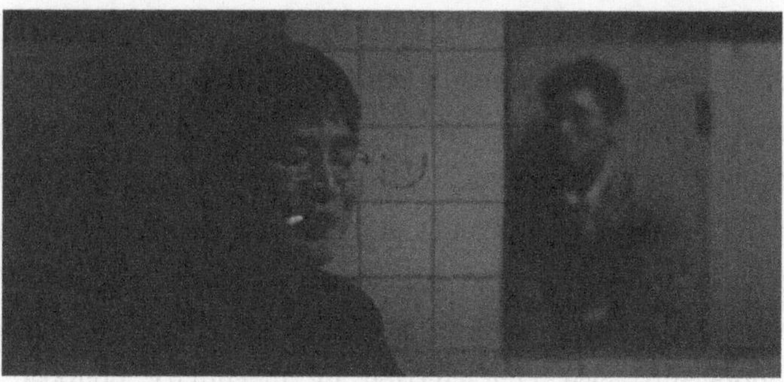

Figure 1 Barking Dogs Never Bite *directed by Bong Joon Ho.* © Cinema Service *2000. All rights reserved.*

Figure 2 Barking Dogs Never Bite *directed by Bong Joon Ho. © Cinema Service 2000. All rights reserved.*

cutting to the quick of what cinema is. For whatever cinema shows, however realistically it shows what it shows, it inevitably distorts simply by calling attention to it, wresting it from the ordinary context of lived experience, projecting it onto the big screen; cinema's realism is allegorical, expressionist, surreal. Even the bathroom itself, with its row of urinals, becomes an exhibition chamber where the world's dirty secrets are flushed out into the open, but then—like Marcel Duchamp's "Fountain"—metabolized back into art.

Hierarchy matters in this scene because it is hardly inevitable, let alone essentially Korean or Asian. Least inevitable of all are those hierarchies that, pretending to be meritocratic, are at once rigidly institutionalized and continually reinforced through semi-ritualized expressions of humiliation and obsequiousness. Late Chosŏn Korea was doubtless a rigidly hierarchical society, featuring an ossified caste system replete with slaves and outcastes. But this hierarchy never ceased to be problematic, and indeed the *Sattelzeit*—Song Ho-Keun's apt expression for the transitional period between the Chosŏn dynasty and modernity—was characterized by incendiary political and religious movements such as the Tonghak peasant revolution, which, rebelling against corrupt elites while rejecting Westernization, sought a return to a purified Neo-Confucianism.[23] Following liberation from Japanese colonial rule and the catastrophe of the Korean War, which left the peninsula divided and technically without peace, the 1970s saw the rise of the Minjung movement. Regarding oppressed and marginalized members of Korean society as the essence of the Korean nation, Minjung provided the main ideological framework for the democracy movement in which Bong actively participated.[24]

Bong shows a society where hierarchies not only still play a role but where nothing conceals their violence, ugliness, and cruelty. He refuses to naturalize them by hiding them behind striking physical differences. And indeed, despite being a comedy, if darkly, *Barking Dogs Never Bite* rigorously avoids the comical depotentialization of the hierarchical. In contrast, the overwhelming tendency of so much American film and TV is both to naturalize and depotentialize, as if to say: here in America, everyone is equal under the law, more or less, but people are so wildly different that natural hierarchies exist, and yet, through a constant exercise of humor, we can pretend that they don't even while they do.

Octopus Girl

The original Korean title—*p'ŭllandasŭŭi kae*—translates to "The Dog of Flanders," the name of an 1872 novel by the English writer Marie Louise de la Ramée, writing under the pen name Ouida, about a boy who aspires to be a great painter but, following his grandfather's death, is left alone in the world with only his dog. There is no triumph over adversity, no heartwarming happy ending: evoking H. C. Andersen's *Den lille Pige med Svovlstikkerne* (The Little Matchgirl), the boy and his dog, left penniless, freeze to death on Christmas Eve.[25] The more immediate reference for the film, however, is a 1975 Japanese TV series closely based on the book and widely broadcast in Korea.[26] The closing credit music is indeed a jazz version of the cartoon's theme song.

The comedic dimension of the film, this suggests, is *cartoonish*, as suggested by the combination of slow and normal-speed shots. Also telling is his decision to cast Bae Doona as Hyun-nam—the rather ignorant bookkeeper—based on not only her plain way of speaking but also her gestures, which resembled an "octopus girl [*nakchisonyŏ*]."[27] This seemingly casual remark—small octopuses (*nakchi*), eaten still wriggling, are a prized delicacy in Korea—connects the film's cartoonish aesthetics to Eisenstein's extraordinary reflections on Walt Disney. Referring to the "silly symphony" *Merbabies* (1938), Eisenstein writes:

> As an unforgettable symbol of his whole creative work, there stands before me a family of octopuses on four legs, with a fifth serving as a tail, and a sixth—a trunk. How much (imaginary) divine omnipotence there is in this! What magic of reconstructing the world according to one's fantasy and will! [. . .] You tell a mountain: move, and it moves. You tell an octopus: be an elephant, and the octopus becomes an elephant. You ask the sun to stop, and it stops.[28]

The protean octopus—changing shape, color, and skin texture to mimic its surroundings—becomes the symbol for the art of animation, whose magic rests in absolute command over appearances. Its very plasticity is a revolt, if ultimately lyrical and futile, against the regimented space-time of capitalist modernity:

> Disney is a marvelous lullaby for the suffering and unfortunate, the oppressed and deprived. For those who are shackled by hours of work and regulated moments of rest, by a mathematical precision

of time, whose lives are graphed by the cent and the dollar. Whose lives are divided up into little squares, like a chess board, [. . .] all of a protective grey colour, day and day. Grey, grey, grey. From birth to death. Grey squares of city blocks. Grey prison cells of city streets. Grey faces of endless street crowds. The grey, empty eyes of those who are forever at the mercy of a pitiless process of laws, not of their own making, laws that divide up the soul, feelings, thoughts, just as the carcasses of pigs are dismembered by the conveyor belts of Chicago slaughterhouses, and the separate pieces of cars are assembled into mechanical organisms by Ford's conveyor belts.[29]

Cut to the apartment complex with its precise grid. Cut to the subway. Cut to *Okja*. Hyun-nam is the *Urform* of Bong's cinematic revolt against the contemporary world's Procrustean order. *Octopus girl against the world*. She resists not by mockery, not by mastering social codes, not by ironizing hierarchy to the point of dissolution, but by refusing, in her primordial cluelessness, to understand the world at all. But this lets her live in it as if in a cartoon. Chasing the bad guy she runs into a door, a military aircraft flies overhead, she falls backward—perhaps the purest instance of Einsteinian dialectical montage in all Bong's oeuvre. The deepest site of resistance is the fluid movement of limbs, the "triumph over the fetters of form," a bendy, twisty way.[30] The corporeal fluidity of the cartoon finds an analogue in *aegyo*, cute displays of affection expressed through vocal and physical plasticity: pouting, duck faces, a babyish voice with an accentuated wah-wah-like melody, silly gestures, even a slumping or slouching posture. And also in body modification through plastic surgery, pursuing an aesthetic idea that finds its archetype in Minnie Mouse's large eyes, moon-shaped mouth, and button nose.[31] What is so striking about Bae Doona, however, is a kind of natural, unforced *aegyo*, perfectly suited to playing a character whose pliant resistance has something mythic about it.

Such cartoonish comedy, again, is altogether different from the kind of comedy, now so characteristic of American film and television, that takes hierarchy as natural and inevitable yet seeks to strip it of its potency, ironizing hierarchical relations through virtuoso displays of wit.[32] Such wit shows that the established conceptual, political, social, ideological order forms on a void, yet far from undermining the order, ironizing wit upholds it by allowing a temporary escape into the revelry of its absurdity—a comedic saturnalia. Cartoonish comedy, in contrast, shows us a radical, originary realm of freedom: a freedom prior to the constituted bourgeois individual, prior to the self, prior to the ego; the protean fluidity of the body, of movement itself, of a form of life hovering between the human and the animal. Above all: the potency of fire: "Not light, but precisely flame. The variability of its living forms."[33] Disney's animation reveals the flame imprisoned in the projector's electric bulb, the flame behind the light. Returning to Plato's cave, our heads are turned around the other way: toward the fire. Here we find another freedom, another liberation. Perhaps it's only because the captives never have the chance to look back to the fire that they are forced to venture upward, searching for the sun.

Fire finds its way back into Hollywood as explosion. The final message of so many Hollywood blockbuster films, when all the layers of transient meaning are sloughed off, boils down to this: we can worship fire only in the machinery of weaponized death—only as death star, Oppenheimer's gadget, an endless procession of exploding cars, buildings, gunfire; sensuous flames bursting from the muzzle of a machine gun. Even David Fincher's *Fight Club* (1999), an homage to hand-to-hand combat, ends with a gunshot and explosions, skyscrapers collapsing in eerie anticipation of 9/11. The gun becomes the counterpart to the *caméra-stylo*. Quintessential hand tool—grasped, clutched, fingered—it becomes the locus of an identification that, not emotional or cognitive but praxiological, concerns what the characters can *do*, how they can exploit the concrete physical potential of the situation to achieve their ends. Identifying with on-screen characters who can only destroy, we simultaneously identify with the auteur-director, whose creative work—its organizational and interpersonal (social) dimension utterly obscured—now appears as a procession of memorable, stylish *shots*. Stylized violence is the altar on which we worship a Moloch, allowing us fire only as the means of sacrifice, self-immolation.

No director is so closely identified with stylized violence as Quentin Tarantino. But as much as he was an early influence on Bong, stylized violence is the exact opposite of cartoonish violence.[34] What makes for stylized violence is not the presence of style but the absence of emotional identification and affective resonance. Stylized losers are gangsters. Style shields them like body armor, making an empathic connection impossible, not least since, if they are vulnerable enough to get killed, this is due to an aesthetic failure: they weren't cool enough to hide from the world the losers that they are. When Vincent Vega (John Travolta) accidentally shoots Marvin (Phil LaMarr) after their car hits a bump, splattering his brains over the windows and upholstered seats, we laugh because Marvin, despite his vulnerability, can elicit no sympathy within a cinematic universe that, closed in upon itself, only refers to cinema. The very lack of emotional gravitas allows the viewer to celebrate mastery of the closed universe of cinematic references. Marsellus Wallace (Ving Rhames)'s suitcase, the sublime object of desire around which *Pulp Fiction* (1994) revolves, opens to reveal a mysterious, obscenely beautiful radiance. What is this radiance if not style itself, the saturated technicolor surface that peels off from the world after its substance, its heart and its brains and its courage, have been scrupulously cleaned up by the impeccably dapper "cleaner" Winston Wolfe (Harvey Keitel), the only voice of fatherly authority that still commands respect.

Bong takes the style of Tarantino—the cleverly asynchronous narrative, the playful appropriation of genre conventions—but he applies them to turn-of-the-millennium Korean society. These devices clash jarringly with the radical sincerity of a world whose emotional palette is anchored in *han* and *chŏng* (情) and whose quintessential cultural form is melodrama with its roots in *p'ansori*, musical narratives performed with a singer and drum.[35] With a deftness and integrity verging on miraculous, Bong not only negotiates this contradiction, even revels in it, but brings it to the highest pitch of dialectical expressiveness.

Incoherence

Pulp Fiction weaves together four different asynchronous storylines that converge in the final scene. Bong attempted something similar in *Incoherence* (1994), yet in this short-format student film, the deep sincerity of Bong's worldview, nourished in his days of student radicalism, is as much on display as his intuitive grasp of cinematic language. The incoherence of the title is real rather than formal: the three storylines converge as all three protagonists, having committed various trivial yet shameful acts, appear on a talk show to discuss the moral crisis of today's youth. Far from inviting us to take aesthetic pleasure in a dissonant, unresolved narrative, we are presented, in rather didactic fashion, with an almost Rousseauian jeremiad against the moral incoherence of a society that invests a compromised human/all-too-human elite with moral authority.

This is very much an inside critique. Bong—grandson of an important writer, son of a professor of graphic design, alumnus of one of the three so-called SKY universities—was destined to become a member of the intellectual and moral elite that he parodies. Yet we shouldn't interpret it merely as a transient expression of generational conflict, doomed to succumb to the hypocrisy it decries. The significance of the class of ethically authoritative, socially and politically enfranchised intellectuals traces back to the Chosŏn dynasty. As Song explains:

> Joseon [Chosŏn] was a nation of *mun* (文). Mun was at once its worldview and character as well as its religion and philosophy of governance. [. . .] To Joseon scholars and bureaucrats, *mun* revealed the source of truth, as well as its means of fulfillment and manner of execution. Their lives began and ended with *mun*. *Mun* was that which conveyed the Way (*jaedojigi*). To say that one was "skilled at writing" meant that one's scope of knowledge of the world was deep and wide, that one had achieved self-introspection and fulfilled the essence of one's nature, and thus that the character of a writer was such that one was qualified to be a leader of men. Self-cultivation was a precondition for the craft of writing (*munjang*), [which] provided a measure indicating the level of one's self-discipline, as well as a sign representing to what extent one maintained a grasp of Heavenly *i*.[36]

Song's larger argument hinges on the role of intellectuals in modern Korea's political consciousness, which demanded recognizing the people no longer merely as the passive object of governance but as politically enfranchised, as the subject of politics, leading eventually to notions of civil society and of an individually enfranchised citizen conducive to Western-style liberal democracy. Of special importance is the emergence of a public sphere in the vernacular language (the phonetically written *han'gŭl*), effectively taking the place of the elite *wen/mun* (文), the literature written in Chinese characters mastered only by the Confucian scholarly and administrative elite. His own account ends during the thwarted modernity of the colonial period, and with a civic literature that, despite its political pretensions, was "produced by a society stripped of autonomy . . . citizens in a cave."[37]

Song's conclusion suggests that nearly a century later, these issues remain unresolved, despite Korea having become an economic success story, a soft-power powerhouse, and one of East Asia's most flourishing, if chaotic, democracies. But if its citizens are still in the cave, it is precisely because they have not been liberated from their Neo-Confucian, quasi-Platonic philosopher-kings—their would-be liberators—who, despite having switched to the vernacular, have never ceased to speak for the people by speaking about them and around them, excluding their voice in the very moment they become their mouthpiece.

Bong's radical ethical sincerity, this suggests, is the sincerity of the artist, the intellectual, who recognizes that artists and intellectuals still have a role to play in society, however contradictory and doomed to failure this role may be. Yet perhaps what is impossible in the element of words is not impossible in the visual-kinetic medium of film. Once again, Eisenstein's theory of montage offers a suggestive hint. During the nineteen twenties, Eisenstein spent time in Japan, studying Kabuki theater and becoming intrigued with the seemingly ideographic Chinese characters incorporated into written Japanese, eventually learning several hundred glyphs.[38] In his essay "The Cinematographic Principle and the Ideogram," he argues that, though the fledgling Japanese cinema lacked montage, "the principle of montage can be identified as the basic element of Japanese representational culture."[39] This montage, however, consists not merely in combining ideas into a new unity or the imagistic layering of feelings, but in bringing together the rational and the sensual, concept and image, abstract and concrete. Alluding to Heinrich von Kleist's essay "Über das Marionettentheater" (On the Marionette Theater), he writes:

> And, just as the two outspreading wings of a hyperbola meet, as we say, at infinity (though no one has visited so distant a region!), so the principle of hieroglyphics, infinitely splitting into two parts (in accordance with the function of symbols), unexpectedly unites again from this dual estrangement, in yet a fourth sphere—in the theater.[40]

Each ideograph is a dialectical image, an image of conflict: conflict frozen into an image, unfolding from the image.

In Korea, a vernacular literary culture was achieved with *han'gŭl*, a phonetic syllabic script.[41] Introduced in 1443 by King Sejong, *han'gŭl* did not come into extensive and comprehensive use until the modern era; now it is not only used for morphological elements of Korean and "pure Korean" vocabulary but also for Sino-Korean words traditionally represented through *hanja*. While the marginalization of *hanja* facilitated literacy among common people, this came at a cost. A given phonetic representation may correspond to several distinct characters—more even than already the case with Chinese, since the Korean phonetic system cannot distinguish different tones or the final /r/.[42] While most Sino-Korean words are formed from two or more Chinese characters, a bewildering degree of homophony remains. Interpretation becomes heavily context-dependent, and even highly educated Koreans struggle to recognize the root meanings from which words are built, while the nuances of meaning conveyed graphically by *hanja*, not to speak of the rich system of associations upon which Chinese literacy had traditionally depended, fall into oblivion. Having lost access to the deepest element of montage— the montage-power, or even the dialectical power of language—the

Korean public sphere is deprived of a powerful expressive means for developing a discourse around the richly articulated, nuanced concept of the people. The situation is only made worse with the importation of Western learning, which soon became another token of prestige, a signifier of elite status. Cinema, with its native command of the deep power of visual montage, has a special social and political vocation. It brings *mun* to the masses.

The Tripartite Soul

In *Barking Dogs Never Bite*, Bong again weaves together multiple narrative strands. His approach, however, is more subtle, less obviously imitative of *Pulp Fiction*. For while the different narrative strands converge at the conclusion of the movie, they also intersect along the way. Furthermore, they are unified through the cinematic space of the apartment complex. Bong's deepened understanding of cinema, moreover, becomes clear in the narrative threads themselves. These are as follows:

(1)　An unemployed academic (Ko Yun-ju) who seeks to secure a permanent position as professor. His wife, Eun-sil (Kim Ho-jung), is eight months pregnant.

(2)　(Hyun-nam), a bookkeeper at the apartment complex who pursues the dog-killer. Yoon Jang-mi, her friend, owns a toy and stationery store in the complex.

(3)　The janitor/guard (Byun Hee-Bong), who likes to eat dog stew.

There are also several characters weaving in and out of these primary threads. The most important of these "shifters" is the homeless man who lives in the basement of the apartment, stealing the janitor's stew, and who is eventually apprehended by Hyun-nam as he tries to kill Eun-sil's dog. It seems significant, moreover, that the "shifters" represent the most subaltern characters: a widowed, family-less woman, a beggar with a child, and a homeless man—the truly marginalized outsiders of Korean society. Finally, there are two abstract or anonymous characters: the "boss" (=the dean, and the bosses at the bank and the apartment management office) and the "dog" (The Shih Tzu, Min Pin, and Toy Poodle). These characters represent extreme limits of the social order: the absolute oppressor and the absolutely oppressed.

These three main narrative threads correspond to the Platonic threefold division of the soul—the contemplative, the spirited, and the appetitive—and, accordingly, to the threefold social division of labor that it both justifies and mirrors.[43] Yet all three tendencies of the soul assume a parodic form. The janitor carries abandoned junk into his basement, practices his swing with a tossed-away golf club, and covets the traditional Korean dog-meat stew—*poshint'ang*—believed by *ajŏssi* (middle-aged men) to promote virility and sexual stamina. The ambition of the "spirited" part of the soul, desiring fame and honor, finds absurd expression in Hyun-nam. Inspired by a news report glorifying the heroism of a bank teller who beat up a would-be robber, she pursues the dog-murderer in the hope of television fame, only to find herself left out when the dog-killer's arrest makes the news. Finally, there is Yun-ju himself, whose struggle to become a professor, forcing him to confront the gap between his naïve ideals and the world's corruption, suggests the plight of the penurious Confucian scholars of yore, whose path to advancement within the putatively meritocratic bureaucracy was often thwarted by corruption and nepotism. As a member of the intelligentsia, he should be hip to the ideologies structuring society. Yet he fails to penetrate its biggest: the myth of meritocracy. He imagines that something could be socially prestigious without the taint of corruption lurking at the heart of all prestige; that "the life of the mind" could exist in the world without being of the world.

Atelic Desire/*han*

Because each of these three narrative threads can be identified primarily in terms of a central, clearly articulated desire, each takes the form of a quest—not only the most fundamental narrative form but the basic form of human action (*praxis*) as understood by Aristotle. As animals *having* language, human beings posit goals and pursue them. Even a purely physical desire assumes a human form when put into words, since what is desirable *to me now in this situation* thereby gets recognized as a general "good."[44] Each, moreover, lives out a vision of happiness which is, simultaneously, the vision of fully and happily occupying the social class where such happiness is possible. There can be no radical contradiction between the desire for the social status of professor and the desire to live the *vita contemplativa*; within the class structure of Korean—and, of course, not just Korean—society, the former becomes the condition of the latter, since human activity assumes an irreducibly social form. Our desires are never simply private desires, ensconced within a solipsistic soul, but communicated desires, comprehensible to all.

But is this the only form desire can take? Or is there not, rather, a desire irreducible to teleology, maybe even resistant to all linguistic expression and formalization? Or perhaps even movements of the soul, events of our inner lives, that, no longer able to be characterized as desire, are radically *atelic*. If these express themselves, it is through pure gestures: gestures that, devoid of communicative intention, reveal a mystery of the self that consists not in desire but in resistance to desire. Is there, in other words, a desire, a fundamental movement of the soul, that cannot be situated and oriented within the social order?

Watching *Barking Dogs Never Bite*, one is struck by the depth of its secondary characters. Eun-sil, Yun-ju's wife, certainly serves within *his* narrative as both helper and hinderer, yet an aspect of her cannot be reduced to a functional relation to Yun-ju's desire. Something remains incomprehensible, mysterious. This reveals itself when, already eight months pregnant, she purchases a toy poodle. In a dramatically intense, indeed melodramatic, scene, strikingly at odds with the film's dark-comic tone, Eun-sil is sitting on the floor in traditional Korean fashion, her downcast face mostly obscured, while Yun-ju enters from behind her. She throws walnuts at him—he hurls the hammer at the window. The camera now peers through the gaping hole while, the argument reaching its climax, each reveals their *han*, that quintessentially Korean sense of bitter, resentful sorrow at a life whose promise and potential have been somehow thwarted.

> Him: Ki-jung became a professor. So did Ju-hyun. Who do you
> think you are? I'm desperate for pennies, and you bought that
> dog? And eat walnuts all the time?
> Her: You idiot! Do you know what she is?
> Him: What? What is she?
> Her: I bought her with my severance pay. You think it's easy
> for a pregnant woman to keep a job? Eleven years with the
> company, and all I get is $13,000 [16,480,000 KRW]. Did I buy
> anything I wanted? I paid 300$ [400,000 KRW] for her! And I
> was going to use the rest to make you a professor. What was I
> thinking!

Hers is the typical fate of working women in Korea. From the duration of her employment, we can assume she started working immediately after college, perhaps to support her husband through graduate school, only to sacrifice her own career and independence for her husband's as she enters into her new, socially ordained role as mother to his children.[45] Soon her life will be diapers and nap-times, baby carriages and play dates, and then school, private academies, supplementary tutoring, the CSAT (College Scholastic Ability Test), college admissions: in short, the bitter struggle to reproduce in one's children the class position that she, as a woman in a patriarchal society, is responsible for without ever quite inhabiting. But given this, it seems even more inexplicable that the *one* thing she'd buy herself is a dog: another living being to care for, another mouth to feed. She even gives the dog the name Soon-ja, a seemingly ordinary Korean female name that nevertheless stands out both because Japanese-style women's names ending with *ja* had long fallen from favor, and because the dog would share the name both with the wife of former president Chun Doo-hwan and with a notorious female serial killer, executed a few years before the film's release. Even in Western countries, giving a completely human name to a pet is rather unusual; all the more so in Korea, where complex protocols govern the naming of children. Moreover, the likely Chinese characters of Soon-ja (順子) mean "obey" and "child." It is as if, on the verge of motherhood, Eun-sil split her baby into two: one baby, the dog-baby, the obedient child, belonging to herself alone, obedient to her desire, and the other baby, which, born human into the human world, will eventually belong to the world and not to her.

If the dog obeys her desire, it is because it exists outside the worldly desire of becoming *something*: it is obedient only to the desire to exist, for "bare life." The birth of the human child, as Hannah Arendt argued in *The Human Condition*, represents a radically new beginning, disclosing pure possibility; the child immediately becomes the locus of desire, ambition—first its parents, then its own. A dog, in contrast, will never really become something other than what it already is. It is not a center of narrative desire, of the pursuit of happiness. Happiness, so Aristotle argues, cannot be attributed to animals; animals live outside the horizon of praxis.[46] And yet to the life of each animal belongs a specific kind of pleasure.[47] As pleasure without relation to happiness or unhappiness, the toy dog—a useless dog—hints at a resistance to the desire that captivates us, holding us hostage to the need to become something. Ultimately, what she learned from marriage and work is that her ambitions never belonged to her, were always the ambitions of others; the only desire that can truly be her own is a desire without ambition, without narrative, without purpose—such a desire as might belong to the Daoist sage, who, at times, appears quite like the *cynic*, literally "dog-like," Diogenes.

The "dog," the ultimate "shifter" in the narrative—playing a role in all three threads—gathers all that cannot be assimilated into the teleological frame; its narrative function is to offer a point of resistance to the telic logic of narration. Dog is dog, but also God: a *Higher Animal*—as the movie is also known in English.

Behaviorism

By the end of the film, husband and wife are finally united in a common purpose—his purpose. She carefully arranges a cake filled with the bribe for the dean, around ten thousand dollars in crisp, new bills. He meets the dean at the same room salon, gives him the cake, submits to the same forced drinking that led to Min's death. Meanwhile Jang-mi (Go Su-hee) gets plastered with Hyun-nam, consoling her for her failure to get on television. The juxtaposition of these two scenes reveals alcohol's ambiguous function: a tool of enforcing hierarchy, a mechanism of social violence, but also a tool of forgetting; a *pharmakon* in the double sense, both poison and antidote for *han*.

Yun-ju, however, survives the subway ride and, having made his way home, falls asleep next to his wife. Now he's a professor. He is gazing out a window at the trees, and the camera, after resting on his head, slowly pulls back just as in the opening scene. He's no longer at his apartment but in a small lecture hall. His "cameralization" is complete; he has an official position, and indeed, even if he were teaching at a private university—the view from the window suggests Yonsei, Bong's own alma mater—he is a quasi-bureaucrat, presiding over a privileged interior, public-private, space. Wearing a suit, no longer hunched in upon himself, he exudes confidence, as if he'd become the position he now occupies—through hard work to be sure but also through his wife's sacrifice and his own crime. His assistant lowers the screen. "Today we'll look at some charts on modern behaviorism." He orders his assistant to close the shades; the room succumbs to darkness as the last window, out of which he is looking, is blocked off. His face appears in a dim light, full and round, tilted slightly to the left; his gaze has something weary, melancholy about it. His mouth opens into the slight hint of a smile, and then his eyelids sink. He is certainly not looking at the slides. . . . Perhaps he is dreaming . . . Of Hyun-nam? Of the trees and the forest? And now we see Hyun-nam's head, from behind, a blurry forest of trees in front of her. Birds chirp in the background. She turns to the left, facing the camera, then turns to the right and starts walking, and Jang-mi comes into view, passing her from behind. Jazz music begins to play and the closing credits scroll down the screen. There is no window, no room, no camera. They are outside.

We recall Yun-ju's first words: "Ah, what a nice day! I'd like to go hiking and take a nap on the mountain." His ambition is one thing, his wish another. He realized his ambition, to be sure, but perhaps this ambition, like his wife's, also doesn't really belong to him. Yet now, with his success, it will become impossible for him to recognize this; to see past his ambition, to see through it, to resist the demands society will place on him. This wish was just a whim, a velleity—the very faintest degree of volition—only just happening to come to speech. But it's also a movement of the soul, of his inner life, that eludes the narration's telic logic. Was this wish also speaking when he threw the hammer through the window?

That Yun-ju is lecturing on "modern behaviorism" is fitting. Behaviorism is just another form of determinism—determinism elevated to an empirical method of psychological investigation. The behaviorist denies—either as methodological principle or ontological dogma—that there is radical interiority. The soul, the mind becomes a black box—nature the totality of empirically observable, mathematically measurable events. Neither the soul's inner life nor the outer life of nature survives. Behaviorism thus represents an extreme form of the cinematic apparatus of philosophy: the ordering of movement, the annihilation of pure movement. But the theater darkens around Yun-ju, whereas Hyun-nam and Jang-mi have found, if not freedom, at least a way out.

Lovable Losers

The heroes of *Barking Dogs Never Bite* walk off at the end . . . but into the forest, through the forest: not even, it seems, on a proper path. This evokes the first stanza of Dante's *Inferno*:

> Nel mezzo del cammin di nostra vita
> mi ritrovai per una selva oscura,
> ché la diritta via era smarrita.

> Midway in our life's journey,
> I found myself in a dark forest,
> for the right path had been lost.[48]

For Dante, however, the dark forest preludes the extravagant mapping of the cultural landscape of the late Middle Ages, illuminated by the light of Christianity—Platonism for the "people [*Volk*]," as Friedrich Nietzsche put it in the preface to *Jenseits von Gut und Böse* (Beyond Good and Evil); Platonism as ideology.[49] The epic pretensions to which Hollywood will succumb situate it within the long shadow cast by a crisis afflicting literature since the early modern period. The disintegration of the late Scholastic synthesis, a comprehensive worldview uniting Aristotle and Christianity, calls into question the viability of epic as a literary genre. Epic either survives as an anachronistic atavism, or seeks to wrestle a unifying sense from the real conditions of modern life, or takes flight into fantasy, where world building allows the epic totality disallowed by the real world. Bong's forest wanderers, however, are not disoriented; they have not lost the right path. Nor is the forest, as in Akira Kurosawa's *Roshomon* (1950), the place where a single truth gives way to a multitude of perspectives. Rather, in the forest, another life can be glimpsed, and with this, another politics.

The roots of this will ultimately be found within Eastern philosophical traditions, and, most of all, Daoism. Bong's "lovable losers" are not merely tragic-comic types, nor do they just give a voice to those whom the Miracle on the Han left behind. Rather, they are like the gnarled, winding tree that is saved from the axe by becoming utterly useless to the world, exemplifying, as in Zhuangzi's parable, the very "unusableness that the Holy Man makes use of."[50] But, above all, these lovable losers are would-be wanderers. Drawing attention, from a comparative perspective, to parallels between Daoism and European Dandyism, Thorsten Botz-Bornstein writes:

> The dandy is a *flâneur*, and in the *Zhuangzi, you* (遊) stands for a similarly aimless roaming, rambling, or sauntering.[51] *You* has been translated as "going rambling without a destination" or "free and easy wandering." While Confucians focus on moral and personal duty, the *Zhuangzi* promotes carefree wandering [. . .]. The flâneur never stops but sees men and women pass by while he is walking.[52]

If carefree wandering is still possible in Seoul, even now, it is because the city's mountainous landscape continues to prevail against every project of rational planning, from the Neo-Confucian architecture of Kwanghwamun and Kyŏngbokkung Palace to monotonously ordered apartment complexes. The mesh of roads, forced to follow the contours of the landscape, snake and sprawl; the square edges of dwellings abut against the forests leading up into mountains dotted by temples, whose caves hide offerings to the local gods.

2
Memories of Murder

Distant Familiarity

Memories of Murder (2003) rescued a foundering career. Reaching an audience of over five million during its domestic run, Bong's second feature-length film was the highest-grossing Korean film in the year of its release. It triumphed in local awards and was even screened at several international festivals, including Cannes and the San Sebastian International Film Festival, where Bong won the award for Best Director.[1] Clearly, Bong learned from his mistakes: for all its cleverness and humor and deep insights, *Barking Dogs Never Bite* lacked a necessary ingredient for a successful film.

What was this ingredient? Just compare their opening scenes. The first scene of *Barking Dogs Never Bite* certainly fulfills the most basic narrative functions. It introduces the protagonist and his motivations, setting the plot in motion. Yet the audience is also left confused—unsure what sort of film they're watching—and maybe a bit bored. The scene tacks too close to the prosaic. An apartment, a bark, a professor: so what! In contrast, *Memories of Murder* begins with potent signifiers, starting with the luscious rice field. This already forebodes a body. The hatless man, so we discover, is a local detective, Park Doo-man (Song Kang-ho), the first to arrive at the scene where the body of a murdered woman has just been found—the first victim in a series of killings that took place in Hwasŏng in the late eighties.

The title alone, moreover, tells us that the film is about something: murder. And indeed, real murders, "true crime." In Korea, the Hwasŏng murders are as strongly etched in cultural memory as Son of Sam in the United States. The first domestic instance of a series of murders with an identifiable signature, it remained unsolved at the time of the film's release. Occurring amid feverish economic growth and political unrest—the final years of military dictatorship—the Hwasŏng murders marked Korea's entrance into "psychopathic modernity." Deprived of rational motivations and social function (protecting the community, attacking the enemy, establishing or reinforcing structures of dominance), violence and cruelty become tools of individual expression.

Bong's change in approach from his first film involves introducing a very different kind of familiarity. Replacing the close familiarity of the everyday—the endlessly repeating weft granting substance to everyday life—is the distant familiarity of those contents that, typically encountered from afar, constitute the warp anchoring the monotonous fabric of a community's lifeworld. This contrast resembles that between prosaic and poetic familiarity; whereas the poetic keeps the prosaic from sinking into tedium, the prosaic prevents the poetic from flying off into the "abyss above," the vacuity of the cliché.

However, applying the poetic and prosaic not to verbal language but to photographic media such as film presents a peculiar difficulty: cinema immediately turns even the most prosaic into something poetic. It takes what is most ordinary and makes it into an icon, whose very appearance is meaningful since it says that it *is* this thing that appears. The photographic is always at once ordinary and iconic—not blurring the two extremes together but allowing them to coexist in continual tension.

Barking Dogs Never Bite already hinted at this aspect of the photographic/cinematic: Hyun-nam dreams of being on television, getting a foothold in iconic existence. Yet her personal failure to realize this dream allegorizes the film's failure to enter into the proper element of cinematic experience. Even while evoking this dream, *Barking Dogs Never Bite* failed to achieve a cinematic language giving play to the tension between the prosaic and poetic, the ordinary and the iconic. It inhabits the cinematic tension between prosaic and poetic comically, indeed cartoonishly, through its own comic failure to occupy it. With *Memories of Murder*, however, Bong discovers the means to abide with this tension, to occupy it tragically. Consequently, our first challenge, turning to Bong's second and subsequent feature films, is to avoid peremptorily translating cinematic language into the aesthetic categories of verbal language. Thus, we must resist the tendency to illuminate the film "retrospectively" in light of its narrative, reducing the film to a "poetic" content: the "distant" familiarity of an iconic type. A movie is over the moment we finally know what it's about. Hence, rather than beginning with an exposition of the plot, I will try to allow the plot to emerge out of, and become comprehensible through, more properly cinematic tensions.

Let's return, then, to the first scene. We must allow it to appear in the bewildering, vertiginous, shocking incomprehensibility of that which is seen for the first time. The most scholarly, thoughtful readings often work against this. Consider, for example, Nam Lee's description:

the film is imbued with national angst from the start . . . [beginning] with a prologue that presents a seemingly idyllic image of a Korean countryside: a golden rice field ready to be harvested under a clear blue sky, boys running around capturing grasshoppers. A golden rice field is a traditional image of peace and prosperity in Korea. However, hidden under this perfect image of a national landscape lies the corpse of a rape and murder victim, the first of many to come. The victim serves as an ominous sign of a looming crisis that is further foreshadowed by the image of grasshoppers. As a common pest in rice fields, these grasshoppers serve as a symbol of the social ills threatening the peace of the nation.[2]

As insightful and nuanced as this reading is, it is literary: the scene becomes an ensemble of tropes, a symbolic complex, offered as its meaning. The irreducibly *cinematic* has been shorn away like a rice husk.

Certainly, the golden rice field can symbolize the national landscape of Korea. Yet what appears before us is neither a golden rice field as such, nor this familiar rice field, but an image of a reality imposing itself upon us in an abundance of rich detail. Are the husks really golden? Aren't they rather a subtle mix of orange and green hues? "Golden" is already a literary abstraction, even an ideological construct, equating the earth's fruit with wealth. Nor do we first see a field but a boy's face surrounded by rice crops. The immediate effect is a peculiar tension between disorientation and orientation: a bewildering forest of stalks—a human face. Our visual perception is oriented toward human faces; we see faces in clouds, trees, or rocks, not rocks or clouds or trees in faces. But the face also orients us through the focus of its eyes. We see the boy focusing on the grasshopper, methodically picking it up, inspecting it. This establishes the importance of the hunter-prey relation; only in these terms does the plot become comprehensible, since both detective and serial murderer are versions of the hunter. Moreover, the very image of the boy hunting an animal feeding off the stalks suggests that, from the outset, this orienting praxeological frame involves a structural complication: the hunter can also be the hunted.

Only when the boy stands up do the stalks become a field, whose defining limits come clearly into view. Now we see the straight dirt road cutting through the field, imposing geometric order but also taking us on an errant path: to the ditch, the body, the scene of the crime. Taken narratively and symbolically, the victim's body represents the disturbance with which the story—a detective story— begins and which should be resolved. Approached cinematically, it is just the opposite: with the discovery of the body, the overwhelming disorientation at the beginning of the scene resolves into the comfortable familiarity of a narrative *topos*, setting in motion the conventions of the detective story, and hence of the detective movie as a subgenre of the thriller.

The Weakly Mythic

To understand the constitutive cinematic tension, we must avail ourselves of a terminology no longer bound up, as are the poetic and prosaic, with literary language. The *mythic*, in the unusual sense I propose, refers in the first instance not to a specific kind of content but to a category of language broadly understood, indeed a "logical" category. The mythic, so conceived, is not pre-discursive, let alone anti-discursive, but involves a certain modification of the discursive function of language. This discursive function of language rests on the ontological distinction, instituted with the metaphysics of Plato and Aristotle, between individual things and general types. Understanding an individual comes down to recognizing the general types—concepts and descriptions—that can apply to it. Socrates— this individual—is a man, a philosopher, a Greek, the husband of

Xanthippe. This is so even if we are talking not about who Socrates was, but about his actions: walking with Phaedrus by the river, drinking hemlock. Description passes through universals.

From this starting point, we may conceive of the mythic as follows: the mythic is where the very possibility of ordering the particular through the universal, subsuming the particular under the universal, breaks down. It gives logical expression to the extra-logical—it speaks to what cannot be spoken. Not only is the mythic riven by paradoxes, but logical paradoxes and contradictions themselves belong to the mythic. Hence, the mythic involves an abiding remnant of ontological incoherence that—having troubled philosophy since its inception— haunts our thinking and world. Take the Greek goddess Aphrodite. From a more conventional philosophical perspective, the mythic formation is a mere stepping stone toward an abstract concept of feminine beauty, love. Yet something about beauty remains irreducible to an abstract category, a universal; there is something that must *appear* to be understood, grasped only through appearance. Beauty only ever appears as *this* or *that* beauty, indicating the universal but refusing to release it from the instance to which it's attached. No mere personification of an abstract category, Aphrodite's very appearance shows how beauty is also tied to the concrete, the individual. It reveals that which is not merely the instantiation of a universal but radically singular, unique; odd to the point of disturbing the natural order—a tyrannical presence demanding even the strange submission of love.[3]

The mythic, so understood, suggests Immanuel Kant's aesthetic experience. For Kant, the feeling of beauty arises when we tarry with a phenomenon that, resisting comprehension, cannot be subsumed under given categories, yet nevertheless seems amenable to understanding, revealing a "purposiveness" without "purpose."[4] Aesthetic judgment demands universal assent, yet since it concerns our subjective experience of the object, saying nothing determinate about what the object—given to us as a possible object of experience—is in itself, it can only claim "subjectively universal validity."[5] Yet the aesthetic is only one form the mythic can assume. Indeed, the mythic exists whenever logical expression is given to what resists logic. Nor should we conceive the mythic as a prelogical form of experience. The very idea of the prelogical—and hence also of the mythical as a stepping stone to rational thought—allows for the ultimate negation, marginalization, and trivialization of everything resisting logic; the counter-logical gets ordered to the logical, such that an ultimate principle of order prevails. By thinking of the mythic, instead, as what gives logical expression to the extra-logical, and consequently understanding the aesthetic as a special case of the mythic, we seek to stress that the phenomenological field of perception does not present as radical immediacy awaiting discursive articulation. Not only is it always already suffused with logical sense, but it allows for the logical expression of what resists logical articulation, countering the "myth of the given" even while remaining open to modes of experience defying logical articulation and opposing scientistic reductionism.

To see better how the mythic applies to cinema, let's turn to the phenomenological field of perception, understood not as prelogical immediacy but as always already invested with logical sense. Here we might identify three different planes: the sentimental, the typical, and the mythic. The typical, encompassing both readiness-to-hand and presence-at-hand, involves the generally recognized purposes and qualities of an object together with characteristic features showing it to belong to a certain "historical" era, locality, social milieu. The typical discloses things in their public existence; whether taken as a mere physical object or regarded in its purposiveness as a tool, the hammer belongs to a world of things that have been categorized in terms of public, worldly meaningfulness. They appear, as it were, in the *agora*, the marketplace of commonly acknowledged values and meanings. Yet while the sentimental, in contrast, involves private meanings, associations, and memories—a "sentimental value" never "cashed out" in the open market—it doesn't unsettle the logical organization of reality through the opposition of the particular and the universal. To experience the sentimental value of a cherished toy or heirloom—to experience it as having a value for me that it could have for no one else—is to feel that it has, for *me*, the same sort of radically private value that other things have for other people. For indeed, the fact that I have my own sentimental attachments makes me just like everyone else. This same thing can also be said for objects of sentimental value for a community.

Only with the mythic does the stable relationship between individual and universal—the ontological structure of the world—become unsettled. The beautiful is mythic but so is a monster, a strange aberrant something, or a corpse—this person, in all his or her individuality, reduced to a mere thing. Celebrities, stars, and icons are mythic. In all these cases, we may speak of the *strongly* mythic: here, the mythic is extraordinary, standing out from the everyday. But there is also another mode of mythic potency. Suppose I am looking at something—a child's teddy bear, for example—that should have sentimental value for someone and yet has none whatsoever for me. A strange tension arises: the teddy bear appears as a typical sentimental object, but as a typical object renouncing its typicalness, at odds with it. Seeing a photograph of a house, we see the typical. But the typical recedes before the absolute singularity that is inherent in the photograph: for it is not just a house of this or that kind—it is this particular house.[6] Now, if it is our house, or a house we are familiar with, then the sentimental dominates. But if we have no special individual relation to what is shown, then the sentimental hollows out into a mere indication of a possible sentimentality.

This is what we shall call the *weakly* mythic, though understanding that the strongly and weakly mythic form a continuum. Since the human world consists mainly of objects endowed with sentimental value, if only because they belong to and compose the familiar spaces wherein everyday life unfolds, the weakly mythic automatically results from the decontextualization inherent to the photographic medium. The mythic inherent to cinema, even when it treats the most mundane, consists above all in this formal indication of a sentimentality that is *not for me*. It is perhaps this strange charisma manifested by cinema that Edgar Morin will understand as *photogénie*, "this quality that is not in life but in the image of life," or that, for Stanley Cavell, constitutes the mystery of things of which cinema serves to remind us.[7] The things that we live with cannot captivate us since their meaningfulness always appears as a meaningfulness, or indifference, *for us*. But just because the camera shows us a world from which *I* am absent—even if it also implies the perspective of a generic viewer—then the lived meaning of things, and especially their sentimental meaning, appears in all its obstinate mystery.[8]

Whereas the logical function of language is to say what and how things are, mythic language discloses. It lets things appear by unfolding a play of proximity and distance. If the gods were the fundamental concern of classical myth—myth more narrowly conceived—it is because the gods can only appear in distant proximity. But the remarkable capacity of film, only possible in a weakly mythic element, is to discover the play of proximity and distance in even the most everyday. The motto of cinema is Heraclitean: *here too there are gods*. Or it is like the "piping of heaven" in the *Zhuangzi*: "the gusting through all the ten thousand differences that yet causes all of them to come only from themselves."[9]

Memories of Murder begins where *Barking Dogs Never Bite* ends: in the mythic element. For the typical Korean, living in a city and working in an office, mid-rise apartment complexes are as everyday as can be, but rice fields belong to another world, however close, in purely physical terms, to one's own. The highways and train tracks pass through them as one travels between urban centers and resorts. And one might even have walked through a dirt road transecting rice fields on the way to the family's burial plot, where, at least for those who keep to traditional ways, rituals are performed on various days throughout the year. Yet, unless one is a farmer, one never enters the field; never loses oneself, hunched down, in stalks of rice. The weakly mythic potency of the rice field consists not in its forceful symbolic value—this would already suggest the strongly mythic—but in being an irreducibly singular instantiation of something encountered in our daily lives, to varying degrees, but mostly off-limits, proscribed. A similar quality of mythic distance attends other elements of the scene as well. Mountains and hills, in the looming presence of their outlines, promise an escape from quotidian flatness. Yet should one go hiking, the mountain, appearing from afar through a synoptic and totalizing image, disappears into a multitude of new perspectives; even upon reaching the summit, the mountain doesn't offer *itself* to view but makes visible the surroundings in their distant potency. We pass by the same houses every day, catch fugitive glimpses of the same living rooms, yet never enter them even once. They remain the mysterious promise of a life off-limits to us. But perhaps most weakly mythic of all is the human face: neither in its immediate emotional expressiveness or its descriptive valences, nor as the time-transcending iconic *countenance*—Akim Volynsky's *lik*—but in the mysterious, yet utterly palpable, immediate uniqueness of this face as it is given to us in the moment *beyond* the moment.[10] The face is always a promise, and even the greatest intimacy never completely overcomes the distance holding off from its comprehension. The initial disorientation of the rice stalks converges with this weak mythic presence.

With the discovery of the first body, this fog of cinematic disorientation lifts. The strongly mythic has dispersed it: the body of a murdered victim, an obsession of popular culture that few have seen with their own eyes from up close, is indeed among the most paradigmatic strongly mythic objectifications. Not merely symbolic of murder, it is murder—indeed, through the uniqueness of the face, it is murder not as a "statistic," lost in the endless traffic of life and death, but as the unique taking of a unique life.

This, moreover, suggests the close relation between cinematic genre and the strongly mythic. Cinematic genre is almost always announced through a strongly mythic moment, be it a space alien, monster, explosion, the open Western frontier, the gunfight, eroticized murder, piles of gold ingots, or even the so-called meet-cute, which, ideally taking place among mysteriously connected strangers, represents the fulfillment of the erotico-Romantic promise of everyday metropolitan life, where we mostly only ever encounter passing strangers at a distance that cannot be bridged. Whereas this strongly mythic moment returns cinema to the literary, the weakly mythic develops a more properly cinematic domain.

Serial Killer as Flâneur

A careful analysis of the conclusion of the first scene of *Memories of Murder*, when the detective approaches the discarded corpse, reveals a functional inversion—a "negative"—of the first scene of *Barking Dogs Never Bite*. The detective walks toward an irrigation ditch partially covered with a concrete slab, crouches down and looks inside. We follow his gaze inside the tunneled ditch. Without a flashlight, he grabs a shiny piece of metal and begins to peer within: first, we see a cricket, then a woman's legs come dimly into view, buttocks hidden in shadows, with the man crouched above at the entrance. Finally, the sun's light, reflected off the metal shard into the ditch, reveals wrists bound tightly together.

Instead of someone looking out from a camera-like room into a thick, claustrophobic forest, we find someone in an *open field*—a field of vision—gazing into the chamber formed by the covered ditch. By grabbing a metal shard resembling an SLR camera mirror, the detective improvises a photographic apparatus (Figure 3). The detective is no longer caught within the "cameral" rationality of modernity but approaches it awkwardly from the outside. The open space of the field, moreover, appears as a communal space where a crowd can mingle—a far cry from Yun-ju's hermetically sealed apartment. Yet this crowd is no mere anonymous mass: whereas Yun-ju first appears *alone* but from behind—the plot indeed will hinge on him not being recognized from behind—the frontal view of the face dominates the opening scene of *Memories of Murder*.

More than anything, this last change reveals the transformation in Bong's approach. Among the most characteristic and shocking

Figure 3 Memories of Murder *directed by Bong Joon Ho. © CJ Entertainment 2003. All rights reserved.*

experiences of modernity is the anonymity of life in the city. Korea, whose modernization was compressed into barely a century of colonialism, civil war, authoritarianism, and compulsory neoliberalism, experienced this shock in a particularly traumatic way.[11] It is not merely that, having moved from the countryside, people find themselves bereft of the traditional communal ties, surrounded by hustle and bustle—the endless flow of traffic—and forced to submit to an impersonal and rational order. Even more shocking is the endless multitude of faces: richly individuated, unique, yet straining recognition. Presenting an excess of signification rather than a lack, every face discloses a world ripe with possibilities—possibilities appearing forcefully because they haven't yet been tied down to a name, a social position, a family. One receives hints, clues, but these demand interpretation; ambiguity always remains. The typical response to this bewildering, disorienting multitude is to retreat into an intimate community—a work-family, friend-family, or actual family. But one could also try to live in and through the crowd. Such an extreme form of life is no less inflected with meaning—artistic, social, political, even theological—than the life of the hermit or pilgrim. Thus, the *flâneur* emerges as the quintessential protagonist of urban modernity.

Walter Benjamin, following Baudelaire, recognized the significance of this new experience made possible by urban modernity. Poe's "The Man of the Crowd," he explains, is

> like an X-ray picture of a detective story. It does away with all the drapery that a crime represents. Only the armature remains: the pursuer, the crowd, and an unknown man who manages to walk through London in such a way that he always remains in the middle of the crowd. This unknown man is the flâneur.[12]

The detective is a version of the flâneur. But so too is the serial killer—the most exalted object of the detective's attention. Both detective and serial killer relate to the urban multitude but in opposite ways: whereas the detective seeks to conquer the multitude by submitting it to an improvised system of knowledge and classification, the serial killer destroys the actuality of life, ruins its everyday happiness and future potential, yet salvages the irreducible singularity of existence. Turning life into a memorial of life, the serial killer collects "trophies" of lives cut short. Facing off, the serial killer and the detective function together as a single apparatus that, not only anticipating but enacting the camera, faces up to the singular faces of the multitude. The face of the victim, frozen in death—its eyes staring off in uncanny fixity—becomes the mystery that the detective explains by returning it to its official place among the multitude; identifying the victim, making sense of what happened, telling the abridged story of a truncated life. The crowd still does not appear as such, in all its bewildering immediacy, but nevertheless comes into view through the gazes of its protagonist and antagonist, turned as they are to the multitude, but above all through the gaze of the victim.

The Time of Suspense

Cinema is most in its element when it has naturalized the wandering, way-making gaze, showing us things and their movements. Even people appear to us first as things: faces and bodies, movements, gestures, miens. But if the world appears as a world of things, things are riven with the distinction, stressed by Arendt, between the cyclical time of everydayness and the linear time of biography.[13] Movement is already space and time in dialectical interplay, so the distinction between cyclical and biographical time is best understood as between the becoming-space of time and the becoming-time of space. Life's everyday cycles close it off into a spatial order; the biographical opens it up to the event.

The weakly mythic in cinema is precisely that which opens things, in their appearance, up to time; the mythic disclosure is first of all the sense of temporality.[14] Ozu Yasujirō's Tokyo Story (1953) offers a striking example: catching our eye before we grasp its significance, the portrait of the daughter-in-law's deceased husband haunts us with its presence by discovering a life story, interwoven with Japanese history, that, occluded by the ordinary rhythms of life, nevertheless resonates with the main narrative event: the mother's death. Even more than the close-up or freeze frame, the filmed photograph manifests the tension between still photography and cinema: between the *trace of lost time* and the *re-presentation of presence*.[15]

This again suggests how *Barking Dogs Never Bite* not only undermines and occludes the mythic element of cinema but presents a world cartoonishly resistant to cinema's very possibility. It is about the apartment complex itself, yet what the complex itself achieves, as the paradigmatic utopian space of Korean modernity, is the cyclical spatialized time of everyday life—the near-perfect conquering of biographical, evental time through the labor time of metabolic exchanges, symbolized by the centrally placed recycling bins. Residency in these complexes is itself transient. With ritual regularity, moving trucks arrive to vacate some of the units; boxed-up belongings are carried out through the balcony window, descend on specially designed cranes, and, a few days later, after some hasty redecoration, a new family arrives. Old and broken furniture, gunked-up kitchen appliances, obsolete computers, stereos, TVs, unloved art in loveless frames, maybe even a grandiose family portrait lie piled up next to the recycling containers for a few days, picked through by scavengers, until a hydraulic arm smashes them apart and hauls them away. The individual units, standardized and almost generic, resist the accumulation of time, of memory: as if they flush themselves, periodically, of their human residences, expunge accumulated biographical time as if stripping away old wallpaper, reject the palimpsestic accumulation of historical memory. Even the buildings themselves, never aging gracefully or acquiring vintage allure, are condemned to predictable obsolescence. But the most striking indication of this collapse of biographical time into cyclical time is the double paring of human life and death with dog life and death; not only is the human baby anticipated by the puppy, but the old woman, having collapsed upon seeing her dead dog, dies in the hospital. Segregated off into a special administrative space, human death no longer interrupts the cyclical time of everyday life; the dog, already deprived of biographical time, dies in *our* place. Perhaps for this reason, the age-old rites designed to keep ancestral ghosts at bay by acknowledging their presence and offering them food and drink seem so void of meaning: the ghosts have already taken flight. It is only in the basement, in the boiler room—the circulating heart of the mid-rise complex—that ghosts still haunt. And, these days, even the boiler systems are being replaced by high-efficiency individual units.

In *Memories of Murder*, biographical time—the time of the event, of history—floods back into Bong's cinematic universe.[16] Bong's films, while no less the work of an auteur, will henceforth be marked by an eclectic deployment of recognizable cinematic genres. Genres, to be sure, are inherently conventional. A genre is that which, to an exemplary degree, allows for classification, since it is only through repetition that historically emergent phenomena gain enough reality to permit classification. But genres are not, for this, lazy clichés that must be rescued from banality by postmodern eclecticism. Whereas clichés offer trite solutions to aesthetic problems, genres are basic structures organizing narration. Orienting the audience, auditor, or reader by unfolding a certain horizon of expectations, they constitute the *classicism*, the basic classification into classical forms, of a given medium. Just as architectural structures organize the lived space of everyday life, constituting quotidian cyclic time, narrative genres are the basic structures organizing and constituting biographical time. There can, indeed, be no biographical time independent of narrative genre. There can be no pure, absolute, anomic time of the event: biographical time takes shape only through the exteriority of writing, convention. But it is also compromised, undone, by the same conventionality; it always risks collapsing into the cyclic time of everyday life. Narrative genres in general can thus be understood as the site of the constant renegotiation, reconstitution, of biographical time. And because of their originary classicism, genres can be clarified, complicated, deepened, radicalized, mixed.

Cinematic genres descend from literary narrative genres, yet there are significant differences. Narrative happens primarily through language, with its most basic elements found in sentence syntax. The moment subject and predicate join, narration has already taken place. The mythic element of cinema, in contrast, is not inherently narrative. Cinema *shows* before it *tells*, before it narrates. And what it shows, more than anything, is the weakly mythic, the indeterminately biographical: it appears to us from the first as the haunting excessive presence of the fragment of a life not yet revealed to us. The mythic objects of cinema brim over with biographical time, and the most fundamental task of cinematic genre is to gather this excess into a constellation of gestures.

In the detective genre, the distinction between cinematic and literary genres appears in the clearest light. The detective story indeed claims a special status among genres because its very conventionality results from the consolidation of the primary functions of literary narration around a stereotypical content. According to Tzvetan Todorov's "The Typology of Detective Fiction," the classic form of detective fiction, the so-called "whodunit," is characterized by a basic duality, containing not one but two stories, the crime and its investigation.[17] Indeed, there are not only two stories but two murders: the first murderer, in the words of mystery author George Burton, becomes "the victim of the pure and unpunishable murderer, the detective."[18] Living embodiment of the power of justice and law, the detective acts with immunity, and this immunity is at the crux of the second story—the investigation. Detection is a purely theoretical activity, isolated from the realm of praxis: "The characters of this second story, the story of the investigation, do not act, they learn. Nothing can happen to them: a rule of the genre postulates the detective's immunity."[19] The "whodunit" is thus opposed to the *série-noire* or "thriller," which came to prominence after the Second World War. Here the crime is no longer anterior to the narrative but coincides with it: "No thriller is presented in the form of memoirs: there is no point reached where the narrator comprehends all past events, we do not even know if he will reach the end of the story alive. Prospection takes the place of retrospection."[20]

The opposition between the whodunit and the thriller hinges on two quite different forms of "interest": curiosity and suspense. The former moves from *effect* to *cause*, the latter from *cause* to *effect*. We see gangsters preparing a heist and wonder what will happen. "This type of interest," says Todorov, "was inconceivable in the whodunit, for its chief characters (the detective and his friend the narrator) were, by definition, immunized: nothing could happen to them. The situation is reversed in the thriller: everything is possible, and the detective risks his health, if not his life."[21] While Todorov is principally concerned with literature, it's clear that the literary genres, which came of age during the golden years of cinema, can hardly be understood in the isolation that formal literary analysis demands. The development from the whodunit to the thriller suggests the transformation of the genre from a literary to a cinematographic form. Whereas the whodunit represents a defiant last stand of popular literature against the onslaught of new media, doubling down on literature's capacity to negate the actuality of the event through its narration, the thriller already anticipates cinema.

This, in turn, may be understood in terms of the difference between curiosity and suspense—a difference that eludes purely formal narratological analysis. By raising questions and seeking answers, curiosity exhibits the most basic structure of language as discourse, whose primary function is to describe the world. Thus, the typical whodunit begins with the discovery of a body. The body *asserts* only one thing—a death has taken place. But this leads to a series of questions: Who is the victim? When did he or she die? Where? How? Was it murder? If so, by means of what weapon, what tool? These first questions are typically resolved by the coroner, whose purview limits itself to the natural, rather than moral, reality of death. The detective's work begins when the natural fact of an unnatural death has been established, and it concludes with answers to the most basic questions: who, how, why? The investigation finished, the detective now narrates the crime. Presenting the crime in the clear light of reason and often confirmed by a confession, this narration is possible because the crime has been transfigured through its investigation; transformed from something horrible and unspeakable to something completely comprehensible—as if the investigation served only to destroy all wonder at the event of death, or life. The corpse of the whodunit, this is to say, signifies the event of a movement from life to death. The point of the investigation, and hence the genre itself, is to situate this event within a twofold rational frame: the order of nature, with its mechanistic relations of cause and effect, together with the order of free will, of intention and motive. The genre of the whodunit thus exemplifies the cinematic apparatus of philosophy; movement captured in this double order, the nature-freedom duality.

Curiosity drives toward an end—and is exhausted in this end. The catharsis produced is the catharsis of a crossword puzzle: the elemental satisfaction of untangling a knot. It solicits admiration for its clever construction—a cleverness resembling the criminal's cleverness in the first instance, the detective's in the second. Suspense, in contrast, involves the suspension of resolution, the suspension of the end. Suspense hovers in the unresolved moment. Suspense originates from the suspension of the satisfaction of curiosity. But the suspension of this satisfaction continues to refer to curiosity. It is not yet a radical suspension but merely a temporary postponement. A more radical form of suspense, however, is possible within the cinematic medium through its photographic capacity to present simple objects from everyday life isolated from the concrete world of living relations and sentimental attachments to which they refer and hence haunted by an unsatisfied reference. The weakly mythic is always already full of suspense, and a strong mood of suspense is created not so much by special narrative intrigues as simply by refusing to allow the weakly mythic presence to dissipate or be channeled. All cinematic genres involve a fundamental relation to what we might call the suspense of things, or perhaps even following the French sinologist François Jullien, the "propensity of things," the name by which, translating *shi/se* (勢), he seeks to render comprehensible the radical a-causality of indigenous Chinese thought.[22] The suspense of things is the time they are pregnant with; the time bursting from them. Every cinematic genre thus involves a dispensation of suspense—an ordering and regulation of time.

The Bland Gaze

In *Memories of Murder*, the case is never solved, just as in reality the Hwasŏng murders were only solved long after the film's release. Bong thus upsets a basic feature of the whodunit: we never find out who did it. This transforms the detective genre into a thoroughly cinematic form—pure suspense. The thriller's suspense is no longer merely the shadow that the world of crime casts on the detective, who, neither morally impeccable nor physically immune, is pulled into the nexus of crime and violence. Rather, the crime, and the curiosity it arouses, is merely a pretext for suspense.

The transformation of the curiosity of the whodunit into pure suspense reaches its pinnacle in the two-scene epilogue to *Memories of Murder*, set in 2003, a decade and a half after the main events of the film. Park, the lead investigating detective, has married his girlfriend and settled down into the dream of upward mobility. At home with his family, he chides his son for playing video games rather than studying. Previously occupying a prominent position within the political order of the small rural community, he is now a travelling salesman, having joined the lowest ranks of the merchants conducting trade between the industrial/urban centers and the countryside. His apartment is spacious and modern but on the ground floor—traffic visible through the window. Returning to the country roads, it is as a stranger, passing through with a minivan full of merchandise. Finding himself at the site of the first murder, he stops abruptly and walks out into the field. The harvest is over now; the rice stalks bent down, bereft of their bounty. He walks up to where the first body was found and stoops down to look inside. The camera reaches into the covered ditch, as if he were wriggling through, as if he had himself become camera, hoping, as the audience will hope, that he could thus finally reveal the killer, that the killer would appear at the end of the lens-tunnel. And then suddenly, stooped over, utterly vulnerable, he hears a voice: "Is someone down there?" A young girl is standing behind him. A while back, she tells him, she saw another man looking in the hole, and she then also asked *him* what he was doing. "What did he say," Park asks.

> "What was it . . . Right. He remembered doing something here, long ago, so he came back to take a look."
> "Did you see his face? What did he look like?"
> "Well . . . a plain face (*ppŏnhan ŏlgurinde*)."
> "In what way?"
> "Just . . . ordinary (*p'yŏngbŏmhaeyo*)."

By shooting this dialogue, itself an exchange of questions, in the manner of Ozu, with only the one who is speaking facing the camera, Bong emphasizes the individual face, without relationship to a world and to other faces: the face in its weakly mythic presence. And it is precisely the individual isolated face—the killer's face—at issue in this final scene. An extraordinary tension thus emerges between the face's appearance, its overflowing mysterious presence, and the logical function of language, which begins with questions and ends with answers. The logic of curiosity, of the whodunit, demands the killer's face be identified. This identification is the ultimate, absolute neutralization of the mythic potency of the face. Once the girl is revealed as a possible eyewitness—not to the crime but to its remembrance—the crucial question becomes: what did this man (*ajŏssi*) look like? The girl should be able to answer the question, helping put a name to a face. But the answer, which promises to resolve everything, resolves nothing: the putative killer looks plain, ordinary. His only identifying feature is having nothing identifiable about him. In the final shot, the former detective Park looks directly at the camera, which lingers on his face until fading to black.

When a dialogue is filmed in this manner, slight deviations of the face and the eyes from the viewer's implicit gaze assume great significance, suggesting the presence of other characters. Only when the actor's gaze meets the gaze of the audience does the diegetic world disappear. This comes close to a *parabasis*—the moment in Greek tragedy where the chorus speaks to the audience directly. One is reminded of the conclusion of Kim Ki-young's *The Housemaid* (1960), a film much admired by Bong: the actor playing the husband, his happy family restored, warns the men in the audience not to think themselves exempt from the desires leading the protagonist to ruin. *Così fan tutte. So do they all.*[23] *Memories of Murder*'s final shot certainly suggests that the murderer could be anyone, even someone in the audience. In fact, the actual murderer did watch the film. But it also carries a more disturbing message: the potential for sadistic sexual violence is not an extravagant exception to human nature; it's not extraordinary, but ordinary, plain, bland. The human face thus becomes the site, and sight, of mythic tension. Far from revealing the soul's depths, it conceals them. Every human face hints at the existence of a moral character that remains yet unknown, at powerful drives hidden beneath the surface. For as Deleuze notes, the close-up is the essence of the "affect-image"—of the affective potency of cinema— while the essential subject of the close-up is the human face.[24]

In his foreword to the second edition of *For They Know Not What They Do: Enjoyment as a Political Factor*, Slavoj Žižek cites a remarkable scene from Tarkovsky's *Mirror*:

his father Arseny Tarkovsky recites his own lines: "A soul is sinful without a body, / like a body without clothes"—with no project, no aim; a riddle without an answer. "Death-drive" is this dislocated soul without body, a pure insistence that ignores the constraints of reality.[25]

The ultimate suspense of the face is an absolute plainness pointing toward the soul without body—a soul detached from worldly purposes and worldly belonging. And perhaps there is an even deeper horizon from which this might be understood. As Jullien writes:

> According to the Daoists of antiquity, the very foundation of reality, in its infinite fullness and renewal, reveals itself to us as "bland" and "flavorless."[26]

With the detective genre, the close-up of the criminal's face assumes special significance, revealing the physiognomic mystery of an evil that cannot help but betray itself through facial expressions. Here, however, the face that appears is not the face that is sought. Yet the seeker's face itself now exemplifies the sought-after face in its blandness—its very lack of exemplarity.

The fundamental question of politics, as Aristotle already understood, is human plurality.[27] The face's blandness, suggesting a nonidentity marked only by rather subtle differences, thus also points toward the most central problem of politics: the lack of a "natural-born leader" distinguished by natural signs. The difference between tyranny and democracy, as Deleuze explains, is that the former "makes the slight difference between men into the instrument of an infinite distance between situations," whereas the latter "would make the slight difference between men the variable of a great situation of community and communality."[28] Precisely this difference in the meaning of difference is at stake in the historical moment during which *Memories of Murder* takes place. The serial killer's bland face reveals the ambiguity of a situation in which both democracy and tyranny are possible.

Violent History

Memories of Murder is a police procedural, and it features a serial killer. These two traits, which we've barely touched on, delineate subgenres of the detective genre that are largely orthogonal to the distinction between the whodunit and the thriller, or the corresponding opposition between curiosity and suspense. Rather, the serial killer subgenre and the procedural invoke a concrete antagonism between the agents of state power, seeking to maintain order against possible threats, and a defiantly antisocial individual, intent on realizing private desires for which the existing order has no room.

Moreover, the very shift from an epistemological/meta-philosophical to a political problematic is itself characteristic of a deepened understanding of the danger posed by capitalist modernity. The detectives of the pure whodunit seek to demonstrate that their knowledge always trumps the criminal's, typically a half-clever pretentious bungler. This proves that the extraordinary powers humans have gained through the scientific revolution can remain subject to political control, even if this requires an extraordinary individual, a Sherlock Holmes or Hercule Poirot, to assist the brain-dead official police bureaucracy. Against this, the thriller demonstrates that, even if the state remains sacrosanct and inviolate, the social order has itself been corrupted to the core, and hence the detective—perhaps a representative of the state but always a member of society—is left vulnerable to both physical and moral hazards. With the serial killer/ police procedural plot constellation, however, the entire focus shifts: the question is no longer whether new forces of production can be subsumed within the existing political frame but whether creative, radically transgressive individuality has any place whatsoever within the political order. The serial killer thus emerges as an eminently paradoxical figure: genius and degenerate, the novelty of the event and the tedium of repetition compulsion, outcast and demagogue or cult leader, the serial killer anticipates the dictator of the totalitarian state. Whereas the traditional detective exemplifies a humane order in the face of technological modernity, the detective is now tasked with something entirely new: to show that genial creativity can exist on the side of order, on the side of the good, the just. Of course, the creativity of the detective is reactive: only the criminal can start something new. Consequently, the radically new, the event, can only appear as a criminal rupture of the existing order. Yet the detective can still prove to be ingenious enough.

With a view to the serial killer-procedural constellation, we discover the most radical tendencies of *Memories of Murder* vis-à-vis the detective genre. The serial killer-procedural constellation not only invokes a historical context but is indeed entwined in historical time, laden with historicity. Yet this historical dimension is typically suppressed or distorted: transformed into the endlessly repeating primordial civilizational task, it forecloses the more radical time of the event. For, in a way, the serial killer as trope has already effected this transformation, and with the serial killer-procedural genre constellation, further layers of historical time are shorn away, till nothing remains but the endlessly repeated confrontation of a disruptive originality with a civilizational order responding to it by neutralizing not only the actual threat but, more importantly, the ideological threat: the hint that the killer, however evil, condemns the world itself.

It is precisely this neutralization of historicity into a routinized metastable order that *Memories of Murder* resists. This suggests the significance of Alan Moore's graphic novel *From Hell*—from which Bong drew inspiration while working on the screenplay.[29] In *From Hell*, the murders attributed to Jack the Ripper are embedded not only within a richly woven portrait of English society, reaching up to Queen Victoria and the profligate Edward, but also within a historical frame. London of the 1880s appears not as a self-contained "world"—a historical context providing hermeneutic closure by allowing crime to be read symptomatically—but as a time riven with dialectical tension; a time of becoming, of transformation, with mysterious tendrils stretching both into the archaic past (invoked via Freemasonry, exposing the contradictions of the Enlightenment) as well as the coming catastrophe of the Second World War and the technological innovations shaping the present. One scene, disconnected from the rest of the narrative, imagines Hitler's mother having a nightmarish premonition of the Shoah at the moment of his conception.[30]

Without following *From Hell* down its more conspiratorial paths, nor indulging in its esoteric obsessions, Bong also seeks to recover historical time from its effacement through the serial killer/police procedural genre. This is achieved not merely by pointing to the political situation through a few impressionistic gestures but by deftly developing a coherent, if schematic, picture of the specific relation between politics and crime that existed at the time. The relationship between crime and politics, indeed, is inherently dialectical. Crime is only possible if a political order exists and a law (even if mere custom) has been established. The continuing existence of crime implies that lawlessness still prevails within the domain to which the law applies. Hence, the law remains abstract vis-à-vis reality. But if every crime signals an intrusion of extra-political lawlessness (lawless violence) into the political domain, the law can only achieve concrete subsumption by incorporating violence. This violence is formally legitimated, and precisely this formal legitimation characterizes the opposition between the state with its government apparatus, on the one hand, and, on the other, the people *qua* multitude subjected to a governance that, even if ultimately done in the name of the people, confronts it as an alien power. The symbol of this formal legitimation is the badge.

Yet it is not so much this general relationship that interests Bong as the specific character it assumed in the Korea of the Hwasŏng murders. Chun Doo-hwan came to power in 1980 in a military coup d'état against Choi Kyu-hah, acting president after the assassination of Park Chung Hee. Whereas Choi had at least held out the promise of democratic elections, Chun quickly reestablished an authoritarian order. Promising continued rapid economic development while playing on the fear of North Korea, he intensified the suppression of organized labor and left-wing movements.[31]

The main events of *Memories of Murder* take place during the last year of Chun Doo-hwan's regime, when tensions between the burgeoning pro-democratic activists and the military regime exploded into the 1987 June democracy movement. Throughout the film, Bong calls attention to the militarization of society and the mobilization of patriotic sentiment. In a striking example of dialectical montage, Bong opposes shots of the police managing an adoring crowd awaiting a presidential drive-by—*hanbok*-clad mothers waving Korean flags—to footage of police brutality at a violent protest, with the local detective Cho Yong-koo (Kim Roe-ha) stomping on a young woman.[32] All the while plays the song that becomes identified with the killer, who, later that night, as police attempt a sting, strikes again.

During this failed sting, the detectives meet two schoolgirls, who tell a story about a crazy guy living under an old toilet at the middle school. When detective Seo Tae-yoon (Kim Sang-kyung) visits the school to follow up, he finds the girls dressed in medic uniforms in front of the school: the playground is now a staging ground for military exercises, and the girl he hoped to talk with is being carried away by her friends on a stretcher. Playing the injured, she got injured, and so the detective takes her to the nurse's office, applying a

Band-Aid to her lower back. Soon she will become the film's final and youngest victim, and in a moment of *anagnorisis*—a nod, Karen Han suggests, to Stanley Kubrick's *Lolita* (1962)—the detective recognizes her corpse from the faded, peeling Band-Aid.[33]

While Seo's interest in her seems paternal and protective, her embarrassment in his presence, her seeming schoolgirl crush on him, lends a certain ambiguity to the scene, anticipating the murderer's pedophilic turn. Likewise, the small wound anticipates her ultimate vulnerability and victimhood. Bong thus shows how the very militarization of society—done in the name of protecting the vulnerable—wounds the children that it should protect, destroying the future with which it justifies itself by claiming to serve. By establishing a strong emotional involvement with the victim among both detective and audience, this constellation of scenes would seem not only to verge on sentimentality, but to reinforce the affective identification of the audience with the detective, promoting the idea that police violence is necessary to "protect and serve," to keep chaos at bay. In truth, it inverts such a narrative: the violence of the militarized state anticipates, indeed precipitates the violence of the criminal. The final murder—a crime against a child—is no longer merely the crime of the asocial individual but of the state itself; authoritarianism is a war against children and the future they embody.

This was already clear when the sadistic Cho brutally interrogated the first suspect, the feeble-minded Baek Gwang-ho (Park No-shik), who spends his time playing video games at the arcade or stalking local women. The state-sanctioned violence of the police is first directed against someone too childlike to carry out such a crime, lacking even the manual dexterity to tie the knots binding the victim's hands. But it is precisely the most vulnerable who are the primary targets of social violence. Baek's scarred face reveals him as a victim of past abuse. Yet by the time the detectives realize that Baek is not the murderer but their only witness to the crime, it is too late.

This, at least, is the message of the madly energetic scene where all the everyday social violence, gathering into a cloud, explodes into a dramatic climax. It begins with detectives Park and Seo arriving at the *samgyŏpsal* restaurant owned by Baek's parents, where they find Cho drinking himself into a stupor. Other patrons are watching a television report about the corruption of a district judge in Incheon. The patrons' voices, interlaced with the announcer's, form a chorus of reproach, which, even threatening castration ("You gotta chop the dicks off those damn detectives"), seems aimed at the TV and local cops alike. Cho stands up, changes the channel, but it's just more of the same. Then, after throwing a beer bottle through the television, he slams a patron's head against a table. A brawl breaks out, during which Cho grabs the hair of a young woman—"You did it with the professor, didn't you?" Finally, Baek appears at the door, and seeing Cho stomp on the woman, picks up the broken-off plank and slams it into Cho's leg. Detectives Park and Seo then chase Baek to the railway tracks, where he scrambles up an electrical pole. Coaxing him down, they get him to begin remembering the murder that he witnessed. But just as he's on the verge of identifying the third suspect, he begins to recall his own abuse, seeming to identify his father, who comes running up, as the person who threw him in the fire, scarring his face. More fighting ensues, and the younger Baek runs off and stands in the middle of the tracks in front of an oncoming train, refusing to budge, even as Detective Park runs to save him.

With the young Baek's suicide, these different modalities of violence—domestic violence, police violence, the violence maintaining social and institutional hierarchies, sadistic sexual violence, even the violence of modern technology, of the inexorable machines with their inhuman speed and scale—are drawn together into a single intractable knot. It is this, above all, that makes the identification of the killer, and hence the very work of the detective, impossible. Waving the picture of the third suspect in front of the only true eyewitness, the detectives hope finally to identify the killer, to match the crime with a culprit. Yet the suspect can only see all the violence done to him all at once; the photo, far from allowing for a rational identification, unleashes its weak mythic potency, appearing as nothing else than the bland face behind which all violence is hidden.

The Tunnel

The police procedural represents both the tension between different investigative methods and the tensions within the institutional structure as a partial microcosm of the social order. Unlike more formulaic procedurals, where interpersonal conflict is minimized, a single investigative methodology prevails, and solving the crime is the foregone conclusion, *Memories of Murder* not only fully develops these axes of tension but endows them with historical significance. The present moment thus appears riven by historical tensions, potent with the possibility of change and transformation. Such tensions converge in the conflict, at the film's crux, between the local detective Park and the "outsider" Seo, who came from the metropolis, at his own request, specifically to work on this case. These two detectives at first appear as polar opposites, with the opposition falling along lines familiar to police procedurals, playing out as the conflict between the "primitive" versus the "modern," the country and the city; "a familiar clash," as Jeon puts it, "between a streetwise detective and a scientific technocrat."[34] We can't help but laugh when Park boasts he can see innocence or guilt just by looking into the suspect's eyes, spends a day in the sauna hunting a man without pubic hair, or enlists the help of a fortune teller. With no more than a high school education, he cannot comprehend the scientific forensic techniques that have become the cornerstone of modern criminology. His primary source of leads is his girlfriend's gossip. In contrast, Seo is college-educated, committed to a modern forensic method, and scandalized by Cho's sadistic interrogations.

While certainly showing the incompetence and corruption of the local police, Bong never allows Park to appear as a mere bumpkin or fool; his face exudes tortured dignity. Moreover, Bong situates the conflict between forensic methods in the relationship between the countryside and the urban center. Seen in this light, Park's approach is not as absurd as it might seem. For a detective in a relatively small rural community, it might suffice to know who is who and what is what; crimes afflicting the local community belong to the natural order of things, and policing is largely a matter of identifying and controlling the local riff-raff and ne'er-do-wells, the perverts, half-wits, drunkards, petty thieves that spring up, ever anew, like weeds in the field. Even Cho's violence and sadism—he does Park's dirty work, after all—is of a piece with the paternalistic governance of the local community; an extension of the domestic violence that pervades all aspects of life. The line between justice and ritualized scapegoating becomes blurry.

Such methods, however, are inadequate for the new crimes that modernity brings in its wake. Modern criminology, with its putative empirical and rational methods, responds to the challenge posed by urbanization. Local knowledge is at a loss faced with anonymous and transient masses. A new kind of crime emerges—the random crime. Dislodged from all local knowledge, from all folk psychology, and in the absence of confessions at first or second hand, the random crime can be solved only by means of the physical traces it leaves behind. Without an obvious suspect given through a dense network of social relations, the random crime must be solved rigorously. It is the crime of the total stranger, a social type that itself becomes possible with modernity. While serial killers murder repeatedly, this doesn't make their crimes less random: rather, it is repetition that allows randomness to appear as such, since, paradoxically, the random event can only appear through repetition—a random event that happens only once either falls below the threshold of observation or appears as monstrosity and miracle. The serial killer's "signature" constitutes a higher-level randomness.

If Seo must come from Seoul, it's precisely because this new kind of crime is a stranger to the local community, which has been invaded by the city, wounded by the city. It's not just a matter of political domination or the expropriation of the agricultural surplus but of the incursion of a specifically modern form of urbanism, characterized by capitalist industrial production, into the countryside. The foremost symptoms of this, jarringly juxtaposed with the rice fields and rolling hills, are the gypsum mine, a grotesque gash in the landscape feeding the construction boom of the urban centers, and the train tunneling through the mountain.[35]

The tunnel is a particularly potent symbol of modernity, and not just because it contributes to the "shrinking" of the world by reducing travel times and bringing the metropolis to the provinces. Because trains demand gentle grades and turns, the railway cannot follow the natural terrain. The tracks fall over the landscape like an iron frame, imposing their rigidity; tunnels get dug through the mountains, bridges stretch over dry land. In the small, mountainous Korean Peninsula, the railway's disfiguring effects are keenly felt, not least because as a poor country modernizing quickly, little thought was put into aesthetic integration. This is despite Korea's long and rich tradition of geomancy, exemplified by Yi Chunghwan's *T'aengniji*, and the value that traditional architecture attached to harmony with nature. And just as the railway imposes a new spatial order, it also imposes a new temporal order, signified by the timetable's inexorable precision. Refusing to wait, poor at slowing down, the train becomes a symbol at once of modern progress and fate, and hence of progress as fateful if not altogether disastrous.

Scientific Rationality

The opposition between Park and Seo ultimately involves the historical collision between two regimes of violent ordering. The local order—a hierarchy upheld through domesticated violence and micro-aggressions, keeping everyone in their place while repressing wayward individual desire—clashes with the new order of capitalist modernity, with its rationalized time and space, its networks of production and distribution. Seo's rational method duplicates the precision of the railways. Just as modernity will subsume Korea within global flows of commodities, capital, and people, Seo pins his final hope on the newly developed technology of forensic DNA testing, provided from a laboratory in the United States.

Yet his hope is disappointed: the modern world remains helpless before the new form of criminality to which it has given rise. Seo's science founders, just as had Park's intuitive gaze and Cho's brutality. The test is inconclusive. This is the properly tragic content of *Memories of Murder*. Tragedy, as understood here, involves the entanglement of the different forms of violence that politics tries to keep separate through the imposition of order. The deepest root of *noir* suspense, the moral vulnerability of the detective, is tragic, as can be seen from Sophocles's *Oedipus Rex*. Neither the specific mythological framework invoked by Greek tragedy—concepts of fate, pollution, inherited guilt, hubris—are essential to tragedy, nor the specific emotions of fear and pity, not to speak of the sad, horrifying, outrageous. Rather, tragedy's innermost core consists in the recognition of an absolute, radical vulnerability to all the dangers against which the political should protect us. In view of this concept of the tragic, moreover, the opposition between the whodunit and the thriller achieves its most rigorous formulation: the whodunit excludes tragic insight—the thriller leads toward it. The absolute thriller transforms into tragedy.

At the center of *Memories of Murder*'s tragic denouement is the outsider, Seo. In contrast, Cho and Park, standing for an old order already in decline, are comical figures who, like Don Quixote, seem absurd in their anachronism. Even the epilogue has a comic quality: the political landscape has changed, but Park still lands on his feet. Married with children, he becomes *pater familias*—as if spun off into a sitcom. In contrast, Seo dreams of a new order. He sees the existing institutions of Korean society, themselves the result of a modernization imposed under outside pressure and internal constraints, as still devoid of the animating spirit of scientific modernity; the new god that will save us. This new god will finally identify the killer, and hence locate the violence, which threatens to contaminate everything, in a specific site, which can then be extracted, isolated, or destroyed.

Montage

While *Memories of Murder* combines elements of both whodunit and thriller, this is no mere blurring of elements, with slapstick comedy and horror thrown in for good measure. Rather, a dialectical development takes place: the whodunit, with its cathartic promise of a final answer and absolute justice, gives way to a suspense that, gaining ever greater intensity, debouches in tragedy. This is possible because the crime in question is serial; with each new iteration of the same crime, with each new victim, Bong reveals the crime in a more suspenseful fashion.

Whereas the first two victims are introduced as corpses, the third victim appears, if briefly, in the flesh. Walking across a field during the rain, carrying a flashlight and an umbrella, she sings a Korean love song. Suddenly, there is the sound of whistling, as if in imitation. She pauses, walks a bit further, there's more whistling, and then suspenseful extradiegetic music begins: the camera dances around her, changing focus from her hand to her face, which, turning around, reveals the gypsum mine's monstrous silhouette bathed in pale light. She has just started running—as if responding to the suspense of the filmed scene rather than the diegetic situation—when the killer jumps out at her from the side of the path. Curiously, the attacker's face blurs across the screen for about half a second: a tantalizing tease of identification.

With the fourth and final victim, the crime appears in an even more radically suspenseful fashion. The scene begins with the sole female detective Kwon Kwi-ok (Ko Seo-hie) walking across a dark and desolate dirt path. She pauses anxiously, then moves forward again. The camera now looks down at her from the trees surrounding the path, and, moving rightward, reveals the completely darkened partial silhouette of a man watching her, his hands pressing against the bark. We are again looking at the detective from the front, and just as she approaches the camera, another silhouette appears on the right side of the screen and then passes behind her—the schoolgirl Kim So-hyeon (Woo Go-na), walking alone at night. The camera pans back and forth between the two as they walk apart—suggesting, if momentarily, the viewpoint of the lurker, as if deciding between victims—and then refocuses on the girl: we see her from the front, from above, and then from behind for about a second. Suddenly, a man jumps out from the side and seizes her. The detective pauses and turns back, then continues on her way.

What follows is not a graphic depiction of the murder but a lyrical montage that, introduced by the air-raid siren, weaves together fragmentary intimations of the crime with scenes of the local shopkeepers preparing for a North Korean attack. As the pharmacist and real estate office close and turn off their lights, the murderer carries off his victim like a felled deer, calmly removing implements of torture from a pencil case. As the town turns dark, the girl's face comes into view, her eyes looking straight into the camera, quivering with fear. The metal door of a butcher shop closes, hiding bloodied animal carcasses—the man strokes the girl's hair as she looks pleadingly toward him, his own face hidden from view. When we do see a man's face, it is not the killer but Seo: standing outside in front of some stores, alarm flashing over his face, he dashes off. The murderer crouches over his victim, her feet twitching. The screen blackens.

This is a perfect example of Bong's masterful, if sparing, use of dialectical montage—and not only because the animal carcass bears homage to Eisenstein's *Strike* (1925). The coherence of the local community, organized around occupations, unified in common emotion and action, is juxtaposed to a crime appearing only through *disjecta membra*: the hand, the feet, the face. The political system of fear and control, exemplified by the citizens' dutiful response to the air-raid siren, is powerless against a crime whose perpetrator doesn't belong to any of the customary occupations of the community, indeed doesn't seem part of the community at all, but—absolute stranger, appearing only as shadowy silhouette save for his hands—haunts its dark periphery. Yet the hands—they are soft, we learn—appear as an artist's hands, carefully removing the tools from their box: a striking contrast to the townspeople's automatism.

Because the victim is a young girl, representing sexual innocence and future fertility, her death, more than the others, traumatizes the whole community, which is gathering as Seo strides, facing the camera, toward the body. Whereas the people behind him are holding black umbrellas, he, without even a hat, is completely exposed to the rain. Indeed, the only ones without head protection are him, Park (whom Seo passes silently), two mourning women—and the victim's corpse. This establishes an elegant opposition between the multitude, still protected from the cataclysmic element by conventional group morality, and those, such as the two detectives, who are somehow set apart. Most set apart, indeed, is Seo himself, the outsider from Seoul who, with his faith in the new god of scientific reason, stands at the furthest remove from the community.

Care

Scientific objectivity demands taking distance from the community with its gossip and its prejudices. Yet this scientific hubris becomes the crux of tragedy, as we begin to sense when Seo approaches the body as it is worked over by a forensic team. The chief forensic examiner, after mentioning the foreign objects inserted in her vagina, peels away the Band-Aid. Seo then does something unexpected: he draws her clothing over the exposed skin. This forensically improper insistence on propriety shows he can no longer maintain objectivity with *this* victim whom he had already met, feeling an affection for her not entirely innocent of sexual desire, having touched the very part of her body he now wishes to conceal.

Is he protecting her body, in fatherly fashion, from a prurient gaze? Or hiding his own shame? Only as an outsider to the community could he begin to comprehend this new kind of crime, brought into the community from the outside. Being a stranger grants him the objectivity to identify a killer no longer identifiable as a member of the community—not a local weirdo, outcast, or deviant but a perfect stranger. Yet he can't investigate the community without becoming part of it. Only an absolute psychopath could live among the community without starting to belong. There is a perfect crime, but no perfect detective. The detective must care, and he must be compromised by care. This is the subjective side of Seo's tragedy.

Furthermore, satisfying the community's demand for justice also becomes impossible when the perpetrator is an outsider. Because Seo has begun to care, he demands a form of justice—a justice comprehensible to the community—that the new scientific methods cannot provide. This is the objective dimension of his tragedy. The two previous suspects, members of the community, were released after exculpatory evidence emerged. The first was a truly marginal member, while the second, Jo Byeong-soon (Ryu Tae-ho)—a churchgoing father—would have escaped notice had the detectives not nabbed him masturbating in women's panties near the crime scene. Given the emphasis placed on the murderer's hands and handiwork, it is significant that the first two suspects were both released because they had the wrong kind of hands: Baek's hands were too maladroit, Jo's too rough. For the one surviving victim, a witness not by vision but only by touch, mentioned that her attacker's hands were soft. Everything points to the third suspect, Park Hyeon-gyu (Park Hae-il)—a soft-handed white-collar worker at the factory, an outsider to the community. When they apprehend him, he's reading a book at his desk, suggesting a daydreaming inner life and aspirations beyond the ordinary. But the most damning evidence comes from the one genuine forensic lead: he had sent in the postcard to the radio station requesting to play the song played whenever the murders took place.

Despite this, the detectives fail to get a confession and must let him go. This latest murder, committed after his release from police custody, not only further confirms his guilt but suggests the failure of Seo's scientific approach. Even if it succeeds in identifying the perpetrator, selecting him from the multitude, it can never reach the absolute certainty of the confession. This certainty, which may certainly be disputed from the perspective of forensic science, especially when made under duress if not outright torture, belongs to a different order than empirical-scientific truth. The confession's truth is absolute not because it can't be false or coerced but because the suspect identifies with the crime, takes responsibility for it. Ultimately a spiritual act, confession takes guilt for the crime upon oneself, opening the way to both judgment and forgiveness, in this world or the next; at its crux, in Michel Foucault's words, is "the veridiction of oneself [...] the obligation to tell the truth about oneself."[36] The ultimate ground of the absolute truth of confession is the tragic condition: the radical guilt of all human beings; original sin. If the third suspect does not confess, however, it is perhaps because confession also registers a sense of guilt not merely individual but communal—a guilt before the community. An outsider to the community, Hyeon-gyu is without guilt, without conscience. His crime remains incomprehensible to the community.

These two tragic threads—subjective and objective—converge in the final scene before the prologue. Seo walks off from the gathered crowd and then drags Hyeon-gyu out from his dwelling onto the railroad tracks where Baek had committed suicide. He starts beating him while cursing, then points his revolver at Hyeon-gyu's head, demanding a confession: "Say it. Say you killed her. Say it! Come on and say it all!" But then Park comes running up with a letter from America. As Seo reads it, a grim expression falls over his face; his lips begin to twitch:

> Since the DNA fingerprint of the suspect Park Hyun Kyu does not correspond exactly to that semen sample found in the victim's body, it cannot be said conclusively that the suspect is the murderer.

A tear falling from his eye, Seo tosses the papers down, murmuring, "Something's not right. This is all a lie. I don't need this." While Seo retrieves his gun from the ground, Park starts looking at the papers but needs Seo to translate. Park then picks the suspect up and clutches his face, staring into his blank eyes, while Seo comes up from behind him, pointing his revolver right at Hyeon-gyu's head. Thrusting Seo's weapon away, he continues to apply his own method. But this proves no more conclusive than the DNA. His gaze is helpless against the expressionless, dead eyes of the affectless psychopath, a stranger to the local community and perhaps to human community in its entirety.

"I said straight in the eyes."

"Damn it. I can't tell."

"Do you even eat?"

"Go!"

"Go, you son of a bitch!"

Suddenly, a train bursts through the tunnel, and the two detectives, together with the suspect, duck off at the last minute, the papers torn under the train's wheel. Seo fires his gun straight into the tunnel, bullets ricocheting off the wall. Park mutters: "It's time to stop." The camera, positioned deep within the tunnel, now shows both Park and Seo, tiny black silhouettes against the tunnel's aperture, no wider than a ninth of the screen, with the silvery rails carving a subtle, mysterious arc (Figure 4). Meanwhile, Hyeon-gyu crawls off deeper into the tunnel.

The English translation of Park's last words hardly captures the nuance of the Korean: *kŭmanhaera, ije.* Literally: "Stop, now." This is not a statement but an imperative, intending a relation to the addressee given the order. But *who* is this someone? Park himself? Seo? Hyeon-gyu? The audience? The world? The gods presiding over human fate? The director? Or, rather than commanding someone

Figure 4 Memories of Murder *directed by Bong Joon Ho. © CJ Entertainment 2003. All rights reserved.*

to stop something, something is itself being told to stop. But then the command runs up against its own impossibility: what must stop, now, is what cannot ever heed a command. It is not a *who* to whom a command could be spoken, but a thing, an *it*. Yet by putting it this way, we already succumb to the grammatical prejudice of English and other Indo-European languages. Regarding this prejudice, Nietzsche writes: "[p]hilosophers of the Ural-Altaic language group (where the concept of the subject is the most poorly developed) are more likely to 'see the world' differently."[37] The very existence of the "it" as a stand-in for the subject suggests that, in languages like English, the grammatical subject can never be absent, thus demanding a clear distinction between personal and impersonal expressions. No such necessity exists in Korean, where verbs are declined neither for number or person, and a subject can be omitted altogether or presented only as the topic of the sentence rather than the subject predicated through the verb. What must stop, what is commanded to stop, is not even *it*, but everything and yet no single thing: the entire world with its endless proliferation of violence. And what must stop is what cannot stop; what comes to word only to run up against the futility of words.

Murderous Civilization

The peculiar suspense sounding in this command resonates with the scene's setting. The train symbolizes modernity and progress but also archaic fate; the inexorable power to which the individual succumbs. It symbolizes the triumph of the mechanical—of logical reasoning inching toward its conclusion—but also the inexorable forward flow of time, the temporal order that cinema itself imposes.[38] Not so much an iron horse as a monstrous mechanical serpent, the train is the phallic symbol par excellence. The cave, likewise, is opposed to the train in all respects: darkness to the train's piercing light; depth opposed to a surface framed with tracks. It is the intuitive, irrational—as vaginal as the train is phallic. But it thus also complements the train, enables the train by yielding to it.

The tunnel is an artificial cave—the product of civil engineering, made possible with dynamite and diamond-tipped mechanical drills. Piercing the mountains, it imposes mechanical straightness on nature's errant lines while also producing depth and darkness. And the train, in turn, passes through the tunnel, again and again—a rhythm born of repetition—piercing the darkness with its light: the Enlightenment in its danger, its brutality. With the conjuncture of artificial phallus and artificial vagina, the sexual act itself—the play of *yin* and *yang*, the original binary articulation of chaos—becomes mechanism. Or likewise the tragic plot, the decree of fate, has been transformed into a mechanical machination. This suggests an analogy with the serial killer, who, driven by repetition compulsion, turns the sexual act, this primal rite of nature—of springtime, of new life—

into the work of death, having replaced the natural act of copulation, living flesh against living flesh, with the insertion of foreign bodies into the vaginal cavity.

The murderer, we might conclude, is neither an element that—bestial or perverse—remains forever resistant to the progress of civilization, nor a diabolical outsider inflicted on the local community. Rather, the murderer ultimately signifies civilizational violence itself, which seeks to reproduce nature as a human work, a work of freedom or at least of human order. This recalls Kant's third proposition from his "Idee zu einer allgemeinen Geschichte in weltbürgerlicher Absicht [Idea for a Universal History from a Cosmopolitan Perspective]."[39] "[N]ature wills that" human beings except themselves from the natural order; that they produce everything beyond "the mechanical organization of their animal existence" not merely through the capacities of their inborn mechanical organization but through their reason, and hence freely: following a principle that radically transcends the natural order. In short, nature wills that human beings transform nature into a work of freedom. The human being is nature's own self-willed self-overcoming: the announcement, within nature, of a will surpassing nature. Hence nature wills that human beings never just be happy, never naturally happy: that happiness should never be a gift.

The insistence on ends over means, the rejection of immediacy, appears even more forcefully with Kant's second formulation of the categorical imperative in the *Grundlegung zur Metaphysik der Sitten* (Groundwork of the Metaphysics of Morals): "*So act that you use humanity in your own person as well as in the person of any other, always at the same time as an end, never merely as a means.*"[40] The psychopathic serial killer, however, does just the opposite: he treats others, and even himself, as pure means. Civilizational violence is, for Kant, nothing else than the negation of the originary violence of nature; the transformation of nature into an order fully harmonizing with human rationality. By sacrificing the end for the means, the serial killer would work against this. It seems, then, as if the serial killer is at once the embodiment of civilizational violence and its destitution.

Precisely this tension reveals the monstrosity of Bong's serial killer: The serial killer is a monster because he "monstrates": he shows off, demonstrates, that there is only violence—all the way down and all the way up—and that the project of civilization, of re-creating nature as a work of freedom, must be understood in the last instance as a higher order of violence. The serial killer thus shows that there can be no end to violence, no solution and final solution. Violence is always with us, since "it" is with us; or simply, it is us. The absence of the idyllic appears in Bong through the total exclusion of the Romantic idyll of sexualized sensuality and sensualized sexuality: people don't "make love"—they fuck. "It" can't stop, won't stop. The local community is already suffused by violence, just as are the forces of modernization and Seo's more sober science.

Into the Darkness

Returning to Detective Park's closing stare, we should understand this in its paradigmatic relation to other stares and gazes, especially those of the young victim and the third suspect. The human gaze and visage are privileged sites of the weakly mythic—the facticity of the generically singular. The weakly mythic is thus akin to the aura, of which, in a passage from *Über einige Motive bei Baudelaire* (On Some Motifs in Baudelaire), Walter Benjamin writes: "The glance is inhabited by the expectation to be answered by the one to whom it offers itself. [. . .] To experience the aura of an appearance means to lend it the capacity to take a glance."[41] This deeply phenomenological formulation describes the glance as a gift expecting reciprocation: we look at something, we grant it the capacity to "open up" our glance by returning it to us—becoming open to our openness. Yet, whereas for Benjamin, the aura is destroyed by cinema as media, even if cinema vainly seeks to recover it again through the "cult of the star"—though gaining not the "unique aura of the person" but only "the 'spell of the personality,' the phony spell of a commodity"—the weakly mythic is the gift that cinema at once gives and takes away.[42] It is the aura that appears precisely through its negation; cinema is always haunted by the very aura that it seems to destroy, the *punctum* of singularity. Hence, the serial killer is itself the monstrous, strongly mythic personification of an aspect of cinema as medium.

In the climax of *Memories of Murder*, the apparent killer, as if taking Park's place, crawls into the tunnel. But in the epilogue, Park repeats, as if compulsively, this gesture of tunneling by climbing into the camera-ditch. *Not even cinema offers a "way out."* Or indeed it traps ever more; we tunnel and tunnel, drawn deeper and deeper into the ditch. Everyone's heard of the cliché of the hero walking off into a horizon lit by the setting sun. Not just a thematic trope—a metaphor for life's journey or the solitude of the hero—this offers an "ideology" of cinema, a vision of cinema as a vehicle of liberation. Cinema gives us the world as a boundless frontier; if the movie industry is centered in California, it is not because here the frontier ends but because here it cannot, must not end. *Memories of Murder* reverses this trope: the serial killer crawls off into the darkened tunnel. The "ideology" of cinema is nothing else than the dream of the world that it gives to us. The serial killer destroys this dream—forecloses every opening, kills the aura: but only because the serial killer is the other side of the camera; the camera turned inward, in upon itself; the moment, repeating endlessly, of the shutter, guillotine-like, cutting off the light. And hence the serial killer also preserves everything he kills. Murder is memory.

Memory

For Bong, the serial killer-procedural constellation reveals the characteristic tensions of a historical era. Yet while this historical moment appears as a conflict between progress and regression, it nevertheless dissolves into a repetition of the same violence. The serial killer, ad infinitum and ad nauseam, demonstrates that progress is mere appearance. Still, he will not have the last word. History retreats into a mythic order of repetition for both Park and Seo because both remain oblivious to depth, seeking only surface mastery. The local knowledge of the community and the scientific method of modern forensics both remain on the surface of things. But there is also another detective, apart from the violent, buffoonish Cho: the sole female officer, Kwon. Disregarded by her male colleagues, working on her own initiative, she discovers that the same song was played at the local radio station during the murders. This leads to the postcard with the address of the third suspect—the only real lead in the case.

This discovery's significance rests on the deep connection between the modern media of radio and the modern crime of serial murder. Music radio joins two domains that, in the world of the film, appear utterly disjoint: the intimate realm of feelings, love, private passions on the one hand, and on the other, a public space commanded by the air-raid siren, mobilized in constant readiness for war. An extraordinary intuition guides Kwon. This new form of crime, she senses, can belong neither to the public space (war, political repression, terrorism, indeed the whole state apparatus) nor to the private, intimate, domestic sphere. Transpiring at the strange invisible skein where public and private meet, the crime's traces can only be found in music radio. Music radio mediates between the concrete particularity of family life and the abstract universality of the state.[43] This suggests not only the Hegelian concept of civil society (*die bürgerliche Gesellschaft*) but also guiding intuitions of East Asian thought into the social and political function of music, which, interior rather than exterior, harmonizing in oneness rather than ordering in difference, complements the rites.[44]

For Song, the mediation of concrete particularity and abstract universality constitutes the basic project of Korean modernity. During the Chosŏn era, the people were regarded merely as objects of governance, subsumed under the bureaucratic apparatus of the state and governed primarily through analogical action rather than efficient causality. Consequently, they could enter history only through "deviance, resistance and force," since their own moral deviations revealed a failure in the moral authority of the ruling class.[45] The fundamental task undertaken by a new class of intellectuals, begun during the final decades of Chosŏn, was the creation of a "new people," endowed with inherent freedom and ultimately capable of democratic self-governance.[46]

Whereas the authority's "music"—exemplified by the air-raid siren—imposes fear and docility, the radio lets people decide the music accompanying their lives. While music radio only gives public expression to inner desires, dreams, and fantasies, it at least anticipates the emergence of a public sphere. It is this anticipation that the serial killer seeks to preempt. Consider the song that the suspected killer requested on nights when the murders took place— "The Woman in the Rain" (1967) by Shin Joong Hyun.[47] The lyrical I sings of his not being able to forget "that woman" who, it seems, he saw only once, entering a fleeting union as she offered her umbrella to him without words spoken or exchanged. She is smiling sweetly—he is looking at the falling rain; their glances might not have even met. Perhaps the very absence of eye contact—the slightest and subtlest of contacts—grants the memory its compulsive quality. With its bland, generic language—of her appearance we learn nothing, she's just "that woman," literally "that female-person (*kŭ yŏinŭl*)"—the song conveys the characteristic trauma of urbanized modernity. This is the trauma of the onetime encounter with the face of the other, that, in the mysterious potency of its singularity, withdraws from comprehension, understanding, and classification. What the lyrical I cannot forget is the flimmering appearance of a public sphere: two strangers united under the most fleeting, temporary shelter, beyond all social hierarchies; outside the broad umbrella of family, clan, and community ties. The two strangers are distinguished, beyond gender, only by commodities and colors: black umbrella, yellow raincoat. Whereas in Chosŏn Korea color was regulated by sartorial codes and invested with social meaning, in modernity it is submitted to individual choice, gaining a new and mysterious signification.

The murderer, it seems, cannot forget the impossibility of forgetting that the song sings of. His crime consists, then, in finding a strange woman and killing her, as if—by thus identifying her with the once-seen gaze—he could destroy the gaze. The first sign of death, after all, is the freezing of the eyes, the stilling of their constant saccadic movements. The stranger's gaze—promising a new people, a new world, new life—is destroyed, and together with it, if only symbolically, the public sphere, the very possibility of democracy. For what appears in the passerby's strange gaze is nothing else than the people not as homogeneous mass but as multitude. The sweetly smiling gaze resists both the domestic order (she is, after all, walking alone, without female friends or a male protector—father, husband, or "big brother," *oppa*) and the subsuming power of the state. The sexual dimension of the crime, moreover, completes this symbolic destruction by taking the gaze of the other, which declares the moral dignity of the human being as end in itself, for a sexual provocation. The yellow coat—clothing in its primary function as protection against the elements—becomes a red dress, taken as signifier of "hot" femininity, femininity "in heat"—erotic availability.

The One Who Got Away

The English translation "Memories of Murder" hardly does justice to the Korean title of Bong's film—*sarinŭi ch'uŏk*. The Sino-Korean *ch'uŏk* does not just mean "memory" but rather the nostalgic reminiscence of something positive that one had experienced personally. While the movie ostensibly concerns the historical memory of a traumatic event, the title evokes the murderer's own joyful reminiscence of his crime. The public experience of trauma is thus juxtaposed with a private *jouissance*. Can we still claim that the serial killer is trying to eradicate a compulsive memory? Yet the compulsive quality of the memory stems from it being positive—the compulsion consists not simply in an involuntary memory, but in the incapacity to stop wanting to reminisce. Conversely, the true object of reminiscence is not the original glimpse of the song but the crime in which it is at once destroyed and preserved as a frozen gaze, rigid death-mask. The murderer kills the living memory that anticipates the future, transforming it into the deadened object of nostalgia. The woman walking alone in the rain, smiling sweetly perhaps only to herself, only at her thoughts, generously offering an umbrella in an act of purest philanthropy—a symbol for a new and just social order—is perverted into the fodder for a nostalgia that experiences the past as moments that live on not because their deep promise remains unfulfilled but only because they were not seized in the moment when they happened; only because the tawdry opportunity that presented itself back then was not exploited to the fullest. As when one says, wistfully: *she was the one that got away*.

The one who got away is the one who could have been the mother of the children one never had. Just as the first canine execution is haunted by the absent bark, *Memories of Murder*'s extravagant violence unfolds around a lack which barely registers consciously yet fills the film with tension. Its apocalyptic ambience originates in this lack: the serial killer's crime is not just vaguely symbolic of the violence of the times but symptomatic of a crisis at once psychological, sociological, political, and ontological. Girls and women are everywhere—schoolgirls, single women, "hostesses" and whores, even a career woman. But the mother is made to disappear by a crime that, absolutizing the erotic potential of the female body, negates the maternal-reproductive; the female victims have been turned into sex toys, objects for male pleasure, and then discarded. The tension born of this lack reaches its breaking point with the last and youngest victim. Having already been seen through the eyes of the male detectives—through a gaze fetishizing the purity of the adolescent girl as both promised fertility and forbidden fruit—her death alone reminds them of the maternal absence, of that more hidden object of desire. Unsurprisingly, it is only with her death that the Mother comes fully into view; having been briefly introduced with a few words spoken to her daughter on the stoop of her somewhat dilapidated home, the mother appears again, wailing as she is escorted away while villagers and police mass around her daughter's body. Yet the mother's brief return also explains the comic denouement buried in so much tragedy: Detective Park—abandoning the detective's tragic vocation—proposes to his girlfriend, making an "honest woman" of her, and so becomes the best-knowing *pater familias*, presiding like a little king over a middle-class family in a scene that could almost have been lifted from a sitcom pilot.

3
Mother

Mother Murder

Memories of Murder is all about *MOM*, the *mater abscondita* incanted by the initials of the English title. This absence will be crucial for Bong's next film, *The Host*, the focus of Chapter 4: not only is the abducted girl's family motherless, but her aunt, the only adult female, is an archer, the mythic figure for militantly anti-maternal maidenhood. Yet with his fourth feature-length film, released in 2009, the mother, abundantly present rather than absent, takes center stage.

While the English title is simply *Mother*, the original Korean title of the film is not a native word for "mother"—not *ŏmŏni* or *ŏmma* but *madŏ*. Neither proper Korean nor typical Konglish, this is the *han'gŭl* transcription of an English word for a concept that, so seemingly universal, hardly calls for English. As a phonetic syllabary script invented for the Korean language, *han'gŭl* is ill-suited to represent the sounds of most other languages; its dense syllabic typography, joining elements vertically and horizontally, does not allow arbitrary combinations of elements. Neither the voiced dental fricative /ð/ nor /r/-governed vowels belong to Korean's phonetic repertoire—and so, "mother" gets mangled. One mother tongue mutilates another. Moreover, even across non-cognate languages, words for mother often sound similar. The mother of all concepts, "mother" is not only the most universal human concept, but the first to form on the lips—the first probing step away from infancy, away from mother. With the film's Korean title, this very universality is turned against itself: the most universal concept becomes untranslatable. Nothing is less translatable from one language to another than its own words spoken—misspoken—in the other. The most universal concept, the mother of concepts, becomes the scar formed from the collision of mother tongues. And someone stammering *muduh, mudah,* could well be misunderstood. For if this butchered word sounds like "murder," it is no accident: "murder," in *han'gŭl,* would end up looking just the same.

A peculiar chiasmus emerges: *Memories of Murder* is MOM—*Mother* is *murder.* At the crux of the chiasmus is the question of memory. In *Memories of Murder,* memory appears as a terrifying alien power compelling the murderer to his crimes. The male detectives, however much their approaches clash, all stand helpless before the power of memory, which, active and passive at once, is constitutive of historical time. This power, which only the female detective begins to grasp, is akin to the maternal. Just as nostalgic memory, as habitual re-presentation of the past, synthesizes passive and active, the mother transforms the receptive sexual act into a radical productivity, the generation of new life. Without this transforming power, integrating activity and passivity, *yang* and *yin,* the revolutionary movement would devolve into chaos before congealing into a new kind of totalizing order, just as happened following the success of the democracy movement. Hence, the hope of a genuinely revolutionary transformation rests with mom. And indeed, the mother in *Mother* not only runs a small shop selling traditional medicine at inflated prices—cheap Chinese imports passed off as native Korean produce. She is also an unlicensed acupuncturist; her knowledge of the meridians, the channels of vital energy (*qi/ki*), grants her power over traumatic memory.[1]

The figure of the mother is, of course, also the primary object of sentimentality. It's a cliché of pop-psychology criminology, endlessly repeated in films and TV, that, whereas common criminals, bandits, gangsters love their mothers with a devotion poignantly tinged with guilt, sexually deviant criminals—serial killers in particular—have a tortured and unhappy relation to mothers who are either pathologically distant or abusively close.

The mother figure thus contains a contradiction. The sentimentalized mother is itself the accomplishment of a patriarchal social order that renders the mother harmless by identifying the more problematic attributes of the feminine with various "marginal" figures: witch, bitch, harpy, whore. Yet power over sentiment and memory belongs to the *mudang*, shaman, witch. It is, at root, a matriarchal power. In Greek mythology, *Mnemosyne*, the goddess of memory, is herself the mother of the nine muses. The sentimentalized mother is only possible because the mother, alone empowered over memory, sentimentalizes herself. Yet the self-sentimentalizing mother can never be the pure object of sentimentality; self-sentimentalizing, the mother becomes something monstrous—the violent return of all the chthonic powers that the patriarchal order, in the name of reason and order, had tried to suppress.[2]

The Solitary Dance

Bong's *Mother* is tragic in an explicitly classical sense rarely approached by cinema: tragic not because horrible and sad things happen but because it hinges on the contradiction, inhabiting its protagonist, wherein the power of fate plays out.

The opening scene already suggests this tragic dimension: the mother is wandering, as if aimlessly, through a vast rice field, surrounded by forest and mountains. The camera follows her, doubling her errant path. She turns back; her body convulses as if startled by something. We hear only birds, crickets, wind rustling through the stalks. But she pauses, looking almost directly, defiantly, into the camera, and tilts her head slightly, dips her eyes to the side with an expression of quiet sadness. Her posture is almost militant, torso tilted slightly away from the facial plane, feet planted firmly about a foot and a half apart. This is a Brechtian *Gestus*, revealing not the metaphysical posture (e.g., stoic determination) of the solitary, tragic self, but a *social attitude*; the nameless mother's solitude is the solitude of a social position elevated to the absolute, cut off from the actual relations that grant it meaning. For her militant stance, one suspects, has long become second nature. Suddenly, we hear a drumbeat, a march, introducing the instrumental theme: she begins to dance while covering her face—now laughing, now mournful—with her hand, as if still the age when ostentatious modesty and decorum were expected from her. Her dance approaches a restrained ecstasy when suddenly the shot cuts off. Now she is in the same field as before but turned against a barren background, the sky already darkening, her hand tucked in her shirt, resignation on her face. A whole life is compressed into this strange play of gestures.

Bong's films stress the relational dimension of life, with solitude appearing as something unusual, seductively tempting but morally suspect if not disturbing. And no one's existence is more relational than the mother—especially in Korea, where young mothers are often addressed through their child's given name. Nor is any activity more inherently social, un-solitary, than dancing, in which Li Zehou, following Susanne Langer, recognizes an original form of collective existence.[3] We later discover, moreover, that this opening scene is not simply a lyrical dream but flashes forward to after the film's bloody climax. This one moment of asynchronous solitude presents itself as a moment of radical truth, authenticity, around which the rest of the events orbit.

The mother's absolute solitude, however, is also only apparent. The camera is still there, moving with her and against her—dancing with her. We too hear the music that she alone should hear. If the mother's solitude grants her a tragic dignity, tragedy itself is tragically compromised: the camera imposes itself as a moment of exteriority refracting tragic interiority with the presence of the *other*. The mother, who doesn't even have a name—who is only *mother*— can never be alone, since she exists, *qua* mother, only through the other, the child. In just this way, the camera's tragic interruption of tragic solitude reproduces the inner contradiction of the nostalgic memory that the maternal embodies. There can be no nostalgic memory, no sentimentality, without the mother's self-othering, self-sentimentalizing. And just as there can be no solitary voice, there can be no solitary dance; no purely expressive dance without mirrors, cameras, audiences—no dance entirely free of seduction, charm, bewitching magic.

Thus, *Mother* transforms fate from a mythological abstraction— the familial curse introduced by an ancient transgression, the inexorable yet senseless will of Zeus—to a properly mythic content inhabiting cinema without contrivance or artifice: purely through the medium itself. The camera not only grants every object a weakly mythic potency but is itself the fateful self-contradiction of memory, thus anticipating the arrival of the strongly mythic—a content, as we will see, always riven by the contradiction of the origin. With the invention of cinema, all nine muses—the established arts—are gathered into this new mechanized memory, exposing the mother in her tragic contradiction; the mother, who should be the absolute origin, the source, appears simultaneously as a self-sentimentalizing contrivance, a sentimentality apparatus. The self-less relation to the child appears as absolute narcissism: the gift of life—the gift of herself to herself.

The decision to cast Kim Hye-ja as the otherwise nameless mother is integral to the film's tragic dimension.[4] Before *Mother*, she was known primarily as the star of *Chŏnwŏnilgi* (Country Diaries), whose 1,088 episodes, running from 1980 to 2002, set a record for longest running series that still holds. Television not only tends to establish a stronger identification between actor and character, but it also develops an intimate relation between celebrities and viewers, who encounter them weekly or even daily within their home.[5] And indeed, in Kim's role as mother in Korea's most famous television drama of rural life, she came to epitomize the Korean ideal of the unconditionally loving and endlessly self-sacrificing mother.[6] Her iconic mother—transcending history, social and technological change, political revolution— becomes the human personification of all-giving, untiring nature, and, consequently, the deep source of nationalist identity. While nothing is more culturally universal than the mother, the mother also becomes the absolute signifier of ethno-national, even racial, difference. The mother is always this mother or that mother, with this or that kind of face, these gestures, speaking this or that mother tongue. The iconic television mother, personifying the universal mother, nationalizes and particularizes the mother at the same time.

Bong's *Mother* brings this entire field of tensions into play: the national mother, mother nature nationalized, is exposed in the dark contradictions inhabiting it. It's not just a matter of showing that the mother is only human, has ordinary human desires—indeed nothing could be further from the case. Her motherly virtue is absolute but also absolutely ambiguous. Absolute self-sacrifice is absolute narcissism through the detour of the Other with which one identifies absolutely.[7]

The power of birth is the power of death, an archaic right of the mother, that, abrogated by the father, then by the sovereign, is still granted to the mother, if at all, only in the first months of gestation. Symptomatic of the maternal contradiction is that the absolute mother's absolute son lacks fluency in his own mother tongue; not only does he speak with a stammer, but, recounting his abusive interrogation to his mother, he alludes to the events in a series of Korean words and their English counterparts, pronounced in Korean fashion: "*sagwa appeluh.*" It is, we may suppose, in his mangled tongue that *ŏmŏni* becomes *muduh.*

Mother, moreover, neither glorifies violence as the hero's last word nor treats it aesthetically as a higher, if "evil," form of expression— the creative act that the detective seeks to interpret. Rather, it appears as the inevitable consequence of the failure of speech. This is shown brilliantly in the scene, the culmination of a series of flashbacks, depicting the murder of Moon Ah-jeong (Hee-ra Mun) as remembered by the junk collector. Yoon Do-joon (Won Bin), the mother's son, having followed Ah-jeong through the winding, derelict alleys after a night of drinking, calls out to her: "You don't like guys." She tucks into the abandoned dwelling where the junk collector had been squatting for the night, picks up a rock, and throws it at Do-joon. A short dialogue ensues:

> Her: "Hey! Do you know me?"
> Him: "No"
> Her: "I said, do you know me?"
> Him: "Nope"
> Her: "Then why . . . I hate guys. So don't talk like that, you stupid
> retard."

"Retard (*pabo*)" is a triggering word for him, provoking him to violence, and so he picks up the same rock, throws it back at her, landing a fatal blow to the head.

Faced with the word giving name to his own lack of verbal facility, his failed command even of his own mother tongue, he resorts to violence. Tossed and tossed back, the rock symbolizes the words exchanged, but it also reveals violence as beyond words, containing the word-language within its limits. It intimates, if faintly, the deepest strata of meaning of the pantomimic silent film: the comic struggle with objects, such as we find in Chaplin, "not only reveals their demoniac personality but turns them into equal, even superior, opponents."[8] And thus it reveals an asymmetry: for her, the rock initiates dialogue, for him it ends it by ending her; smashing her head, destroying her capacity for words and speech. While violence is numbingly ubiquitous in movies and television, it is nothing new to art; what cinematic media, compared with literature and other arts, make possible is the total separation of violence either from words (as in epic verse) or even from expressive gestures (as in theater and dance). Violence thus comes to engulf speech, which, in the typical Hollywood action film, appears as little more than formulaic dressing for virtuosic displays of graphic violence; since human beings have already been rendered effectively mute, loss of life is bereft of its moral significance. Remarkably, however, Moon Ah-jeong's murder draws brute violence back into a moral order characterized by language.

One aspect of the scene, nevertheless, remains utterly unrealistic: the rock looks rather large and heavy, between twenty and thirty kilograms by my estimate. Not even the well-built Do-joon, let alone diminutive Ah-jeong, could throw such a rock the distance between them. It is as if, the very moment words begin to fail them, they both acquire a superhuman, magical—or, rather, cartoon-like—strength.

Yet if the cartoonishly stylized, CGI-enabled violence of the typical Hollywood blockbuster action film absolves the human body of its vulnerability, eradicating the last reserve of the interiority on which ethical life depends, this brief lapse of verisimilitude does the opposite: violence is returned to its root in human interiority. The desire to signify, to speak, unable to find words, is translated into physical force whose cartoonish excess betrays its spiritual origin. We are witnessing *han* (恨): that untranslatable word expressing a sorrow, grief, bitterness tinged with the hope of an *otherwise*.

Since this scene depicts the junk dealer's own memory of the events and is shown rigorously from his perspective—looking out through the dirty windows of a darkened room—we don't see the blood streaming from her wound. This is surprising, since the flow of blood and other liquids—suggesting elemental *qi/ki*—is a persistent visual motif, beginning with the very first scene after the titles, when the mother, guillotining medicinal herbs in her shop, cuts her finger as she looks distractedly at her son when a Mercedes—out-of-town professors on a golfing trip—slams into him on the sidewalk opposite her store and drives away. He is struck without being wounded; she bleeds, as if for him. Thus begins a double series of flows paired with violent events: his pee running off on the floor; the water bottle knocked over by the mother after she spies on Do-joon's friend Jin-tae (Jin Goo) and his girlfriend Mi-na (Chun Woo-hee) making love; Ah-jeong's nosebleed; her friend's menstruation; the glue oozing from the tube—the hit-and-run; the comical fight at the golf course; Ah-jeong's murder; the collision with the police car; Do-joon's interrogation; the jail-yard fight; the glue-sniffer's interrogation. The two sides of this series only fully coincide when the mother, hearing the junk dealer's story and learning that he is witness to her son's guilt, smashes his head with a large wrench. Blood, dark and viscous, flows from his head and mixes with dirt. This is, indeed, the only true murder of the film; Ah-jeong's death, the junk dealer's testimony reveals, would rather qualify as "manslaughter." In the mother's crime, sex and violence converge, and indeed violence is rejoined to ethical interiority. Violence is bloodshed precisely because human life depends on the integrity of the skin, which keeps blood from spilling out. Yet as menstruation and childbirth prove, there can be no life without some bloodshed—not without the outflow of fluids. The proximity of sex and violence rests on the absolute integrity of the body being itself illusory; interiority is inherently vulnerable. The body is not self-contained; it flows into broader flows. This suggests an understanding of the body, evinced in the works of Zhuangzi, as of a piece with nature, with life and death belonging to the same process, and the body, on its dissolution, transforming into other bodies.[9]

We again come up against the contradiction of the mother. Indeed, a deep if subtle connection ties these flows back to the problem of nostalgic memory. The Greek word "nostalgia" speaks to the *algos* (pain) of the *nostos* (returning home). *Nostos* comes from the verb *neomai*; meaning "to go or to come back," it is also used to describe the flow of rivers. Every river, after all, flows back to its home, the ocean. Itself a kind of flow, taking us back to the absolute, "immemorial" source of all memories, memory is only possible because the origin, having forgotten itself, tries to remember itself again. Yet at the very moment of absolute memory, the return to the source, there is no memory.

Tragic Flows

Despite all the virtuosic genre mixing and stylistic eclecticism for which Bong is celebrated, *Mother*'s dramatic kernel is a tragic concept of tremendous purity and force. The mother has neither first name nor last name, nor, it seems, any living relations save her grown-up, mentally disabled son. Not only is it unclear if she is widowed or divorced or a single mother, but the father is not mentioned, not even as a figure of absence. In one scene, the mother speaks, while administering acupuncture to her friend, of how she became pregnant with her son. In return for a loan, she offers her friend a supply of the medicines that she used to get pregnant. Facilitated with medicinal-magical herbs and maybe also with the phallus-like acupuncture needle, the mother's own pregnancy appears as parthenogenesis. The alien origin of her child, the impregnating seed—a traumatic sexual encounter, perhaps—has been forgotten. And that she gave birth to a son represents the ultimate triumph of this pseudo-parthenogenesis: even the male isn't beyond her powers. And while her son is slow, he is attractive, even beautiful. Her relation to him borders on incest: when he is peeing against the wall outside as she feeds him, she stares at his genitals. Mother and son share the same bed. He even says he has slept with her, though it's unclear if he knows what this means. What matters here is not the actual possibility of incest, but the ambiguity that follows from the unnatural extension into adulthood of the natural, nonsexual physical intimacy of mother and child.

Desperate for a sexual experience with the local girls, Do-joon, despite his good looks, is thwarted by his status as an "idiot."[10] Do-joon's sexual desire obviously puts him at odds with his mother, who wants nothing more than to keep him as her eternal baby. Like a dog in heat, as one person describes him, he strays from his home, and after getting nowhere with the ladies at the Manhattan Bar, wanders through the alleys of the moon town, stalking the schoolgirl Ah-jeong. When she is found murdered, propped up on the roof—on display for the whole village to see, and with a golf ball marked with his name in plain sight—he becomes the prime suspect.

But her death merely sets up the tragedy: the essential tragic concept involves the mother's quest to vindicate her son of the murder for which he's been accused, and which the police regard as a closed case once they coerce a confession from him. Rejecting a lenient plea deal proposed by the lawyer she hires—seven years in a mental hospital—she takes the matter into her own hands, seeking to discover the true culprit. Her first suspect is her son's ne'er-do-well friend, and after surreptitiously filming him making love to the daughter of the proprietor of the Manhattan Club—cinema, so Jean Cocteau, is an event seen through a keyhole—she absconds with a red-smeared golf club, wearing plastic gloves to preserve the integrity of the evidence, and brings it to the police.[11] This leads nowhere—just lipstick, a female detective observes.

Purely physical evidence, it seems, won't help her; the real work of detection operates through memory. Already during her first visit to her son, in the lawyer's presence, she urged him to rub his temples to facilitate his memory. The memories that emerge, however, not only do nothing to vindicate him but lead him to recall that, when just a boy, she had tried to poison him in a botched murder-suicide. It is only after Jin-tae confronts her, having broken into her home, that her memory-work takes a more fruitful direction: she learns from him that the seemingly innocent Ah-jeong had a "history." She not only sold herself for rice cakes but photographed her johns using a cell phone with the obligatory click disabled. The memories the mother elicits—from her friend with a camera shop, from Ah-jeong's own tech-savvy friend, from two local glue-sniffing boys—lead her to the phone, and this in turn to her own prime suspect. Among the pictures on the phone, Do-joon recognizes the junk dealer from whom she bought a broken umbrella and whose face she would not have even seen had he not insisted on returning her change. She visits his dilapidated hut in the town's outskirts on the pretense of providing free acupuncture to the elderly, and when he begins to describe Ah-jeong's murder—not as the perpetrator but as a witness to her own son's guilt—she bludgeons him to death and sets his dwelling on fire.

Thus, the two series mentioned before—the flowing, seeping liquids and the seemingly random, disjoint acts of violence—flow together with a third: the sequence of recollections that the mother herself produces in her detective work. This marks the culmination of the tragic plot, as rigorous in its logic as Sophocles's *Oedipus Rex*: seeking to vindicate her son, the mother not only discovers her guilt but commits murder herself. Memory, seeping liquids, and violence flow together into a moment of absolute maternity, absolute motherhood: motherly love and motherly hate, birth and death fuse with the symbolic death of the father.

Within *yinyang* thought, the *yin* is identified with the feminine, dark, hidden, yielding. The value of *yin* as feminine is very much at stake in the contestation between Confucianism and Daoism, with the "spontaneous passivity of the *Dao* [. . .] associated with the female body," which often serves as a metaphor for the *dao* in the *Daodejing*.[12] Daoism indeed contributed much to traditional Chinese medicine, which understands the human body in terms of the *qi* that flows, alongside blood, through the body's vessels in a cyclic rhythm, surging back and forth from the center to the extremities.[13] Such a conception of the body underwrites Chinese and Korean acupuncture, in whose development Daoist hygienic practices played an important role. This casts a different, though complementary, light on the mother's tragedy. We recall, again, her dancing—half shaman, half coquette—in the open field. *Wu* (無)—"nothingness," "lack," "emptiness" and, more originally, "hiddenness"—is perhaps the most fundamental concept of philosophical Daoism and appears 101 times in the *Daodejing*. Yet as Wang notes, in the oracle bone script, the oldest attested form of written Chinese, *wu* is the symbol for dancing, and Chinese has three closely related characters all pronounced *wu*: 無 (nothingness), 舞 (dance), 巫 (shaman). Their meanings are connected by the Han dynasty scholar Xu Shen, creator of the first comprehensive Chinese dictionary: shamans are women who can perform service to the shapeless and make the spirits come down by dancing.[14] The same linguistic connection appears in Korean, with the character *mu*—corresponding to the Chinese *wu*—found in such words as *mudang* (shaman), *muyong* (dance), and *mu* (nothingness), a common negating prefix. Shaman-dancer, conjurer of the great void, she is at once absolute mother existing outside—and as if banished from—the patriarchal order, and parthenogenic progenitor of her own son. For all her mastery of the flow of *qi/ki*, the mother cannot restrain, in herself or others, the violence of bloodshed. She is, as it were, patriarchy's monstrous other, its shadow. Or in a word: *muduh*.

Liberation

For all the classical purity of this tragic plot, *Mother* is still not exactly a tragedy. Rather, as the title scene suggests, it is almost a story of liberation and indeed a double liberation: the mother and the son are both freed from each other, the umbilical cord finally cut. This process begins when the son is in prison: the moment he remembers what his mother tried to do to him, his personality changes. He speaks with new confidence and clarity; like a lifting fog, his mental disability starts losing its hold.[15] After he is released from prison, his transformation is even more apparent. For a second time in the film, he is shown eating with his mother. The first time they ate together, having returned from the police station after the golf course scuffle, he stuffed boiled roots into his mouth with his hands as his mother tried to feed him. Now, however, he is using chopsticks with perfect dexterity. Their conversation is also telling; he tells his mother he's been thinking about why the "crazy JP"—who ended up taking the rap—"put her body up on the roof, way up high?" Then he stands up to pour his own glass of water, towering over her—conventional cinematic language for dominance—while speaking in a tone brimming with clever confidence: "So I think, maybe it was so people would see her? She was bleeding. She needed to go to the hospital. So he put her in a place where people could see her fast. I bet that's it." In the next scene, they are lying together in bed when her eyes flash open, as if in sudden recognition of the new truth of their relationship.

These are hardly the words of an imbecile. Even if taken in the most innocent way, they imply a capacity to form an evidence-based hypothesis regarding the motivations of another person. Yet everything in his tone and demeanor, which now resembles Jin-tae, suggests a less innocent interpretation: he is trying to show his mother, without exactly confessing his guilt, that he is responsible for the girl's death. He understands that he gains power over her if she knows that he knows his own guilt and thus hers as well. Not only can he now communicate in full sentences, but he deftly uses language as a tool of manipulation and domination. This becomes clearest in the final scene. Mother and son are sitting in a bus station, waiting for her to board a seniors-only excursion. He hands her a gift: the acupuncture kit that he had recovered, after his release from prison, from the burnt-out ruins of the junk dealer's house. The murder committed by her was not a perfect crime: there are no eyewitnesses, no memory traces save her own, but there is a physical trace, which he now returns to her—revealing both his knowledge of her guilt and her indebtedness to him.

Motherly love is a boundless, unconditional love. Mother and son are alike held captive by this love, literally *retarded* by it. Motherly love retards because unconditional love allows no reciprocation; every return of love would undermine its claim to be absolute. But without reciprocation, there can be no relation: unconditional love is not really love at all but an absolutely alienated absolute narcissism. Opposed to absolute, unconditional love is the explicit contract. This is not only the foundation of capitalist economic relations (the putatively free exchange of labor), but returning to Hobbes, the basis of modern European political philosophy. There can be no transition, however, from maternal love to the social contract. The social contract might perhaps offer an escape from a rationally postulated "state of nature" conceived as a war of all against all, but, regardless of whether it introduces the father-sovereign or fraternal equality, it's helpless against mother nature, nature as mother.

What emerges at the end of the film between the mother and son is neither unconditional love nor an explicit contract but something else: a reciprocal relation wherein each helps exonerate the other of the crime each knows the other to have committed. Only thus do both gain independence. Whereas murder-suicide—mother and son frolicking together in the heavenly flower garden—is the inevitable denouement of the maternal absolute, this criminal exchange allows for a different relationship: they have both grown up. One could think of this, indeed, as a double adoption, replacing purely natural motherhood with an artificial relationship, a proto-juridical relationship premised on knowledge of crime.

This new independence, moreover, rests on the new power gained over memory and forgetting. The bus tour, another gift from the son, has a particular significance: the women in the tour bus, shown dancing in the aisle, will most likely be taken to some tourist spot, where they will meet up with men brought by other buses for an afternoon of carefree pleasure.[16] Yet the mother, after her son's revelation, is distressed, sitting glumly while the other women dance. But then she takes out her acupuncture kit, jabbing the meridian point in her thigh. The camera shows her from the side, the low-hanging sun dancing in and out of the bus's windows. A drum beats out a march, and then we hear the tense, yearning plucks and sensuous rhythm: the music from the title scene when she danced alone in the field—after committing murder, we now understand.

She rises and starts dancing and soon her silhouette loses itself among the other silhouettes—one dancing shadow among others. And the camera, jerking back and forth, up and down, dances with them (Figure 5).

Shadowy optics and wistful music notwithstanding, this seems like a happy ending. The mother is riding off into the sunset in a bus packed with dancing *halmŏni* (grandmothers). She is a survivor. One recalls the end of Bertolt Brecht's *Mutter Courage und ihre Kinder* (Mother Courage and her Children), where the mother, bereft of children, pulls her cart by herself.[17] Just as Brecht's mother is freed in the end for her economic activity in its purest form, no longer justified by the higher purpose of protecting her children, Bong's mother is freed for the only paradise that late-stage capitalism can still promise the laboring multitude: leisure, consumption, and, most of all, sex.

But this is also a Dionysiac bus of maenads, a Daoist dancing ritual, an orgy. . . . The flowing bodies flow with the light into a single cosmic dance. Here, perhaps, we find not just the danger but the saving power too.

Figure 5 Mother *directed by Bong Joon Ho. © CJ Entertainment 2009. All rights reserved.*

The Obscure Camera

In *Mother*, there are no trains, no tunnels. Unlike the rural community in *Memories of Murder*, and despite the more than two decades elapsed, it remains almost entirely off the grid binding the provinces to the metropolitan centers. Though the mother wanders through a rice field, there is otherwise little evidence of productive economic activity: the herbs and roots she sells come from China; the rural has been reduced to a mere scenic backdrop, a commercial ruse. Rather than being subsumed under the central political and economic powers, the rural community of *Mother*, like the mother herself and so many of its residents, has been abandoned, left to go to seed. The patriarchal element itself thus appears only in an attenuated, compromised form; the professors, symbols of central power—the new Neo-Confucian scholarly elite—speed through town in their Mercedes on the way to the golf course, colliding with Do-joon. Ultimately, they are "too important to be here," as one of them imperiously declares at the police station.

This, of course, reflects the situation of Korea post-IMF-crisis along with the broader trend of its economic development, which has led to the marginalization of the rural economy.[18] But it also suggests the special place that *Mother* occupies within the topology of Bong's films. Whereas *Barking Dogs Never Bite*, which begins with camera-space, represents the utopian prospects of modernity, and whereas *Memories of Murder* plays out the tension between the pre-modern and modern spatial orderings while opening into the abyssal depths of memory, *Mother*'s spatiality is predominantly the porous, intertwined, labyrinthine space of memory itself, stretching out into the fields and only loosely contained at its perimeter by various institutional spaces such as the prison, the mental hospital, and the cemetery. Indeed, the best use the city can still find for the countryside is the golf course, a utopian recreational space. This "mnemonic" porosity is evident from how characters violate the boundaries of seemingly private dwellings; houses have not yet become the absolute refuge of the solitary individual or the family unit. And it is also seen with Ah-jeong: just as her vagina has been claimed as communal property by the village men, her murder occurs amid abandoned derelict dwellings that anyone can occupy. Hiding inside one of these, she throws the stone at Do-joon, and from his perspective it appears as if the stone were flying out from a darkened slit. The *camera obscura* and vagina fuse into a single motif. Yet she also has her "pervert phone": if her prostituted and slaughtered body represents passive memory—traumatic memory—the camera, standing in for the cinematic camera, is its active counterpart. Whereas for the mother, these two aspects of nostalgic memory flow together, in Ah-jeong they burst apart. She is a victim, and she bears witness: but she can never bear witness *as* victim.

This diremption between the victim and the witness marks the ethical limit of cinematic representation. Depending on the mediation of genre conventions, technique, artifice, industrial capital, cinema can only bear witness to the suffering and trauma of the *other* as *other*. The mother, however, is the one who can never be other—a pure immanence that claims everything as its own, takes up everything within itself. The *othered* mother is the young girl; Ah-jeong appears as a universal object, and, as soon as she resists, she must die. This suggests, moreover, that the mother herself, even when elevated to the main theme, cannot be thematized. Like the *dao*, the mother eludes representation.

4

The Host

The Monster

Both *Memories of Murder* and *Mother*—and *Barking Dogs Never Bite* as well—are movies about a terrible, monstrous something: the perverse, destructive desires hidden in the human heart. But they aren't monster movies. Never coming fully into view, monstrosity remains always hidden behind the normal, ordinary face—the face of the normal, everyday Korean. There are, of course, other faces: slightly deformed by scars and burns (the first suspect in *Memories of Murder*, the "pervert camera" girl in *Mother*). But these are not the scars of monsters but bear witness to the monstrosity of others.

The hiddenness of monstrosity, the absence of the monster, is itself a characteristic feature of the detective genre. If evil were immediately visible, if it weren't always hidden behind a normal face, there would be no need for the detective, whose basic task is never just to find the obvious but to uncover a hidden truth. For there are two primary heroic archetypes: the epic hero, exemplified by Odysseus, occupies a world of manifest monsters; the tragic hero, exemplified by Oedipus, dwells in a world where monstrosity is a riddle, hidden beneath the surface of things. Odysseus is the progenitor of the action hero, slaying monsters of one or another kind; Oedipus the first detective.

And indeed, the first *noir* detective, since he is utterly exposed to the evil he pursues. It inhabits his being—he catches himself. The lineage of the whodunit detectives, on the other hand, begins with Socrates, practitioner of a rationality that, convinced of the identity of knowledge and virtue, is immunized from moral danger.[1] For the Socratic detective of the whodunit, evil is hidden, but only superficially. *It is only really the material causes of evil that are hidden, not their moral causes.* The doer of evil deeds is first concealed from the detective, only to be discovered after the fact. But evil is not a mystery hidden in the human soul itself.

By combining typical tropes of the *noir* detective genre with both masterful sociopsychological realism and expressionist bathos, Bong conveys the presence of an inner moral reality merely indicated by the scars of the violence and vice plaguing the quotidian world. Both *Memories of Murder* and *Mother*, moreover, juxtapose the familiar, comfortable surface of life—a surface most evident in rural communities not yet completely disarrayed by urban modernity—to the chthonic depths first revealed through memory.

Bong's third movie—a tremendous commercial success, setting a record for domestic box-office sales unsurpassed until James Cameron's *Avatar* (2009)—is something completely different: a bona fide monster movie.[2] The true star of *The Host* (2006) is the *koemul* (怪物, "monster," "freak") itself: a giant slimy cephalopod-reptilian something that mysteriously appears in the Han river years after hundreds of liters of formaldehyde are poured down the drain in a US military pathology clinic. The monster movie differs from other genres, whose elements it may freely incorporate, in this above all else: it shows us the monster.

This suggests that genres are not to be understood as "patterns" of elements that may either be mixed with others or presented in a "classical" purity. Genre involves a decision allowing no middle ground: *either the monster appears in the flesh (the monster genre) or there is only a hidden monstrosity infecting the surface of things (the detective genre).* And indeed, perhaps this is no longer a matter just of genre but something even more fundamental: a decision between two different modes of signification, showing the "thing itself" versus hinting at it; expression versus indication. And yet, if the monster presents itself as the liminal phenomenon wherein this decision reveals itself in the clearest light, we immediately face a problem. For the word *monster*—from the Old French *monster* and the Latin *monstrum*—is related to the Latin *monstrare*, to show, and *monere*, to warn. The monster is a demonstration and admonition: it points something out to us, warns us against it. It shows, warns, portends.[3] Whereas in Medieval Europe, the monster was understood as an aberration from the natural order (say, an animal born with two heads) portending some consequential historical event, the modern monster no longer predicts some specific catastrophe but points toward the deeper contradictions inhabiting the order of things. The relation between the monster and monstrosity now changes: before, we spoke of a monstrosity without the monster—signs of a radical evil not showing its "true face"—but it now becomes clear that the monster points toward a monstrosity that *never shows itself*, that *cannot show itself.*[4] The monster, in all its monstrous presence, is a sign, a mode of signification, signifying nothing else than monstrosity. Yet monstrosity is what is never itself—the original contradiction of the thing itself. Monstrosity is thus at once ontological and semiotic: the originary self-contradictory Being, and a mode of signification that always points beyond the finite, determinate, toward infinite semiosis, the mad, errant, play of signification.

But what does it then mean to "show the monster"?—a formulation no less paradoxical than "showing the money," since money, like the monster, is a sign. The monster is the "face" of monstrosity—of self-contradiction—just as the normal human face, especially with its characteristic ethnic appearance, is the "face" of identity and self-identity. We find ourselves face-to-face with two faces and two ontologies: a double face and a double ontology. Cinema, it now becomes clear, unfolds in the chiasmic relation between two modes of semiosis (finite, infinite) and two Beings (radical self-identity, radical self-contradiction).

We can now clarify the distinction, already alluded to several times, between the weakly and strongly mythic. We previously identified the monster as one form the strongly mythic may assume. This is true, however, only if the monster is taken in a very narrow sense. But not only is the monster, *sensu stricto*, the paradigmatic form of the strongly mythic, but all expressions of the strongly mythic are versions of the monster. The weakly mythic involves a particular instantiation of a general type—*this* face, *this* portrait, *this* house— that consequently creates an enormous tension or suspense and hence an intention toward the full presence of the unique, singular individual. The strongly mythic consists, contrariwise, in a radically singular presence set in relief from the world of individuated forms—*these* things and *these* people—and pointing toward original contradiction, primeval chaos, the subconscious, the Heracleitean "one differentiating from itself." Whereas the weakly mythic puts the aura into play as the trace of the individual's individuated singularity, the strongly mythic beckons toward the absolute singularity of the origin, not the singularity of the individuated *this or that* but the singular ground.

The monster is never in the first instance this or that kind of monster, but simply monster. Accordingly, it has a *unique* appearance, which thus comes to be absolutely identified with this film or series of films or maybe with an iconic monster-type. This doesn't mean that the monster defies all description: a monster can be mammalian, reptilian, cephalopodan, extraterrestrial, or humanoid; it can have this shape, these colors, these features. Yet such descriptions merely compensate for the lack of species and genus. Thus, the very term "monster" functions not as genus but reveals the breakdown of taxonomic ordering, just as, in the scholastic-Aristotelian theory of the transcendentals, *being, unity, truth* are not ultimate genera but transcend the generic by applying to all things whatsoever. Still, there is not just one monster but a multitude. Whereas transcendentals point to an identity beyond the logical articulation of things through genera and species, monsters, *monstrals* as it were, discover a radical nonidentity and irreducible manifoldness through which the logical fabric of the world comes apart. The monster's monstrosity exposes the breakdown of the categorial articulation of the world—of an ontology organized through genera, species, and individuals. And indeed, it signifies through a mode of signification that is anti-categorial. And yet in just this way, it also reveals a modality of being: *beings in their non-identity, in their deviation from the logical articulation through which they submit to language, in their radical in-coherence, incomprehensibility, senselessness—but also novelty, uniqueness.*

Globalization/Signs of Life

It should not surprise us that *The Host* was Bong's first great commercial success. The nearly perfect realization of the "Korean blockbuster," it ended up doing just what one feared Hollywood would do, dominating screen time and stifling competition. For many cinephiles, its success boded ill for the future of Korean cinema: to remain competitive, Korean films would now have to assimilate Hollywood's most problematic tendencies, with a black-and-white vision of good and evil triumphing over moral complexity and nuance, violence taking the place of dialogue, and introspective depth vanishing behind a cartoonish façade.[5] To be sure, the plot of *The Host* is, in its main contours at least, barely more subtle than its featured monster: after running rampage along the banks of the Han river, killing and eating many, the *koemul* absconds into the sewer mains with a young girl, whose family, once they discover she is alive, try to save her. Meanwhile the Korean government, acting in league with the United States, endeavors to cover up the incident by concocting a story about a virus. For all its psychological, sociological, and historical nuance, and despite its unconventional ending, *The Host* mostly consists in the stock in trade of the Hollywood action film: fights, chases, escapes. Indeed, while *The Host* was criticized for its anti-Americanism, even its anti-American messaging is very much *à l'américaine*. Bong, in his own words, was simply turning the tables on Hollywood's representations of the evil Other.[6]

This cartoonishly unsubtle depiction of Americans, however, is not deployed naively. Rather, it suggests a subtle engagement with the question of globalism. The cartoonish evil other represents the threat of globalization while simultaneously neutralizing it. For if globalization threatens the erasure of boundaries, distinctions, solidity, and materiality—the liquefaction of everything solid—then any representation of the global as this or that concrete threat has already cut against the grain.[7] The threat of globalism is represented as the threat of Americanism: the natively Korean is mutated by an American pollutant, which almost literally poisons the blood of the people. The threat of "miscegenation" is indeed obliquely indicated by the appearance of an interracial couple—the absurdly heroic American soldier and his pretty Korean girlfriend—early in the film. And yet this very representation of globalism—moving entirely within a virulently nationalist imaginary—is itself the result of the self-conscious, deliberate assimilation of a "Hollywood" style to represent the threat of globalism faced by Korea. Deleuze observes that cinema, as an industrial art, exists in a permanent relation to the conspiracy of money, an "international conspiracy which conditions it from within, as the most intimate and most indispensable enemy."[8] Regarded both as a commercial event and as a work of industrial art—comprehensible through its plot—*The Host* is at once plot with and counterplot against this conspiracy.

Given Bong's penchant for material representations of the mechanisms of the cinematic apparatus, one could even argue that the flowing river represents film, and hence the Han, the quintessential Korean river, is Korean film. Born of the polluted river, the monster would signify Korean film exposed through globalism to the corrupting power of the "Hollywood" style—a mutant monstrosity born from the confluence of Korean cinema and Hollywood, Korea and America. But this, in turn, implies that the representation of monstrosity is itself the monstrosity. The representation of monstrosity converges with the monstrosity of representation. The monstrous effect of globalization is allowing globalization to appear *as* monster. Precisely by exposing the dialectic of cinematic monstrosity in all its monstrous paradox, *The Host* achieves nothing less than an immunization against the contagion of American-style globalization. In a word: it brings Hollywood to the point of irony. Not the superficial, self-celebrating irony that Hollywood itself revels in, but the deep irony of the idea, the unifying concept brought to the point of absolute self-contradiction, "an absolute synthesis of absolute antitheses, the continual self-creating interchange of two conflicting thoughts."[9]

We might be tempted, then, to conclude that *The Host* demonstrates nothing less than the monstrous absurdity of the monster. Going back all the way to *Don Quixote*, this is the one fundamental theme of the Romantic work of art. The "classical" monster—the monster of epic—is a "real" monster; the monstrosity of the real—primordial nature in the threat it poses to human life. The "Romantic" monster, on the other hand, is the creation of the would-be hero who, at sea in a monster-less world, needs monsters to be the very hero he would be.

Yet things are not so simple. As an allegory of representation, *The Host* represents the monstrous absurdity of representation. But globalization is not just a matter of "ideology"; it has a material existence, whose ultimate form is the metabolic exchange between human beings and the "natural" environment.[10] *The Host* may allegorize the impossibility of representing the ecological threat of global capitalism save in terms of a neofascist imaginary, but it concerns the very real threat to the real. Just as Marx stood Hegel back on his feet, the Romantic monster, the product of the heroic imagination, again becomes real. Far from negating the dialectic of monstrosity, this brings it full circle.

This is how we can understand the somewhat convoluted subplot: the US Military's and Korean government's concerted attempt to cover up what happened by concocting a story about a virus. If we spoke earlier of immunization, this is not without irony; immunization against a viral contagion suggests the very biopolitical regime that Bong challenges.[11] But the dialectic of the film, unfolding in two parallel series—the real and the ideal, "material" substructure and ideology—does not reach a simple verdict against the biopolitical. If the monster is taken as *real*, then the virus is a cover-up; biopolitics will be nothing more than an "ideological" apparatus that captures and subjects the real. But if the monster is the monstrosity of representation, then the viral cover-up must in fact reveal the truth. The monstrous logic of representation is itself a viral logic.

These two dialectical series not only coexist but contaminate each other as they flow together and apart again. The culmination of this convergence is the genetic, which is both real and ideal, or, rather, neither and both at once. Genetic code is both material reality and information—materialized code. Life is mutation, monstrosity—the originary monstrosity of a monstration that, not simply representing an abstract structure, signifies the paradoxical fusion of signifier and signified, intertwining and disentangling. *The Host* immunizes against the contagion of Hollywood but only by returning cinema, in its endlessly unfolding double series, to its origin in what we might call mutant life, becoming-life; *natura naturans* in the only sense in which it can now be understood: the pure virulence of an emerging, monstrously self-replicating order. We might speak of life as sign of life, since life is the sign: not as formal structure, but as materiality-ideality.

A city map of contemporary Seoul suggests a curious resemblance to Saussure's famous diagram of the "sign" in his *Cours de linguistique générale* (General Course in Linguistics): a circle halved by a line—written in the top half, *signifié*, and in the bottom half, *signifiant*. Signified and signifier—the two halves into which the original, radical unity of the sign splits. Lee Hyuk-rae's documentary *Yellow Door: '90s Lo-fi Film Club* (2023) refers to this almost iconic image of the sign, suggesting the importance for Bong's early formation of a serious study of the semiotic dimension of film. Perhaps this strangely significant, strangely signifying series of divisions and resemblances also struck Bong. The river is the sign, dividing signifier and signified, superstructure and substructure, culture and nature. But it is sign *as* genetic power of mutation, the mobile sign, the sign of mobility: the cinematic sign. Cine? And we might also recall Hölderlin's sententious line from "Der Ister" (*The Ister*): "Denn Ströme machen urbar / Das Land. [Because streams make the land arable]."[12]

It is a sign not as the abstract structure of an immobile order of things from which the diachronic, the flow of time, has been banished, but as the power of origination accomplishing itself through the diremptive coincidence of the emerging and the emerged. Signification signifies as the tension between the synchronic and diachronic—the city/state (*Stadt, Staat*) and the river that runs through it.

The Vertical and Horizontal City

Cities organize human life horizontally and vertically through an artificial environment that, built into the preexisting natural environment, joins the two together. This achieves a totality, or rather a semblance of totality; the city remains dependent on the countryside just as human life depends on wider nature, however much this dependence is denied and repressed. Because the vertical organization is determined by the interaction of the artificial/ historical with the natural, it assumes strikingly different forms; different cities are organized in dramatically different ways.

Whereas the quantity of land is conceived horizontally, as surface area, the quality of land is determined primarily by the vertical: by the shape of its surface, the vegetation growing out of it, and its climate, which implies a relation to the meteorological. Even soil quality, geology, and access to water involve a downward verticality. With the city, moreover, the vertical, at once given through nature and conquered through artifice, is symbolically potent. The tall cathedral at the heart of a European city establishes a theological order; the bird's-eye view, taking in the surrounding space, belongs to the Church and not to the State. The winding steps leading to the belfry suggest that access to commanding heights demands a diligent effort of which few are capable, the discipline of a spiritual calling. In the nineteenth century, the impoverished artist, confined to dingy, suffocating garrets, will assume this lofty discipline, partaking of a vocation at once worldly and spiritual. However, a different kind of poverty—sepulchral and debased—belongs to damp basements and the cavernous world beneath the city; the underground (*podpol'e*) of Dostoevsky's spiteful ex-civil servant.

But this all changes with high-rises and elevators; now affluence commands the heights, whether as the opulent palaces of managerial and financial capital, the private abodes of the wealthy, or the quasi-public spaces selling a few hours of panoptic vision to the masses. At both the juridical and ideological levels, capitalism depends on maintaining the illusion of the social transparency of wealth. Stashed away or dispatched for obscure purposes, wealth becomes Plutonic, hellish. Gold's radiance is a symbol of affluence, but it also makes wealth visible, promoting its transparency: only when returned to the bowels of the earth, locked away in vaults, does gold become evil.

With Seoul, the vertical dimension unfolds along several lines of tension. Even Chosŏn Seoul was organized around two quite different attitudes toward the city's mountainous terrain. Exemplifying Neo-Confucian ideas of harmonious order, the palace complex at the heart of the old city follows simple geometric lines; the surrounding mountains rise behind the palace, solidifying the palace in the austere purpose of its "heavenly mandate" without submitting it to the mountain's crumpled topology. On the other side of Inwangsan, a syncretic Buddhist-shamanist temple has been built into the mountain, enlivened by its crazy verticality, with a perilous stairway leading up to a sacred boulder where women pray for pregnancy. Pongwŏnsa, a more sedate temple belonging to the T'aego order of Korean Buddhism, rests calmly on the placid slope of Ansan. Finally, the fortress wall running along the mountains offers military outlooks.

These features persist in the modern city; there are still active military fortifications dotting the mountain alongside the rebuilt ruins of the old wall. But another level of verticality has also been superimposed: the city's planar spaces have become the privileged locations for mid-rise and high-rise developments. This results in an odd topological contradiction: while wealth builds *up*, with skyscrapers becoming the visual sign of capitalism, the poorer residents are crowded into the hills, which are not only less suitable for large complexes but also cut off from the main thoroughfares and the subway system. There are also a few affluent neighborhoods in the hills, but, for the most part, the typical *nouveaux riches* dwell in mid-rise complexes, with skyscrapers such as Lotte Tower reserved for the ultra-rich among them. And unlike in New York or Paris, there is nothing equivalent to an old, distinguished, elegant apartment building. Newer, shinier, and sleeker is almost always better, more expensive, more prestigious.

With these antagonistic orders of verticality, the city offers numerous conflicting points of privileged yet partial vision. If these can be united under a single symbolic order, rendering the city transparent to itself, it is through the strange convergence of the mountain moon town (where ascent requires effort, a punishment imposed on the poor) and the skyscraper (rewarding wealth with an effortless sovereign view). What results is the vision of an absolute meritocracy constantly imperiled by absolute unfairness, vividly dramatized in the Netflix series *Squid Games* (2021–). Happiness is possible in a fair society because effort is rewarded with a flourishing life. Happiness is possible in an unfair society because it has been given over to fate, chance. But a society that holds on tenaciously to meritocracy, regarding failure as not only shameful but culpable, even while acknowledging its impossibility, is a society that has made happiness impossible; a society that, all its affluence notwithstanding, has turned itself into a hell.

And yet . . . gently flowing out into the Yellow Sea, the Han not only cuts through the mountainous terrain with its flatness but invites to a leisurely recreation at odds with a city otherwise so tensely charged.

Its banks serve a special function, hard to grasp until you've spent enough time in the city to begin to feel it, for all its vastness, closing in around you, as does every metropolis once the vibrant, intoxicating façade encountered by the tourist gives way to the routine circuits carved by the day-to-day. Here families and friends lounge about, picnic, and drink, young couples walk holding hands, ride tandem bikes, or make out in the rented tents. The Han's banks, in other words, mark out a utopian space, belonging to the present and not the future: the *realized utopia* existing within the city and upon which its order depends—a kind of "Sabbath space." The banks of the Han are where happiness happens. Running through "Hell Chosŏn" is a sliver of heaven. Nevertheless, this utopia is more apparent than real: work, extreme poverty, and class division persist, together with the hidden violence upholding the whole system.

Silent Flows the Han/Monster as Sign

The Han is the dynamic origin: the originative and generative logic of the sign as the paradoxical coincidence of nature and culture, as site of transformation and mutation. It is time and history, the irrevocable forward flow that is also always a flowing back, a return to the oceanic. And while every city is the product of the origin and the work of history, contemporary Seoul, with its relentless dynamism, is especially so. Yet only on the banks of the Han does the originative signification of the river, along with the vertical dynamism of the city, flicker into view in a flash of radical transparency. The monster must invade the banks of the Han, turning an earthly heaven into an earthly hell. But conversely, if the monster seems very much to be something, it is revealed as nothing, the pure power of negation. The monster is a sign for signification, but the originative, infinite power of signification negates itself the very moment that it represents itself through a finite sign. If, even so, one must battle the monster, defeat the monster, it is only to show that the monster is always already nothing: that *signification* is everything, the *finite sign* nothing—and yet, nevertheless, a nothing that signifies everything.[13] Here too we recall the yielding emptiness of the *dao*; the nameless "fetal beginnings of everything that is happening."[14]

In every monster film, it is important how the monster becomes manifest. There is often even an eroticism of the monster; a play of veils—a dance of intimations, hints—before the obscene *thing itself* arrives on scene. Bong, however, emphatically rejects this monstrous strip tease, remarking in an interview that he "hated the monster film's convention or tradition that we have to wait for more than an hour just to see the tip of the monster's tail."[15] From the moment the monster surfaces, Bong shows us everything, the "full monsty."

In this, he is guided by a deep creative and philosophical intuition. If the monster were to remain mostly hidden, bathed in darkness, shimmering in obscurity, or were only to slowly, teasingly reveal itself, we would remain entangled in the veiled dance of signification, the play of truth as un-concealment, *alētheia*. This truth-play would appear through the monster but only because the teasingly concealing/un-concealing monster appears as a concrete sign of truth—of truth "set into work" in an earthly materiality.[16] Instead of the play of signification, however, what Bong's monster shows is an exhausted, fulfilled, saturated signification—signification *as such*, not just of this or that—that accomplishes itself through the negation of the finite sign.

Replacing this gradual erotic unveiling of the monster is a series of anticipations which, rather than showing us progressively more of the monster, show its development as a structure of signification. These appear after the formaldehyde release but before the opening credits:

first, a man wading and fishing in the Han catches and releases a mutant swimming critter; second, a businessman, before jumping to his death, stares down from the bridge at a monstrous something. With the first anticipation, the monster manifests as something real—something that could still be captured, grasped, destroyed. With the second, it manifests in its absolute, ineffable, impalpable meaning—the Han itself as pure becoming, the movement between life and death, the unspeakable horror of the original contradiction in all things. This meaning is neither signifier nor signified nor sign but originative signification.

The prologue thus presents, first, a finite sign bereft of signification, and, secondly, signification bereft of a sign. When the monster finally bursts on the scene, sign and signification, each having appeared separately, are reunited. This not only restores the sign but brings it to the point of saturation. Meaning is only possible through a system of signs, each signifying through its difference with others—through the differential nexus of the entire system of signification. Yet each sign also signifies signification as such, though only when its finite signification has been suspended. This suspension is possible because the sign, separated from signification, appears as a mere thing— something that can be destroyed.

The monster appears at once inside and outside the entire system of signification; in the world as what doesn't belong to this world. The monster's physical body, vulnerable to destruction, appears as the this-worldliness of the sign, whose destruction relegates the finite to the nonexistence that belongs to it as such even while unleashing the un-worldliness of the monster—signification as such. This separation of sign and signification, however, is only possible if the monster appears all at once from the first, bathed in the full light of day.

The Absent Mother

But this is only half the story. The monster appears and is destroyed. Nearly every monster film reenacts this same passion of the sign, and like the Passion of Christ is also a family drama. Yet the family belongs to the nation and the state, and the nation is part of a global economic and political order, situated within the total metabolism between human beings and non-human nature.[17] While the passion play of the sign, the birth and death of the monster, seems to exhaust itself in an ultimately vacuous dialectic, the monster remains entangled with the world, the system of finite meanings. The monster doesn't just appear as if against a void; it bursts into the world. The negation of the monster, revealing the finite sign's nullity, not only illuminates the world in a flash but transforms it. The substantial truth of the monster passion play rests in this transformation.

Born from the origin, representing the origin, the finite monster cancels the origin's infinitude, only to restore it by perishing, negating its own negation. The monster's sudden appearance makes the world transparent to itself, revealing it as a total order. But the monster is nonetheless precisely what has no place in the world, contradicting its claim to totality. The world's totality cannot contain its own representation. Hence, the monster's destruction restores totality but also transforms it. It opens the world; transforms a closed totality, whose own representation cannot be contained within it, into an open, infinite whole, suffused with self-understanding, cognizant of its own historicity, hence open to the event. The monster is dead, but the world has opened itself to the monster event—the monstrosity of the event.

This half of the story, moreover, assumes an irreducibly concrete form: it is a story about "real" people, painted in broad strokes, to be sure, but not merely vapid caricatures; not superheroes, abstract and devoid of substance as the monsters they battle against. The openness to the event, if not to become a fetish—the narcissistic glorification of alterity as an end in itself—must appear not only draped in the clothing of everyday life but as this life and nothing else, culminating in an irreducibly concrete, specific ethical act.

This family drama centers around the Parks, whose patriarch Park Hie-bong (Byun Hee-Bong) owns a river-bank bodega, selling light snacks, alcohol, and grilled squid with the help of his elder son, Gang-du (Song Kang-ho), a clumsy, narcoleptic, slow-witted oddball who, as if stuck in adolescence, dyes his hair blond. The other son, Nam-il (Park Hae-il), is an unemployed university graduate and former student activist, while the daughter Nam-joo (Bae Doona) is an elite archer and national medalist. The youngest member of the family is Gang-du's adolescent daughter, Hyun-seo (Ko Ah-sung).

Like most girls her age, she is embarrassed by her family and especially by her father. More than mere adolescent petulance, her embarrassment registers the spirit of the times; it's the voice of the new, shiny, glitzy Korea of Gangnam to which she herself—the bodega is located on the southern bank of the river—marginally belongs. Dressed in her school uniform, she already has a toehold in the future world from which her own father has been ejected, and to which the rest of her family aspires. All she needs is a new cell phone! Her father is saving to purchase one, squirreling away loose change in a jar like a child. While the "smart phone" had only just become a thing, the cellular phone, with its miniaturized screen, is already the exemplary signifier of capitalist hypermodernity, wrapping together the most potent dreams of consumer capitalism—total connectivity, perfect integration into contemporary society's information flow— into a gadget that, held in hand, is simultaneously on display to others.

Whereas Hyun-seo, somewhat devoid of character let alone eccentricity, suggests the new Gangnam-style Korea that will appear once the old city with its crazy winding alleys and haphazard piles of trash, its war-grizzled *haraboji* and trash-haulers, its half-rotted shanties and crumbling concrete have been razed to the ground, the three siblings are at once realistic portraits full of sociological nuance and mythic stereotypes. Gang-du is the country bumpkin, the clown—all brawn, no brains; Nam-il the frustrated Confucian scholar whose success was thwarted by a corrupt system pretending meritocracy while favoring the privileged; and finally Nam-joo, practitioner of the most quintessentially Korean sport, deeply invested with cultural significance and a source of great national pride, suggests both a new, liberated woman, threatening to the Neo-Confucian social order, and the archetype of the virginal maiden huntress, recalling the *wŏnhwa* ("original flowers"), female warriors of sixth-century-Shilla.

Conspicuously lacking in all this is the mother. Not only is the matriarch of the family absent, but Hyun-seo's birth mother, following her unintended birth, abandoned her to the care of Gang-du, the presumptive father. Not only are there no moms, but the maternal has ceased operating as a locus of sentimental attachment or nostalgia; the mother's absence is not felt as a lack that in turn becomes the focus of desire but as an absence so deep, so unsettling, that it cannot even be felt or put into words.[18] Meera Lee may be correct in pointing out that, in postmodern Korea, the traditional tragic heroines of Korean cinema—"strictly moralistic, long-suffering, and endlessly patient mothers, wives, or lovers"—no longer appeal to audiences. Yet something can fascinate without appealing, and, however unappealing, these heroines retain their symbolic resonance, as seen with *Mother*, released three years after *The Host*.[19] Changing tastes cannot explain the absence of the mother—and not least because an emphatic absence is an emphatic presence. The absolute mom—

suffocating the family with her m/omnipresence—and the mom's absolute absence are, in fact, two sides of the same coin.

What is lacking, in both cases, is a delicate balance between the two opposed centers of gravity around which family life orbits. The very concept of matriarchy, outside a narrow anthropological application, is misleading because maternal and paternal power operate in fundamentally different ways, make different claims, and only clash in certain artificial tragic situations—the plot of *Antigone*, for example—which arise when both overstep their limits. When family life is marginally functional, these two powers, like *yin* and *yang*, balance and constrain each other, having achieved a subtle and delicate compromise. Korea's condensed modernity upset this compromise, and rather than destroying the ideals attached to the maternal and paternal centers of power, it allowed these ideals to persist in hypertrophied form; what withered away were the complex, concrete cultural protocols that had adjudicated between the terms of an otherwise abstract opposition. If in *Mother* we see the ultimate mom without borders, her son suffocated under a limitless, lawless love, *The Host* shows the sorry spectacle of a patriarchy that persists only in crude gestures of petty violence, incapable of even passing down its values and reproducing itself.

Because the monster, at once in the world and out of the world, signifies signification as the horizon of a world of concrete signs, then, to the extent that the maternal itself has been excluded from this world of concrete signs, the monster, even as it signifies signification, also signifies the maternal *as* signification, signification *as* maternal. The monster, in other words, suggests the *archaic mother*, to use Barbara Creed's terms, and not only as a mythic archetype but as a logic of signification, according to which signification is no longer understood in terms of transcendental signifier or signified but as immanence, originative becoming, "natural" mutation.[20] Or, indeed, the monster is maternal, immanent signification as grasped within the order of transcendental signification. Put another way, it is the yielding creativity of the *dao* seen from the perspective of a repressive apparatus—the Neo-Confucian subordination of *qi/ki* to *li/i*. Hence, the total absence of mom appears as a frightening unworldly presence. Nevertheless, the arrival of the mother is also already anticipated by the presence of Hyun-seo, born to a *mater abscondita* and bequeathed to the—putative—father. Putative: because, in the absence of DNA testing, paternity will always depend, in the last instance, on the purity, the good conscience of the mother. One suspects, then, that the entire Park family, held together by Hyun-seo, depends on a belief that has never really been tested, indeed cannot be tested. They take her for their own, but in fact, she is something foreign: a monstrous birth for whom the fundamental patriarchal claim—to the possession and ownership of female bodies—rings hollow since this very claim depends on the complicity of the departed maternal element.

Hyun-seo's existence among the family anticipates the *monster*, because she, like the monster, doesn't really belong. When the monster snatches her away, it's as if the mother returned to take back what has always been hers. As the two brothers, still believing her dead, bawl and brawl before her image, the father declares that her abduction has finally brought the broken Park family back together. But this is precisely because it has removed the last real, living trace of the real mother even while giving a positive symbolic form to the mother's unsettling absence. And so, finally swallowing Hyun-seo, the monster has returned her symbolically to the womb. Dragged lifeless from the monster's stomach after its final defeat, she has been rebirthed. More than just a "sad ending" defying Hollywood clichés, her stillborn rebirth is necessary because, in truth, she could never have existed. A higher tragic logic prevails. She had to die because the true ground for her existence, the subtle complicity between matriarchy and patriarchy, expired long ago.

Such an interpretation might seem paradoxical. For all his playful irony, Bong certainly doesn't keep the audience from identifying with the family's grief or their desperate quest to save her. Nor does the monster ever do anything to elicit sympathy or even appear morally ambiguous. But this is just the point: one must root for the family, identify with their suffering and struggles, to feel the depth of their renunciation.

There are several subtle but telling signs of Hyun-seo's *surreal* presence. When the monster attacks and she is abducted, it is because of Gang-du's blunder: running away from the monster, he grabs the wrong girl's hand, realizing his mistake only when it's already too late. This mistake reveals a deeper truth: if he can mistake the other child for his own, it is because, ultimately, his own is not really his own; because, in the absence of the mother—the ultimate guarantee of natural belonging, of the natal and native—the child cannot belong absolutely to the family but has only been adopted into it.

One of the film's most striking scenes finds the Parks eating together in their bodega after Hyun-seo's abduction. Hyun-seo appears at the table, eating with them—then disappears. The audience thus experiences her loss not as an abstract crime or tragedy but as the unsettling absence of a familiar presence. Yet this also suggests that, in a way, her presence was always a haunting presence, imagined rather than real, and that she never really belonged. After all, her home—as far as we can tell, she lives in the bodega in the public park—is not really a home but a familiar haunt. Familiar cohabitation becomes co-haunting.

While the Park family is trying to kill the monster and rescue Hyun-seo, we are introduced to another family: the homeless orphan brothers Se-jin (Lee Jae-eung) and Se-joo (Lee Dong-ho). Breaking into the Park bodega, they help themselves to food. Invoking the traditional concept of *sŏri*, the elder brother explains that this is not theft; they are not taking money but only the food they need to survive. Far from merely justifying theft, *sŏri* neutralizes the entire ritual system organizing family life around paternal lineages guaranteed, in the last instance, by the maternal womb. For the orphaned brothers, this patriarchal law, which subsumes maternal productivity through a system of control and distribution, has no meaning—a different law, older perhaps and more just, takes its place. Still, it's not clear that the bodega's fare falls under *sŏri*. Fruit can be snatched away to still one's hunger because, not having been prepared or cooked, it remains the fruit of the earth; it is not yet cultural, only natural. But, perhaps, precisely because the ultra-processed packaged food is only cultural, existing only as commodity, it can also become "fair game" for *sŏri*; it is fruit of the capitalist machine, of exchange value—the patriarchal order of the symbol given over to its own unrelenting growth.

Killing the older brother, the monster snatches off Se-joo. Meanwhile, the Park patriarch Hie-bong is killed by the monster due to another of Gang-du's stupid mistakes. When the siblings finally slaughter the monster, it has already swallowed both Hyun-seo and Se-joo. They draw Hyun-seo, clutching the still living Se-joo, out from its gaping maw. In her death, Hyun-seo, becoming maternal, has *adopted* Se-joo, who in turn is adopted by Gang-du as his own child, taking her place. The monster-belly-womb is not the womb of gestation but adoption. The movie ends with Gang-du and Se-joo eating together as a family in the bodega, changing the channel when the TV news turns to the aftermath of the incident, now blamed on "misinformation" (Figure 6).

His adoption represents not just a consolation for the death of Hyun-seo but the final and unequivocal rejection of the existing vestigial patriarchal order, which, with the mother absent, insists yet

Figure 6 The Host *directed by Bong Joon Ho. © Showbox 2006. All rights reserved.*

more violently on the principle of common blood. A new order takes its place, based on adoption rather than natality. This not only represents a transformation of the family unit but also challenges the entire logic on which the Korean nation-state, with its myth of ethno-racial purity—blood purity—is based. Yet this is not an embrace of a global order where all communal bonds are liquefied into atomic individuals bound together through civil society and the state apparatus, concrete utility and abstract law. It remains a question not of saving the family in general but of saving the Korean family. The only thing that can save the Korean family, however, is a total rejection of the mythic grounding of the family in the conjuncture of the primal potency of the maternal and the symbolic power of the paternal—of mythic nature and mythic culture; the Neo-Confucian synthesis subordinating *yin* to *yang*, *qi*/*ki* to *li*/*i*. The truth of culture, of the family, is not myth, not even language, but food. And food must be shared.

The Sewer

Nah ist
Und schwer zu fassen der Gott.
Wo aber Gefahr ist, wächst
Das Rettende auch.

The god is near, and hard to grasp.
Where danger is, grows the saving power too.

Hölderlin, Patmos[21]

The Han signifies the originative power giving rise both to new forms of life and to meaning. Life and meaning arise as mutations of the inanimate and insignificant. The power of the Han is, in a word, the power of fermentation. This connects the Han with alcohol. While Bong's films are filled with alcoholics and addicts, his abused substances possess an ambiguous potency. They numb suffering—and especially the suffering caused by history's traumas. They quiet the bad conscience of those who've become complicit in evil. But they also bear the explosive power of the event. Precisely this power is rendered palpable, transparent, consumable through soju bottles and beer cans; the ferment of the Han, bottled and canned, itself becomes a monstrous power.

Yet the Han with its tributaries is also juxtaposed to another system of confluences: the sewer system hidden beneath the city. This represents the real networks of "hygienic"—biopolitical—control upon which the modern city and society depend, and which, against the explicit myths organizing everyday life, must not only remain hidden to function but whose very function is removing contaminants, hiding them from view. The hygienic value of modern plumbing and sewage is no less symbolic than real: waste products of all kinds, from human feces to nonbiodegradable plastics, disappear instantly and effortlessly from view, no longer troubling with their obstreperous, obnoxious presence. The same hygienic logic, moreover, is applied to the population as well: criminals are hidden away in prisons, punishment no longer a public spectacle, while hospitals and other institutions house the insane, sick, dying, and indigent. Just as the apartment and the mountains represent two aspects of the vertical dimension characterizing the city as an organization of human life and activity, urban infrastructure plays out as the tension between the Han and the sewers. Whereas the Han embodies the cyclic flow of water—generous like the *dao*, yielding, bland, the originative life-sustaining metabolic flow—the sewers enable urban concentration by draining off waste products . . . into the Han.[22] And then into the sea and the ocean: the broadness of global nature. When the US military coroner, ordering his Korean assistant to dump formaldehyde down the drain, urges him to be as "broad-minded" as the Han is broad, the "watercourse way" of the *dao*, to use Alan Watts' phrase, is twisted into a justification for environmental crimes. But such a justification is implicit in the sewer system itself, which, superficially resembling the *qi*-channels of the Daoist body, in fact represents an entirely different hygienic regime: one based not on rhythmic balance but on a waste disposal premised on an imagined boundlessness.

The sewer system, furthermore, represents the hidden apparatus of control over the city and its inhabitants. Immediately following the monster's attack, this hidden subterranean apparatus kicks into action. Official workers dressed in hazmat suits drag away those who had contact with the monster, sequestering them in a special facility. An army of workers fumigates the tunnels. It is not just the Korean government that kicks into action but an obscure coalition of powerful national and international interests spearheaded by the US military. These bizarre hygienic measures are not directed against the monster but a mysterious virus. The hidden apparatus of power justifies its own obscure existence—a total lack of transparency—through the obscurity of the threats that it combats. The real monster is neither seen nor combated by it.

The monster, this suggests, doesn't simply represent the threat posed by the modern world. For indeed, the most fundamental danger of the modern world is the absence of signs, of manifestations, of demonstrations and monstrations. The danger afflicting the modern world under the regime of technology—as Heidegger shows through his analysis of the *Gestell*—consists in the impossibility of danger appearing as such since the very possibility of truth, as manifestation, has been imperiled.[23] Taking the place of truth is the endless flow of commodities, logistics, and information, together with hygienic/biopolitical control; a total ordering of life around the end of life itself. In the absence of manifest truth, politics also becomes impossible: democracy withers away into a mere pretense—an illusion of transparency—insisted on ever more violently even as everyone knows that the real power lies elsewhere, hidden beneath the surface. In its hidden potency, the monster is not the danger itself but the saving power that grows where the danger is. It symbolizes the power of cinema to expose the modern danger, though, to be sure, always in a form that misrepresents to the extent that its signification assumes concrete, finite form.

Limits of Subversion

From the moment the Park family learns Hyun-seo is still alive, their first instinct is to access the hidden network. The private individual, private detective, or "maverick" secret agent gaming the system is an endlessly satisfying theme of cinema. *The Host* gives us this pleasure in spades: Gang-du escapes from his special medical detention; the Park patriarch, bribing mobsters, equips himself with a fake sanitation truck, a map of the subterranean sanitation system, and even firearms—no small feat given South Korea's strict gun control; the whole family cons their way past a security checkpoint. Sneaking through Seoul's dense urban labyrinth to the central office of a telephone company, Nam-il has his friend Fat Guevara (Yim Pil-sung), a former activist in the democracy movement, triangulate the location of Hyun-seo's last cellphone call. And then as the police close in on him—his erstwhile comrade, gainfully employed but soaked in debt, betrayed him—he evades capture by shorting the building's power grid.

Yet for all this trickery, hacking, and bricolage, *The Host* forbids us to believe that the heroic individual could defeat the repressive system through subversive knowledge. Playing against genre expectations, the film's finale makes this clear. When Gang-du finally finds the monster, it swallows both abducted children—Hyun-seo and the orphaned boy—and then swims off. Frantically running across the bridge traversing the Han as the monster swims below, Gang-du reaches the river's southern bank. Here, a strange yellow apparatus, suspended from a crane, is belching out "Agent Yellow" while a taped voice loop warns people to walk until they can't hear the announcement anymore. The yellow apparatus—the monster's double—is surrounded by an enormous group of protesters, pushing against a phalanx of police in riot gear. Whereas the *koemul* is only seen and engaged by individuals, this second "monster" is recognized by the crowd. Yet as soon as the first monster appears, the crowd, fighting this other "monster," scatters.

This is shown in an ingenious way: the shot focuses on individual members of the crowd, a young man and woman wearing matching red and yellow "Free Park Kang Doo" T-shirts. Looking out toward the shore, their eyes begin to widen, then they climb up and the girl takes out a camera and starts filming; another joins them, and soon all three are screaming and the entire crowd disperses in terror while the girl with the camera is dragged off by her friend. The monster now climbs up to the concrete embankment, and, after a load of Agent Yellow is dumped on it, is left stunned. Arriving in the nick of time, Gang-du can pull his daughter, with Se-joo clutching her, from its hideous gaping maw.

Accompanied by a lugubrious soundtrack—the trumpet lending it a vaguely military feel—Gang-du picks up Hyun-seo's limp body. Writhing in the background as more Agent Yellow is dumped, the monster tosses a sad little fish from its stomach. A policeman in a gas mask films with a small camera while another vomits blood. Finally, the surviving members of the Park family, the three siblings, all gather around Hyun-seo's body, which, surprisingly, has failed to magically revive. Dead is dead.

This is not the happy ending that an audience, habituated to Hollywood conventions, would have expected. Nor is it exactly unhappy. The other child *does* survive. And perhaps what is most important for the family, in the last instance, is not that Hyun-seo should live but that they can mourn her properly; that her body is returned to them. Properly mourning—melodramatically mourning—is the happy ending. Moreover, the siblings have been harmoniously reunited. And perhaps Hyun-seo never really belonged to the family from which she was snatched away. Her death, properly mourned, becomes her rebirth as a proper member of the family.

Immediately after this brief interlude of mourning, the family again takes up arms against the monster, vanquished but not yet destroyed. In a moment of superhuman strength, Gang-du swings at it with a metal post torn up from the ground; then Nam-il throws several soju-bottle Molotov cocktails, which burst into flames around the dazed, flailing monster. A final defeat of the monster appears within tantalizing reach when the homeless man, accompanied by a grandiose musical crescendo, climbs above the monster and showers it with gasoline. Nam-il need only strike again with a Molotov cocktail for it to burst into flames. Yet somehow, just as he is about to throw, the improvised weapon slips from his hand. It is left to his sister to pluck an arrow from her quiver, ignite it, and shoot it right into the monster's eye. The monster bursts into flames and, after Gang-du shoves a metal post down its throat, finally succumbs, tumbling down to the ground with a final lamenting roar. Only then does Gang-du walk over to the younger child, the orphaned and brotherless Se-joo, who has been left for dead on the ground. Gently shaking him, his eyes burst open, and Gang-du carries Se-joo off, staring poignantly into the camera.

The Revolutionary Situation

With his virtuosic mastery of cinematic conventions, Bong encourages emotional identification with the Park family. We can hardly help but rejoice in the monster's defeat. Yet, without being obviously satirical or humorous, the battle scene remains a bit absurd. With the two children already recovered and the Agent Yellow-drenched monster in its death throes, there is something gratuitous, even superfluous, about their violence, which seems primarily cathartic, allowing them to vent their anger at a monster that, no longer posing a real threat, has become a purely symbolic enemy. If, indeed, the Agent Yellow has killed it, then the more dangerous, more subtle monster is still in their midst. The Park family are symbolically united in a battle against a symbolic enemy, and thus the entire fight reveals itself as more ritual than real. Indeed, as the family was waiting in the gymnasium, the family patriarch, waxing philosophic, instructs his children in the "ancient ways":

Her birth was an accident, and so was her death. Old people have always said that an animal which kills a human should be torn limb from limb. That it's a human's duty to do so.

And then he adds, while an official worker in a hazmat suit slips in the background.

Until I slit that beast's stomach, and at least find Hyun-seo's body, I'll never leave this world in peace.

The fundamental duty expressed in these "ancient ways" is to maintain human superiority over the rest of nature. By carrying out their father's pledge, the Park siblings achieve a ritual reassertion of the patriarchal order to which they are subject and under which they suffer.

Yet while the monster's defeat appears ritualistic, representing the merely mythical defeat of a mythic entity, perpetuating the myth of the family and of human dominance, it also has a very different significance. The monster, after all, is not defeated in its subterranean lair but out in the open, in the full light of day, at the very site of a political demonstration. The people are united in open protest in the full light of day rather than intriguing against the intrigues of the system, subverting it through covert knowledge of its hidden operations. The focus of their protest is the bio-toxic Agent Yellow, which is being deployed, under the direction of governmental and extra-governmental entities, putatively against the virus, but in truth against life itself. Agent Yellow thus represents the extreme realization of the underlying tendency of the existing order, which seeks to submit life to its control, destroying it for the sake of life itself. An extreme activist intervention in the natural order, this tendency is precisely the sort of intentional action that Daoism rejects in favor of *wu wei/muwi* (無為), nonaction. Yet hidden and hence monstrous, it also shares the monster's ambiguity. In this final scene, both the *koemul* and the Park family converge at the site of the protest, as if the two monsters are really one monster, and as if the Parks, in their suffering odyssey, have also finally come to represent the people. Nor is it defeated by the Park family alone; a crucial role is played by the homeless man. A former activist, while also representing the abject people of *Minjung* theology, he had the foresight to douse the monster in gasoline. The "revolutionary situation" has already been prepared in a double sense; the siblings need but light the match. With this final battle, therefore, the original utopian space is transformed into a site of protest, and, consequently, the private battle of the Park family against the monster is suffused with a deeper political sense. By refusing to have the people *not* appear, Bong rejects what, for Deleuze, is the most basic condition of a modern political cinema—that "*the people are missing*," that they "no longer exist, or not yet."[24] But it also suggests the transformation of a Daoist opening—a place of wandering and water where a deeper harmony with nature prevails over the more rigid social order—into a site of political action. Perhaps this gives the first hint at a renewed Daoist public sphere, even Daoist democracy.

The Mythic Event

We are confronted with a curious ambiguity: the killing of the monster is both a real confrontation with a real threat and the ritualized killing of a symbolic threat. It is an action of the assembled militant masses, symbolized by the Park siblings, and yet also a merely private affair; the fulfillment of the revolutionary promise of the monster—whose very appearance is an event—but also the counterrevolutionary restoration of the increasingly imperiled myth of the family. This ambiguity suggests a basic problem in activist politics. Protest movements often form around incidents or issues that have a primarily symbolic value. Even when these stand for real injustices demanding redress, the symbolic resonance of an incident often conjures forth powerful associations—deeply rooted in the social and political imaginary—that run interference with reality, misdirecting attention toward a plane of magical thinking. This danger is perhaps greater than usual in Korea, where the mythic conception of ethno-racial unity remains quite powerful, and the relation to the United States has tremendous real as well as symbolic importance. Moreover, precisely because the formation of a nation-state has been continually interrupted through the intervention of foreign powers, the boundary between the symbolic and the real becomes especially problematic. For a nation-state still in the process of forming, the myths of nationhood express an "aspirational" reality; a reality that should exist but doesn't yet—in a word, an idea. As *ideas*—projects, "fragments of the future" as Friedrich Schlegel puts it—national myths have a reality that cannot be dismissed just by pointing to their lack of actuality, which is to say, present reality.[25] For indeed, the lack of actuality corresponds to its virtuality, its potentiality. Perhaps a genuine *event*—an irruption of radical novelty—can never take place without the garb of myth, and yet this mythic garb cannot but draw the event back into the past from which it should escape. One recalls Marx's *Der 18te Brumaire des Louis Bonaparte* (The Eighteenth Brumaire of Louis Bonaparte):

> Hegel remarks somewhere that all great, world-historical facts and personages occur, as it were, twice. He has forgotten to add: the first time as tragedy, the second as farce.[26]

Historical materialism notwithstanding, there is no history without tragedy and hence without myth. Precisely because the political situation in Korea remains in a potent state of ferment, ripe with the event, the mythic remains always in play. The danger of myth, again, announces the saving power—or, maybe, *is* the saving power. So, the question becomes: which myth? The myth of the *demos*? Of *minjok*? Of the paternal king? Of the family? Of globalism? Of Gaia?

The ambiguity, it stands to reason, must be taken differently than before. While the killing of the monster appears within the film as real confrontation with a real threat, the very existence of the monster is mythic rather than real. Indeed, the reality of the monster is nothing else than the reality of myth. The monster is not simply a symbolic representation of one or more real problems afflicting reality but represents the very power of myth as it plays into, and plays out through, the event. Fighting the monster is always fighting *with* myth *against* myth. The monster discloses a field of conflict that takes place on the mythic plane, and thus we could even say that the monster film represents a quintessentially modern form of Greek tragedy. If the Han, as proposed earlier, is the liquid fermenting embodiment of historical time, then the monster is the double manifestation of historical time as it breaks into the cyclic, endlessly repeating present of everyday life. It is both the evental future and the mythic past— the radical indeterminacy of the event that breaks into the present time, disclosing the prospect of a radically different future, and the interpretations that, drawing from the potent reserves of past experience, fill out this indeterminacy, give sense to it, realize it.

It is certainly possible, in this way, to discover something like a message in *The Host*. We noted before that *The Host* culminates in an ethical act: the adoption of the child. This ethical act, already implying a rejection of a concept of nation built on blood purity derived from extended family and clan, corresponds to a correlative political act: the insistence on a public sphere characterized above all by a vibrant culture of political activism. These two acts converge in a powerful—if not unproblematic—vision of democracy as originating in, and guaranteed by, the vital presence of the people as a body that, by protesting, gives voice to their will.

Yet maybe it's not so simple. Here the event is merely the cinematic representation of an event; the event can never exist outside its mediatic representation. Consequently, if the film conjures forth a vision of radical democracy, of a genuinely public sphere, or even of a Daoist politics relinquishing the patriarchal myth of blood, this vision is itself only a mediated vision. It does not seem, in other words, as if the event, conjured through cinema, can ever break free to become anything but entertainment. The monster movie indeed seems like one of the most fertile incubators for a new mythology; the monster almost inevitably returns with a sequel. Sometimes, monsters even pair up. *The Host*, however, treats the tension between media and event thematically rather than pretending to its own neutrality. This can be seen from how, throughout the fight scene, we see people— the activists, then the police—filming the monster with their own cameras. It neither offers a simple myth, nor pretends to have gotten past the mythic.

This tension between event and mythopoetic media once again shows the contestation between the cinematic apparatus of philosophy and the philosophical apparatus of cinema. The event, the irruption of historical becoming, is the most radical, absolute form of movement—the pure movement of historical time. As such, the event does not exist beyond the horizon of human agency and human language but only through this horizon. It is always already interlaced with myth—only comprehensible in mythic terms, even if it is also always betrayed by the mythic residues in which it is clothed.

Precisely this paradox is explored in *Snowpiercer* and *Okja*. *The Host*, *Snowpiercer*, and *Okja*—all various incarnations of the "blockbuster," with each occupying a slightly different position in the space stretching between the Korean and the global—should be regarded as a trilogy. The films are related to one another not through common characters or obvious themes but through a conceptual problematic worked out dialectically. *The Host* poses the problem, *Snowpiercer* develops it to the point of extreme contradiction, and *Okja* suggests a solution.

5
Snowpiercer

The Tentacle

Inhuman in appearance but with a superhuman grasp, the tentacle is human potency released from human control, alienated from the ethical substance of human life, dislocated from every locality. Strong without rigidity, malleable yet not flaccid, it offers a potent symbol for globalization as perceived by the imperiled local community: an insinuating, threatening, incomprehensible power. While Bong's first two feature-length films treated globalization as a tentacle-like peripheral phenomenon, threatening Korean society from the outside, lapping its edges, reaching through the cracks, *The Host* takes this peripheral experience of globalization to the limit. The peripheral now appears simultaneous with the center: the Han, running through Seoul's (and the Korean Peninsula's) heart, also joins it to the outside. And with the *koemul*'s rapacious appendage, globalization's tentacles reach into the very center of the film.

Only with *Snowpiercer* does Bong go beyond such a concept of globalism as peripheral threat to an integral center—an understanding of globalism that, in Korea, has roots in Minjung theology, which, for all its emphasis on the marginalized and subaltern, holds on to the ethno-national idea of the *minjok*.[1] No longer merely a Hollywood-style blockbuster tailored to the local market, *Snowpiercer* is radically global. Loosely based on the French graphic novel *Le Transperceneige* by Jacques Lob and Jean-Marc Rochette, the screenplay, written in collaboration with the American screenwriter Kelly Masterson, is mostly in English. Even the production company is a combined Korea-Czech venture.[2] If *The Host* treats thematically the conditions of its production—the "battle" of Korean filmmakers for survival with the relaxed quota-system—*Snowpiercer* is a fully global film about globalization, a piercing cinematic critique of the lopsided vision of globalism promoted through American hegemony.[3] The struggles surrounding *Snowpiercer*'s release in the United States would only illustrate, if illustration is needed, the pertinence of this critique: having acquired distribution rights, Harvey Weinstein demanded violent cuts and modifications. Standing his ground, Bong had to settle for a limited theatrical release in the United States, with the film opening in just eight theaters.[4]

Snowpiercer is set in a not-too-distant future. A catastrophic attempt to address global warming through geo-engineering caused the earth's temperature to plummet—an even more extreme example than Agent Yellow of the affirmative intentional action that Daoism rejects. Only a tiny remnant of humanity survives aboard a train that, built as the pinnacle of luxury in late capitalism's last gilded age, now unceasingly crisscrosses the desolate frozen globe, passing through the iced-over ruins of the great metropolises that once served as exotic destinations for its passengers.[5] While ticketed passengers live luxuriously in the train's forward cars, the ticketless are crammed into the rear. Kept alive with repellent protein blocks, they are deprived of all but the barest necessities of life while subjected to a brutal regime of control. Workers cater to the needs of the elite and keep the train running while a military regime maintains order. It is as if, bringing American exceptionalism and manifest destiny to its logical culmination, the Western's bleak desert landscape has gone global; there is now only desert. The American dream, the "single fundamental film" that "American cinema constantly shoots and reshoots"—the "birth of a nation-civilization" as "melting pot in which minorities are dissolved" and where "ferment [...] creates leaders capable of reacting to all situations"—has been realized as absolute catastrophe, the preemptive utopia as absolute dystopia.[6]

No mere backdrops for the storyline, Bong's settings gain meaning from how they organize life; they involve a spatiality that is not merely "representative" or "symbolic" but "architectonic." Buildings are built into, or indeed out of, the natural environment, transforming the natural environment into a built environment, orienting human life toward the natural world such that certain habitual relations to nature begin to emerge. A multifaceted relation thus arises between architecture and locality: while architecture follows the local landscape's features, it also determines how the landscape becomes manifest to us. Local architecture and the local terrain fuse together.

It is precisely this unity, however, that modern rapid transportation calls into question, and nowhere more than with the railroad. Neither following the landscape nor soaring above it, the track cuts through the local landscape, deranges it, imposing a geometric precision on the natural contours and gradients of the terrain. Even while ships and airplanes are the primary vehicles of transcontinental globalization, the railway embodies globalization's most uncanny trait: the subordination of earthly life, in its regional variations, to a unifying apparatus of technological control.[7]

Hence the terrifying dreamlike potency of the image of *Snowpiercer*'s train. Powered by an "eternal engine" whose energy source remains mysterious, the train, like all perpetual motion machines, exists at the fringe between technology and magic, science and fantasy. It is the mythical archetype of *technē*. The absolute train, in other words: the train as an image of absolute globalization—the absolute submission of the earth to technology. While the *Snowpiercer* train only assumed its world-salvaging role in response to ecological catastrophe, a deeper perspective suggests that the world froze because of the train—embodiment of an absolute technological regime—and that the "backstory" of ecological catastrophe merely offers a plausible causal account for a higher cinematic truth. The track itself enables gliding: movement with minimum friction; it achieves, by artificial means, the effect of ice, and hence the iced-over earth, with natural life and growth reduced to nothing, suggests the entire earth turned into an artificial track for a train that now holds within—preserves and negates, *aufhebt*—all the earth's life. It is not the *Gestell*, the scaffolding frame, that constitutes the uncanny essence of modern technology but the *Geleise*, the "track." The *Gestell* is still "put up" against nature, which it "puts upon" with its demand to "put out" as standing reserve; but with the absolute *Geleise* of the absolute train, there is no outside whatsoever—nature has been taken up entirely into the system.[8] Only one possibility remains: *for the system itself to derail*. The saving power is nothing else than total delirium, going off the rail.

Nor is the train merely the abstract symbol of modern technology's deranging power, but the concrete setting wherein the film's plot unfolds. There is a visible landscape outside the train—CGI-generated aerial shots show the train from outside, speeding past civilization's frozen relics, disappearing into mountain tunnels—and a physical element that the train contacts. But there is no local setting, no locality; the local setting—the world as an environment we relate to by moving through, manipulating, discovering its possibilities—has collapsed into the length of the train. A mobile building, a built world, the train has subsumed all locality into itself. No mere symbol of globalism, the train is the global order itself as technological accomplishment, artifact: the complete subsumption of earthly life under the domination of *technē*. When one of the tail-dwellers is punished by exposing his arm to the frigid air before shattering it into icy shards, his hand is shown from outside the train, writhing in agony, grasping at nothing.

While the opposition between artificial and natural sets plays an important role in the history of cinema, where it is invested with aesthetic and ideological significance, it itself depends on the noncoincidence of the artificial and natural. It must be possible to experience *technē* and *phusis* in a relation of exteriority to one another. The microcosmic artificial-natural setting of *Snowpiercer*, however, calls just this exteriority into question: the train, as a global ordering of the earth's local settings, converges with the train as a cinematic space. The opposition between a natural setting and a built set—between realism and expressionism—thus loses all significance. The cinematic set becomes nature as artifice, artifice as nature.

The Cameral Train

The settings of Bong's films, as observed before, are not only "architectonic" but "cameral." They represent not the camera's appearance but its essential function. Projecting light into a dark chamber, the camera masters light as a medium of appearance, a mastery only possible since appearance involves both light and darkness. Nowhere is this dialectical "cameralization" of space clearer than with *Snowpiercer*'s train, a gigantic polarizing machine. While the windowless boxcars of the tail are draped in darkness, the engine at the front of the train glows with the mysterious energy of the primal life force that it has harnessed, as if submitting *qi/ki* to the track's rigid law. Yet even while the forward sections of the train have windows, the outside world is buried under a sheet of monochromatic white. There's nothing to see here since outside nature is no longer polychromatic; nothing remains of the warm tonal oppositions through which verdant life reveals itself. The light and life that the train disposes over, submitting to its polarizing order, belong to the interior—as if the train were a camera turned upon itself.

Just as the camera is a tool of memory, keeping traces of the past, the train preserves the last traces of natural and human life. Following the insurgents' forward push, we view the desolate luxury afforded its more fortunate inhabitants. There are dentists, tailor shops, beauty salons; a grey-haired woman peeling an apple amid dolls, cat figurines, family portraits, books; the gaudy elegance of a bar with wood-framed barrel chairs and golden cupids. Even a sauna, a dance club: techno-music blaring, scantily clad young bodies, shirtless studs, heroin-chic women in furs with raccoon eyes, writhing in tedious rhythmic ecstasy or hunched over their drinks and dope. The train's compartments are so many fragments of the human world preserved for perpetuity—as if in amber or celluloid.

As an extreme cameral space, the train also elicits the contradictions of the camera and likewise of memory itself. Memory is either *of* something else than memory—hence creative and radically unfaithful to what is remembered, radically imaginative—or it is merely a memory of memory. The production of new memories—original memory—itself depends on the experience-transcending power of the imagination; absent such imagination, memory can only exist as the memory of what is already remembered; it becomes a trace of a trace of a trace ad infinitum. Hence, if something like true, generative memory is possible, it is only through the complete darkening of "passive" memory, the memory of memory.

Since the train is a camera, a memory machine, it itself contains the contradiction between "active" ("originative") memory and "passive" ("derivative") memory. Active memory, in turn, has its seat in the tail's darkness. Among the tail section's residents is a painter (Clark Middleton), silently sketching the children, chronicling new events as they unfold.[9] While the front-dwelling elite are in control of the train, possessing a seeming monopoly over power-knowledge, the power of representation—the camera-power to chronicle the life of the train—is out of their hands.

The Gun

A self-enclosed, self-referential camera space, the train polarizes into two camera forms. The darkness-drenched tail is an opening only possible when vestigial memory is extinguished; the head is pure vestigial memory, the snapshot of the snapshot of the snapshot . . . The tension between these plays out in the conflicts unfolding within the train. And indeed, if the artist most of all suggests the first camera-form, the second camera-form is embodied by Franco the Elder (Vlad Ivanov), the stone-faced, silent assassin. Like the tail-section artist, he remains almost completely silent throughout the film. This doubled silence—corresponding to the tactile activities, respectively, of the artist's sketching and Vlad's shooting, hitting, stabbing, impaling—creates a striking tension. As if a "silent" film were woven into the "talkie," the film's visual dimension at once counters and complements the dialogue.[10]

The gun's outsized role in cinema, however, owes not just to our obsession with violence. Whether conspicuously present or conspicuously absent, the gun signifies the camera, whose very operation—pointing and shooting—it mirrors. This is, more precisely, the operation of the second camera-form: negative rather than positive, closing rather than opening; gadget violence rather than gadget art. When Franco the Elder goes rogue—shooting a front-end passenger and even a member of the security squad—he does the work of the second camera-form, which can never do more than *snap* off *shots*, breaking the world into fragments which, as soon as broken off, vanish into nothing.

The identification of gun and camera becomes clearest, however, when the gun serves to discover the setting. Just as *mise-en-scène* is revealed through the camera shot, the gun discovers spaces by shooting them up; the gun's tactile manipulation allows for a tactile-kinetic identification with the characters as they eye their surroundings, looking for a clean shot. In a remarkable scene, Franco the Elder catches sight of the insurgents in another compartment as the train bends around a curve. He begins to shoot through the window, and a gunfight with Curtis Everett (Chris Evans) ensues. At precisely this moment, the train, its integrity violently undermined, appears not only as camera-space but—as if come full circle—as a camera turned against itself, shooting itself (Figure 7).

Yet this scene, where the spectator's eye assumes the shooter's perspective, features a strange interlude. The camera pans from a hole

Figure 7 Snowpiercer *directed by Bong Joon Ho.* © Radius-TWC 2013. *All rights reserved.*

in the window over to the face of Namgoong Minsoo (Song Kang-ho), the Korean security specialist enlisted by the tail-dwellers, as he follows a snowflake floating inside. Lasting just a few seconds, this scene seems merely wistful and impressionistic, yet it turns out to have a very concrete significance. Namgoong, as he later tells Curtis, had learned from an Inuit cleaning woman about the various kinds of snow. This single large flake offers a crucial sign that the weather is changing, that the outside world is becoming warmer, even habitable. While the gun—the *camera negativa*—creates an opening, the other camera-form, the *camera positiva*, can alone see through it.

The most striking conflict between these camera polarizations, however, appears in the iconic fight scene occurring soon after the tail-dwellers break Namgoong and his clairvoyant daughter Yona (Ko Ah-sung) out from the prison car, and, bribing them with Kronole, enlist their help. Yona warns not to open the gate, but it's too late: the doors draw apart, revealing a room full of goons, faces and eyes masked, armed with battle-axes, and with one of them holding a silver carp by the tail. He cuts it open from the gills, spilling its slippery blood on the floor; then he and his men rush at the insurgents.

The fight is divided into two halves. The first half, while leavened with Bong's tension-breaking humor, is perversely beautiful: a long slow-motion sequence. Axe swings—abstracted into gestures, accompanied with grunts and swooshing sounds—unfold against Marco Beltrami's elegiac score. Suddenly, a foghorn blares. The film resumes normal speed, and the camera discovers the front of the compartment, with five officers (all Asian, it seems) facing the backs of the goons, who have returned to an ordered array. The leading officer, towering over the others, screams into a megaphone: "Passing Yekaterina bridge!"

Waving their battle-axes, the goons count down the New Year. Then minister Mason enters, declaring that exactly 74 percent of the tail section will die. If her declaration seems both performative command and assertion of fact, it's because she knows something that the tail-dwellers cannot know: the train is just about to enter a long tunnel, throwing the compartment into darkness. The goons, who first uncovered their eyes, now put on night-vision goggles. Having advanced this far because bullets—encapsulated fire—were seemingly extinct, the rebels are again helpless. The train's henchmen have become identical with the camera; alone granted the power of vision, they can execute the order given to them, carrying through the subsumption of the rebellious tail-dwellers under the eternal order of the train. As if seen through the goons' night-vision goggles, everything appears in greenish glowing monochrome, inscribed with a grid and numbers; with visible light temporarily extinct, there is only the vestigial infrared glow, translated by the goggles into the dominant order's vision. But then Edgar, remembering Namgoong's matches, calls out for fire. A boy runs from the back with a flame. Suddenly torches drench the cabin in light. Vision restored to the rebels, they gain the upper hand, leading Minister Mason away in chains. As if the battle weren't just between warriors but between a camera dependent on the last vestige of vestigial light—the shadow of a shadow—and a camera whose illuminating source is fire, the troglodytic tail-dwellers triumph because, even passing into the tunnel-cave, they still possess the archaic power of artificial light.

Plot

More than Bong's other films, *Snowpiercer*'s plot realizes the setting. Recalling the roots of the English word "plot" in a Proto-Germanic word meaning *patch, rag, strip of land, Snowpiercer*'s setting is nothing other than a burial plot: remnant human life preserves itself into an eternal future by entombing itself within a supposedly perfect system, a microcosm of nature. Indeed, this system's very claim to eternal perfection precludes the possibility that it could preserve human life for the event of the future, the future to come; the only future it knows has collapsed into the present. The train is a plot, a patch, a strip, and already the two settings of Christianity's dualistic theology have collapsed into one: this life and the other life—the castle of Boccaccio's *Decameron*, where a group of young men and women secluded themselves in a villa to wait out the Black Death, and Dante's hell, heaven, and purgatory.

The train is thus a theological Mobius strip. While medieval Europe's political-theological vision hinged on the compensatory counterpoint between this life and the other life, both lives, forming a double series, now collapse into one. Within its eternalized economy, the train's tail is literally hell, its front literally heaven. Yet if the tail-dwellers begin by falling into the worst depravity, they also discover Christian virtue in its most extreme form. For as Curtis explains to Namgoong, the denizens of the tail section, starving to death, began eating their own babies, stopping only when Gilliam (John Hurt) cut off his own limbs, giving of his own flesh to eat. And meanwhile the passengers in the front-most sections, some dressed as angels, cavort and frolic in drunken, stony-eyed ecstasy. The reward forever bestowed on the rich—earthly pleasure—is also their eternal punishment, while the punishment of the poor becomes a blessing; they alone, at least, experience human solidarity and hope, whereas the train's idle rich pass life by in a narcotic haze.

This extraordinary collapse of the setting into the plot is not only symbolically significant but also transforms the relation between setting, character, plot, and narration. For as long as there has been a social division of labor, class distinctions, including gender, have been not only reflected in but organized through the built environments wherein human life unfolds. The division and transformation of nature solidify social division; natural barriers separating nations are supplemented by built barriers separating the nation from itself, dividing it against itself. But at the same time, the nation—whose very existence depends on sexual reproduction—can only exist if its parts intermingle. The nation's survival depends both on the legal institution of marriage and the family—exemplified by the walls dividing private spaces—and the transgressive function of radical promiscuity. Barriers must be playfully transgressed, with this transgressive possibility built into the spaces themselves. Plot unfolds just this essential excess of possibility, as Shakespeare's *Romeo and Juliet* demonstrates: faced with the tragic confrontation between an enmity dividing the nation against itself and the young lovers' sensuous nation-unifying promiscuity, the friar seeks, through the ruse of a sleeping draught, to turn the tomb (the plot) into the place of resurrection. This fails, as fail it must: human cunning cannot bring about a sensual, worldly, immanent imitation of the resurrection. Yet this very failure—the young lovers' tragic death, the sacrifice of their bodies and sensual desire—affirms the higher spiritual truth of unifying love. In cinema, however, it is principally the spy, so often a master seducer, who has a special relation to the transgressive eroticism of setting. Consider, for example, Hitchcock's *The Lady Vanishes* (1938): half espionage film, half Romantic comedy, it discovers the train as a space overdetermined with possibility.

Snowpiercer, like *The Lady Vanishes*, is also a train flick. Yet there is no baggage compartment filled with magic boxes, no cunning ruses, nowhere to hide. This is clear from the beginning, when a young boy, hidden under his mother's voluminous dress, is immediately discovered and snatched away. Due to the total absence of all erotic play-space, the plot not only collapses into the setting, determined by it absolutely, but takes the form of loveless sex, sex without *eros*.

The entire plot, in other words, consists of pushing from the back of the train through to the front. It is a single act of penetration—of a space at once absolute phallus and absolute vagina; self-penetration of a space that, collapsed absolutely into itself, is already utterly self-penetrating. Eroticism thus manifests itself as the originative excess of setting over character, plot over character, narrative over plot, and even spectacle, *mise-en-scène* over narration. When this playroom, a nimbus sensuously enveloping the purely physical, disappears, nothing remains but brutal physicality imploding into its own contradictions.

Snowpiercer teems with fetishistic content that, stripped of erotic potential, can only horrify. Hence the grotesque trinity of female functionaries: Minister Mason (Tilda Swinton), the teacher (Alison Pill), and Claude (Emma Levie). Dressed in a bright yellow dress coat, a crucifix hanging from her neck, Claude stands out jarringly against the dark, almost monochrome palette of the tail section, its denizens, and even the guards accompanying her from the front. Measuring the limbs of the children, she leads two of them away by the hand. When a father throws a shoe at her head, she wipes the blood, licks her finger, and then waves away a solicitous officer with the snooty contempt of a petulant, spoiled schoolgirl. Absurdly, glaringly yellow, she is a queen bee; her voluptuous zaftig body exudes a kind of sexuality, leading one to suspect she's not only the assistant but the mistress of Wilford (Ed Harris), the father of the train. And thus she taps into the strong loathing felt toward women who, attached to powerful men, become complicit in their brutality. This visceral hatred might originate in the archaic figure, evoked by Aeschylus's Clytemnestra and Shakespeare's Gertrude, of the treacherous mother: the mother who, succumbing to sexual desires that motherhood has not eradicated, proves disloyal to the original father, replacing him with a wicked substitute. The gnostic opposition between good and evil fathers gets mediated by the ambiguously voluptuous receptivity of the earthy woman who is, at once, mother and whore. Or, in a word: bitch—the expletive hurled at her together with the shoe.

Yet this very voluptuousness is the last reserve of erotic feminine sensuality; stripped away, there's only horror. After the shoe-throwing, Andrew (Ewen Bremner) is immobilized by Franco the Elder and his goons, who prepare him for amputation. Minister Mason arrives to give a speech, waving the shoe in her hand, as Andrew's arm, fixed outside the train, freezes to the bone. Gaunt, androgynous, draped in a shapeless purple dress and ratty brown fur, she screams to the tail-dwellers about order and chaos, lipstick-smeared lips pressing out from her tensed mouth, and, in a final rhetorical flourish, puts the shoe on her head. Lipstick, marking femininity by exaggerating the lips, possesses a powerful fetish-quality. Rubbing off on other surfaces, leaving unseemly traces, it epitomizes those fetish objects that function by offering a detachable, transferable signifier of sexual difference. The most disturbing fetish-form to appear, however, is the amputation, performed as Mason gives her speech. Amputation is a kind of symbolic emasculation, and tellingly, the amputated tail-dwellers are predominantly, perhaps exclusively, male.

After passing through the agricultural sector—this includes an aquarium, where they enjoy fresh sushi, and a freezer car draped with hanging animal carcasses—the rebels, with Mason dragged along in chains, enter the school car. Filled with globes, maps, pictures of animals and flowers, model planes, ships, hot-air balloons, the school car is a polychrome museum to the extinct world. Here they encounter the third white female, perched before a group of screaming children. As if anticipating the debauched reveries awaiting them in the front-most cars, the children's faces are hidden behind construction paper masks. Dressed in an absurdly prim, lace-collared floral dress, the teacher, belly bulging with child, looks every bit the young, fresh, virtuous Sunday school teacher as she shows a video about Wilford and his train—an ingenious way to introduce "back story." Then, accompanying on an organ, she sings "Old MacDonald" with her charges, repurposed with new lyrics: "What happens when the engine stops. We all freeze and die."

She too suggests an erotic type—the almost virginal young mother—turned into something grotesque. Indeed, while they are in the school car, a bald obsequious eunuch-like creature (Tómas Lemarquis) brings a cart full of eggs, boiled in the engine's warmth-giving waters, distributing these to the passengers. Curtis's egg has a capsule and another message: "Blood." Hidden in an egg basket are machine guns, and the teacher and egg-headed egg-man immediately start shooting at the rebels. The symbol of fertility, of new life, the egg becomes bullet, gun; milk becomes blood; the nurturing maternal womb is only the gift of death, and the amputated phallus-limb returns, in the hands of woman and eunuch, as prosthetic weapon.

The Extinction Event/Film and Literature

Only two things ever really happen to us: we lose and we find. All experience is the experience of finding or losing. Things are mislaid, forgotten, stolen, taken by force, hunted, chased, produced, grown, won, excavated, and researched, or simply hit upon by chance. And not only mere things but also the soul, thought and conscience, truth, words—and, maybe most of all, the self itself. This helps explain something as enigmatic as it is obvious: the enormous difference between film and literature as narrative art forms.

Languages live and die, but within language as synchronic structure—the language in which we dwell—nothing can ever become extinct. There may not be dinosaurs or unicorns, but there are "dinosaurs" and "unicorns." This is not just because *extinction* is a temporal category but because, while language can develop and expand, we can never experience the absence of a feature of language we possess. Even when a word slips out of mind, it is like a missing jigsaw piece—known through the empty space it fills. And if I try to remember what it was like not to know *this* word, I do so from within the horizon of a language in which this word already exists. I only remember not having the word that now I have—maybe through symptoms of my ignorance or an embarrassing mistake I made hearing it for the first time; the true lack of the word eludes me. I cannot experience the unnamable absence of this name. As Wittgenstein put it, the limits of my language are the limits of my world.[11] Thus, while experience only becomes comprehensible and communicable through language, language, as the horizon of experience, withdraws from experience, since experience, in essence, is the experience of losing and finding, and, in language, this can never be experienced. The very comprehension of experience, in language, thus destroys it. The more absolute the loss, the clearer this becomes. The mother tongue can speak of the death of the mother, but, as mother tongue, it always holds on to the mother, even as it mourns her passing, her loss.

Thus, literature faces a fundamental struggle against language as its element; it can only recover the radical original experience of losing and finding by working tirelessly against its own dis-experience. The crux of this struggle is the plot; the plot becomes open to experience by allowing the event of finding and losing to appear. Thus, time, irreducible to structure, emerges. Time is experienced as mood.

The camera, in contrast, can only show what is already extinct: this flash of light off this surface. Cinema assembles and arranges the traces of these flashes of luminescence—it replays them *ad perpetuum*—but they never cease, for this, to be less gone. Whereas literature can only recover the original experience of losing and finding by tirelessly battling against itself, cinema need only to allow the camera to speak—poignantly, piercingly, devastatingly. But, of course, this is just what so much narrative film refuses to let happen. Whereas literary plot wrests free from language and thus enables experience, the cinematic plot counters the camera, erasing experience.

It is this very refusal that *Snowpiercer* allegorizes. Unceasingly looping around the extinct earth, the train exists as the perpetual denial not only of the specific extinction event, which it denies by allowing a remnant of the human world to survive intact, but of the very fact that every event, just for having happened, is already an extinction event, given over to the radical transience of becoming. *Snowpiercer* thus allows us to glimpse the ideology of cinema—the cinematic effacement of cinematic truth—in its moment of genesis. Whereas Plato's cave-allegory already presents the cinematic apparatus of philosophy, Bong's train-camera offers a counter-Platonic allegory. The Eternal Engine is an ideal republic engineered after Plato's heart, according to the most time-worn political metaphor—the identification of classes with the parts of the body. A living imitation of eternity, it nevertheless reverses Platonic emancipation. Because the Platonic sun, realized as technology, has blocked off the actual living sun, the republic, turned into a perpetually rolling cave, is no longer an ideal, a desideratum, but a stopgap and refuge. Philosophy— rather than imperfectly imitating absolute, eternal truth—becomes ideology, the eternal repetition of a lie that exists only for the sake of allowing eternal repetition. Plato's cave-allegory shows how the natural life of the "natural" state—together with natural, ordinary language—produces the spectacle that holds people captive, keeping them from philosophy. With *Snowpiercer*'s train, Platonic philosophy has been processed into the ideology sustaining the system, driving it forward in endless repetition of the same.

Appearing near the middle of the film, the schoolroom car—we recall the schoolteacher's protruding belly—is the very navel of the train, whose organization is so laden with meaning. Separating the train's productive centers from the residential and administrative, it marks the precise point where the *ideological state apparatus* and the *repressive state apparatus* fuse together into one. This is made absurdly clear when the schoolteacher, after singing a nursery rhyme, whips out a machine gun.

The first thing we see the children being taught is the basic doctrine, expressed in a song. One is reminded of Plato's *Laws*, where a song serves as a preamble (*prooimion*) to the laws, and indeed a charm—a tonic, in Minister Mason's words—to render the bitter doctrine more palatable.[12]

> What happens if the engine stops? We all freeze and die.
> But will it stop, oh, will it stop? No, no. Can you tell us why?
> The engine is eternal, yes, the engine is eternal,
> The engine is forever, yes. Rumble, rumble, rattle, rattle,
> Who is the reason why?
> Wilford. Wilford! Wilford! Hip hip! Hooray!

The train's doctrine comes down to this: the absolute state of emergency requires absolute submission to the eternal order of the train, personified by its visionary founder and leader, Wilford, whom the children hail, arm outstretched. It thus becomes a preamble for laws that can no longer exist, since Wilford's executive decrees have taken their place. The train has teachers (who serve as pastors), doctors (or at least dentists), engineers, security personnel, police/soldiers, farmers, cooks, cleaners, ministers, executioners, but not a single jurist. There is no longer a normal order—only an exceptional order achieved through perpetual acts of violence.[13]

But the train's teachings are not just a matter of explicit doctrine. The most fundamental lesson is that there can be nothing new under the sun, nothing new in the world, since the train itself is not a thing in the world but the ark preserving existing forms, existing contents, for eternity as the only world that could exist. And so, the school car is stuffed with the effigies of everything that's become extinct—and yet, despite the video celebrating the sacred engine, there is nary a single model train. Whereas the mythological and hence ideological function of children's toys, Roland Barthes argues, is to reveal the exhaustive absolute reality of the conventional forms of everyday life, now it is no longer even actual historically emergent reality that is eternalized and naturalized but the extinct world preserved in memory. The present world—with its eternal, sacred engine and ever-depleting stocks of actual goods—is a mere vehicle for eternal preservation.[14] A fixed and settled order, it can no longer yield anything new.

The schoolroom car thus suggests nothing else than the cinematic apparatus of philosophy itself: the negation of radical movement. The most radical form of movement is historicity—the event, the opening of time to becoming—while the most extreme negation of the event is its dissolution and resolution into the self-same order of eternal forms. These eternal forms might seem like objects of the most esoteric inquiry. Yet once we have language and language has us, they force themselves upon us—we are already captivated by them, imprisoned by them. Our world collapses into the self-same meaning of our words. Moreover, with the school car, the cinematic apparatus of philosophy, itself anticipating the actual development of cinema, now appears not only as pure ideology, existing to sustain the system, but as a mythopoetic tendency inhabiting cinema—one of the two tendencies in constant battle.

The school car, tellingly, has taken the place of the graphic novel's cinema car, which is showing *Casablanca* and *Star Wars VII*.[15] As in the graphic novel, the advancing characters tarry here, captivated by a show promising to reveal the truth of the system wherein they are imprisoned. And indeed, it does show the system's truth by revealing the lie—the ideological mechanism, the spectacular function—at the very heart of its functioning. This spectacular-ideological function—with "ideology" understood not just as message but as the mode of truth it allows—involves negating the trace of the extinction event that appears with every flash of light, resolving it into the experience-less element of language, its eternal forms, its myths. This tendency assumes its most extravagant form when the teacher calls attention to the seven rebels, whose frozen corpses illustrate the principle of order they violated by trying to escape. The school car's windows flash in mechanical rhythm to the images of the frozen outside, the vestigial traces of the world and even of history. Yet these are resolved, one and all, into the monotonous incantation of order—into the colorful forms, effigies of extinct things, that fill out the car.

Fire

The match light, at once incendiary and self-extinguishing, hints at the deeper significance of the machine gun fire breaking out within the train. The train's ideological apparatus cannot do without violence; its eternal order must be preserved through direct interventions of a violence that, consecrated only to the principle of order as such, is utterly lawless. This violence expresses itself through actual gunfire. The symbolic gun, empty of real bullets, is not enough. But while the gun, as remarked earlier, signifies the extreme form of the negative polarization of the camera, it is also a *firearm*, harnessing an incendiary element encapsulated in the bullet casing. The specific function of the gun, indeed, consists in translating the luminescent power of the explosive into propulsive energy. Consequently, the use of firearms cannot but put into play the positive polarization of the camera. The moment the gun fires, the cinematic apparatus of philosophy appears utterly vulnerable. The philosophical apparatus of cinema flashes into view.

The two camera forms—the camera's positive and negative polarizations—are ultimately stitched back together through a constellation of intertwined symbols. Throughout the movie, the rebel tail-dwellers, led by Curtis and his second-in-command Edgar (Jamie Bell), are guided by mysterious messages written on little pieces of paper stuck inside metal capsules. The bullet-like metal capsules, at first hidden in the protein bars, thus serve as conduits for messages seemingly guiding toward an evental rupture. But at the same time, the insurgency only becomes possible after the tail-dwellers realize that the guards' guns are useless—reduced to merely symbolic utility—since bullets have become extinct. The evental potency of the hollow bullet-like capsules speaks to the absence of actual bullets and the gunpowder granting them lethal power. While the ordinary bullet, filled with explosive powder, symbolizes the monopoly of violence sustaining the existing order of the train, the empty bullet breaks open this closed order. Likewise, the capsules with their messages to the tail-dwellers exist in a close symbolic relation to Kronole, the industrial waste that is not only the front dwellers' drug of choice, coveted for its hallucinogenic powers, but also a powerful explosive. Both functions are connected: as hallucinogen it allows imagination to pass beyond the train's limits; as explosive it makes it possible to destroy the train and even escape, if only into the icy void.[16] The refuse of the engine, the excrement of the head rather than the tail, Kronole is precisely the excess of signification upon which the closed system of signs depends. It is the originary surplus, the originative excess, the "accursed share," in Georges Bataille's expression, whose frenzied sacrifice, expelling it from the quotidian order, rescues this order from destruction.[17]

Polarization is, of course, the radical principle of the Idealist dialectic of Fichte, Hölderlin, Schelling, and Hegel. Dialectic is opposed to all linear and finite thinking, all fixed hierarchies. Having sidelined natural language, which—forever torn between myth and reason—persists in its natural but limited dialectic, cinema is potentially both the least and the most dialectical art form. This may well be cinema's most fundamental ambiguity, captured in the distinction between the cinematic apparatus of philosophy and the philosophical apparatus of cinema. Eisenstein was the first to discover, in montage, the vast wordless dialectical potential of cinema.[18] Montage is dialectic through images. To the dialectical image is opposed the radically undialectical mythic image, what Barthes will understand as mythology.[19] The mythic image congeals the fecund dialectical power of polarization into naturalized oppositions. Yet if the train embodies an anti-dialectical, linear, purely formal order, it cannot totally dispense with the dialectic. Literally a montage, the train's cars are coupled together just like strips of film, and this montage indeed realizes itself immediately in the setting of the movie, with the jarring juxtapositions of the individual cars within the total ordering of the train. Thus, the movie director, master of montage, appears as the double of the "Satanic" capitalist visionary—a conjunction that, implicit in the industrial nature of cinema as art, has haunted it from the beginning. "At the time of *Citizen Kane*," Metz notes, "Orson Welles [. . .] would go into raptures [. . .] at all the apparatus he had been made master of: 'That was the finest electric toy ever given to a boy.' Erector set, electric train: both montage toys."[20]

With this last observation, our argument, like the train itself, has come full circle. As total globalization, the train involves the absolute subordination of *physis* to *technē*—the total incorporation of the fermenting, yielding, originative power of life within the closed order of an endlessly self-reproducing machine. The train thus constitutes an absolute cameral space, and this cameral space *polarizes* into a positive and negative camera, giving the impression that, whereas the negative camera forecloses on the event, the positive can become open to it. Yet just as the two polarizations of the camera fuse back into one, it becomes clear that, if a relation to radical exteriority—to the temporal rupture of the event—is still possible, it could only be by way of the absolute realization of both cameras in their absolute identity. The only opening, that is to say, is explosion. The only way that the camera system can capture the outside is by exploding itself, shooting itself, shooting itself up . . . The complete dialectic of the train—of complete globalization—now comes into view.

The system of the train excludes earthly nature. Yet this exclusion is possible precisely because the train encloses nature within itself, submitting it to its technical ordering. And indeed, the animating, fermenting "fiery" power that the system seeks to lock up within itself is not just the life force of *qi/ki* or *yinyang* duality, but the power of systematic rupture, of nonidentity, of radical spontaneity, *ziran*; of the yielding way of the *dao*, of a nonaction (*wu wei*) deeper and more active than any action. The system can only achieve absolute closure by bursting open, becoming identical with its own nonidentity. But the explosion into nonidentity is, simultaneously, the implosion of the false identity, the false form of the system, into the nullity to which it has already been consigned.

The Hero's Quest

Precisely because *Snowpiercer*'s plot fulfills the logic of its setting, it appears, in most respects, quite simple: as a literal passage through the train, from tail to front. There can be no digressions, no real plot twists, only obstacles that must be overcome—battles that must be fought to press through. But while there are no twists, deviations from the straight plot, there are surprises. Indeed, everything that happens as they push forward to the head, discovering a world they've never yet glimpsed, is a surprise, though, to be sure, some surprises are more surprising than others.

Snowpiercer's plot is not only ploddingly simple in its linear advance through the train, but it also conforms to the most archetypal plot form—the quest. There is, however, not a single quest, but several quests, all united in a single complex action, each of which may itself involve multiple protagonists with diverging motivations. The first quest centers around the leading figures of the tail portion: the thrice-amputated and elderly Gilliam—the tail-dwellers' spiritual leader—and the muscular warrior Curtis and his second-in-command Edgar, who, guided by mysterious messages hidden in capsules in their protein blocks, have long been plotting revolution. The most recent message, recovered in the first scene after the preamble, suggests both a new strategy and a new ambition. They will now seek nothing less than to reach the engine, to take over the train itself; all other revolts have failed since they have not gone far enough. But since the train is partitioned with locked gates, they will need to free the Kronole-addicted Namgoong from his prison cell and enlist his help in opening the doors separating the different sections of the train.

This all suggests a well-defined revolutionary project: they will gain control of the entire system by seizing the engine, which—reflecting the collapse of the opposition of ideal and real, substructure and superstructure—is both the root of all productive forces and the head of the state apparatus. This will be possible, moreover, because of the inherent vulnerability of the security system. Depending on hidden mechanisms of control, it can be subverted from within by the specialists in charge of it, who, creatures of flesh and blood, can be bribed and corrupted. What the security apparatus reveals, in other words, is the impossibility of a total identification of real and ideal; of the total subsumption of *phusis* by *technē*. There remains a mysterious intransigent remainder, an essential hiddenness, which paradoxically is both absolute *technē*—the security system as hidden code—and absolute nature, the residual evental character of nature that Namgoong has longed to observe. This also suggests the significance of his daughter's clairvoyance—attributed in part to her being a "train baby." Whether through genetic mutations or epigenesis or cognitive adaptation, human nature seems to be transforming in ways the system cannot anticipate. In essence, then, Curtis's quest comes down to this: he seeks to gain control of the subversive power, that mysterious potential on which the system somehow depends but that it cannot control. It is, as it were, another quest for the holy grail.

Curtis's actual motivations, however, are rather more prosaic. Whereas Gilliam pontificates in a stilted language conveying epic gravitas and a mysterious insight into the root of things, Curtis and Edgar talk bluntly, dreaming of steak. This obsession with meat is especially striking given that he became Gilliam's disciple after Gilliam offered his own flesh in place of a baby Curtis was about to eat. Curtis wishes to take control of the system, civilization in its totality. Yet civilization in the last instance is nothing but the total organization of consumption—a system for determining what gets to eat what. In the state of nature, in contrast, there prevails the anarchy of first come first serve; man is not only a wolf to man but a buffet. The essence of the train's civilizational order, moreover, is carnivorism—the total submission of natural life to human consumption. Yet humans are still part of the closed system; they are the summit of the system but hardly exceptions to it. While the belief in the train as perfect closed ecological system forms the ideology, indeed the political theology of the train, this theology is fully secularized. This is because the real basis of transcendence is an Other to whom sacrifice is possible. Here there is no other; only the same consuming the same; pure autophagy. For just this reason, Gilliam's act, offering his own flesh, assumes mysterious power: since the entire natural order, at its limits, is autophagic, the gift of one's flesh suggests a power that is simultaneously immanent and transcendent to nature. Giving of itself, nature is outside itself. The gift of flesh nullifies the autophagic logic of natural metabolism.

The second quest, in contrast, involves members of the tail who are not among its elite. These are Tanya (Octavia Spencer) and Andrew. They seek to retrieve their children, who have been snatched away for obscure purposes by Wilford's assistant. Whereas the first quest is initiated by finding something, the second is initiated by losing; the first is a quest to change the existing order, the second to restore this existing order, as terrible as it was. The significance of this is compounded by the existence of a hierarchy of tail-dwellers, duplicating the order of the entire train. By separating these two quests, Bong suggests that, despite the apparent unity of the tail-dwellers' mission, there is an abiding tension in their motivations.

It often happens in Hollywood action films that the hero, while fighting neither for ideals nor duty but for the sake of his (or, rarely, her) family, nevertheless ends up serving the common good. Draped over the hero's neck like an amulet, wholesome familial love wards off the danger of the idealistic abstract fanaticism that characterizes totalitarian movements right or left, religious or secular. There is a kind of Burkeanism to this, a fear of Jacobin extremism: the American hero may fight on behalf of the existing order, the state, maybe even an ideal. Yet he is not fighting for an abstraction but for something vitally concrete. It is as if the truth of the state were perfectly realized and expressed through the nuclear family and the affections that bind it together. The most fanatical hero becomes the most concrete, with antagonism no longer assuming the form of real conflict between family or civil society and the ideals of the state but appearing merely as a conflict between the concrete substance of the state, which has already achieved a perfect subsumption of content and form, and the residual deviant elements, be they criminality, ideological fanaticism, or even bureaucratic formalism.

Bong's films refuse this gesture, and *Snowpiercer* offers an especially trenchant critique of the identification of the interests of family and state by separating the two quests of the tail-dwellers—suggesting that they don't coincide. What distinguishes the tail from the front, moreover, is that in the tail such noncoincidence is still possible. In the front, in contrast, this coincidence is enforced through the ideological state apparatus. Indeed, one of the most disturbing moments in the whole film comes when we see how deeply the children—playfully learning, surrounded by colors, toys, arts and crafts—have already internalized the ideology of the train with its hierarchy. For indeed, the identification of family and state is only possible to the extent that the family is organized around exclusionary violence; the state affirms the family by affirming and doubling its constitutive violence and above all the violence of property. But in the case of the train, where life revolves around consumption, what the ideology excludes—what the family must exclude to coincide with the state, and what the state excludes for the sake of the family—is biological reproduction, life itself, even work. The train survives by excluding the tail-dwellers, but what it excludes, in this way, is the very possibility of its own survival. For the tail-dwellers are the proletariat in the literal, etymological sense: those who exist only for the sake of reproducing. The tail's children are like stem cells: they are not yet formed by ideology. They alone can replenish the train, serving the lowly functions needed for its survival—even taking the place of mere parts.

Yet there is also a third quest: that of Namgoong and his daughter.[21] This third quest differs from the other two in several crucial respects. First, it is not introduced at the absolute tail of the train but only when Namgoong, freed from the prison car, joins the band of insurgents. Not beginning at the train's tail, neither does it end at its head but right before, though Yona does briefly enter the final compartment. Consequently, the passage through the train assumes an entirely different meaning. It is not a question of pushing through to the end but of gaining the requisite supplies and knowledge. But what does this quest involve? What is its goal?

Action and Event

No longer confined by the physical limitations of stage and actors, cinema can stray further from the canonic neoclassical unities of time, place, and action than even the most extravagant plays of Shakespeare, Calderón, Brecht, or Kleist. It is telling, then, that *Snowpiercer* comes so close to a perfect realization of the three unities in their most reductive form. Not only does the entire film take place within the train, but the various strands of its plot converge in a single action—the movement from rear to front—articulated into three parts, a beginning, middle, and end. There is even an approximate convergence of diegetic and narrative time. The train is ten miles long, meaning that it would take about three hours—only an hour more than the film—to walk through the train at a normal pace. Even though most of the action takes place during pauses in the forward advance, with progress through the train merely indicated following a typical cinematic convention, and while there are a few flashbacks and asynchronous scenes, the duration of the movie is not too far off from the duration of the events depicted within.

Yet this extravagant classicism is nevertheless contradicted in no less extravagant fashion: the train is a single unified place—long and narrow, allowing no diverging paths or lateral motion, with no place to hide—and yet it is also racing across the earth, covering hundreds of miles during the film's duration. The action collapses into a single insurgent movement from head to tail, but it not only unfolds into various quests but also develops a radical contradiction between action and event. And as compressed as the film's time is, this compressed time appears as a hyphen connecting a forgotten past and an unknown future—the future opened up by the event—through a present moment of time. While the film's actions begin within this cyclic and repetitive present time, they also call it into question or indeed finish it off. The tension between action and event—or between the negative and positive camera-apparatus, or between the cinematic apparatus of philosophy and the philosophical apparatus of cinema—plays out in the peculiar tension between radical classicism and radical anticlassicism.

This contradiction between action and event achieves the most spectacular form in the final third of the film. While presenting the denouement of the action—drawing together the various threads of the plot, gathering the action into unity—this also brings it to the point of internal contradiction, causing it to explode into the event. Crucial to this unfolding dialectic between action and event is Curtis, who represents the idealized type of the action hero. Resourceful, clever, charismatic, handsome, a physical virtuoso, he nevertheless lacks a deep and solid sense of purpose. He is a follower, a vessel filled with goals and dreams not exactly his own—a convert, a fanatic, thus also a wild card.

The typical Hollywood action film has the audience share in the fanaticism of the action hero, which thus comes to appear as the natural, ordinary human response to the situation in which he finds himself. Indeed, what the action hero so fanatically desires is often nothing else than the preservation of the existing order against various nefarious forces. At its limit, the action hero's empty fanaticism becomes the fanaticism of the existing world for itself. Film indeed has a special relation to this sort of fanaticism; presenting the world without the mediation of verbal description, it lets it appear as the pure object of fascination and desire. The weakly mythic is closely related to this: stripped of context, suspended in potency, things appear not as the finite meaning of the world but as its very existence. In *Snowpiercer*, however, Curtis's fanaticism appears problematic from the beginning. His rebellion is a pure insurgency; an assault against the existing order, which has relegated his own people to the last place or even a non-place. It has nothing to defend and hence cannot justify itself as a defense of what is its own. There is no pastoral moment juxtaposed to threatening powers.

Curtis is not simply a rebel without a cause but one who needs a cause, though the nature of this cause remains indeterminate. The action of the final third of the film hinges on Curtis, but only as the vessel for the conflict between different causes, different quests. For indeed, while Curtis, as Gilliam's follower and disciple, is driven forward by his quest, its very nature remains obscure to him: mostly he just seeks to push forward to the head of the train. He dreams of steak, to be sure, but this is not so much his quest's goal as its motivation, its "inspiration." The goal is not his own, but Gilliam's. Therefore, we may identify three moments within the final third of the film where Curtis's own sense of mission develops and transforms decisively.

The first takes place in the sauna car, during the final fight scene before the insurgents reach the final door leading to the engine. Having just shot Tanya and killed Edward, Franco the Elder, opening the doors to private rooms, discovers Namgoong hiding behind an obese woman. After Namgoong leaps out and seems to kill Franco the Elder,

Curtis comes up to the dying Tanya, takes out the picture of Timmy (Marcanthonee Reis), and promises to find him: Tanya's quest has now become his own. Now only three insurgents remain: Curtis passes through the techno-club and Jacuzzi with Namgoong and Yona, as the latter snatch up gobs of Kronole and fur coats worn by the revelers.

About two-thirds of the way through the film, the throbbing dance music and the deranged ecstasy of the doped-out front-cabin revelers give way to total silence as the insurgents pass through the control car, marching past train engineers staring at terminals and walls of buttons, levers, and flashing lights. And then, just as suddenly, the silence yields to noise, and we see a metal gangway leading over churning gears and smoke. The insurgents have reached the door to the head of the train and the eternal engine. These rapid transitions exemplify how the train, as cinematic setting, itself prefigures the montage effect, with montage, no longer an artifice of editing, generated in a seemingly natural way through the characters' forward movement. As radical *artifice*—marking an absolute break with mimesis—montage thus constitutes the basic organizing principle of the train, the microcosm of the world, and precisely because this microcosm, understanding itself as a natural totality, is itself a contrivance. While the train's hierarchy represents itself as a seemingly natural system of organization derived from organic structure, it is revealed as pure parataxis and artifice.

This exposition of the principle of montage prepares the second moment, which takes place right before the final gate leading to the engine. At stake above all is this: the very meaning of the gate as a physical representation of the paratactic principle of montage. Looking beyond even the concrete dialectical potency of montage, which depends on relations between interconnected elements, we are left with the enigmatic significance of the paratactic conjunction: the moment of passage from one film fragment to another. This passage always has a double sense, representing a moment in which two possibilities emerge. For while it is the possibility of a movement forward—through time, through the plot, through a sequence of elements arranged according to a certain dramatic logic—culminating in the exhaustion of the film's content, it also marks a break, a moment of rupture, bringing into view the radical incoherence of the elements, the senselessness of their arrangement.

It is tempting to say: *at the same time*. Yet it's not the same time but a difference in time that emerges within what seems to be the same time. The time of the *now*, the moment, breaks from the time of the continuum, the spatialized time wherein the now vanishes between the receding past and the arriving future. This *now* no longer has to do with the plot's telic fulfillment; it is a matter of *pleasure* rather than *happiness*. Film's vertiginous pleasures have nothing to do with the happy ending demanded by the more prosaic taste of the audience.

The meaning of the gate—the meaning of montage—is at issue in the conversation between Curtis and Namgoong. After Namgoong demands all the Kronole from Curtis before opening the last gate, a scuffle breaks out between them. He then tosses Curtis a cigarette— the world's last—and takes out his translation device as, meanwhile, Yona moans in the background.

This last cigarette is a fitting prop for Curtis's long monologue, where he recounts his "conversion" from the leader of a baby-devouring gang to a disciple of Gilliam, revealing that Edgar was the baby rescued through Gilliam's sacrifice. Whereas the time of the train is—or at least should be—eternity approximated through endless circular movement, the cigarette, burning from beginning to end, marks time consumed, exhausted, spent. Even the mass-produced cigarette maintains a trace of the contemplative function of the philosopher's pipe, the hookah, and North America's indigenous tobacco ceremonies; smoking a cigarette, submitting to this vanishing linear time, also allows for a moment's reflection, a pause from life's racing course. The cigarette not only implies, as with Kronole, the explosive-narcotic duality, but the last trace of that very finitude that alone could allow a break from both the forward push through the train and its circular revolutions, thereby gaining the perspective needed to end the existing order. In a word: the last cigarette—cigarettes were believed long extinct—is nothing else than the very possibility of experiencing extinction itself; of extinction, the extinguishing time, as experience. Namgoong is an addict, but his remarkable restraint with this last cigarette, which he saves and then gives away, reveals his power to break from an order that is, to its core, addictive. Where danger is, grows the saving power too.

Hanging in his hand, unsmoked, its ashes growing long, the cigarette poignantly exhibits the emotional intensity of Curtis's monologue, which describes the early days in the tail section and the rise of Gilliam's cult. Namgoong responds by challenging the most basic assumption of Curtis's account: that there is only one gate that matters—the gate leading to the head of the train, to Wilford. What Namgoong disputes, in other words, is that the only possibilities are possibilities within the system. The gate that Namgoong wants to open is not the train's final gate but the gate to the outside world: "It's been frozen shut for 18 years. You might as well call it a wall. But it's a fucking gate. Let's open it and just get the hell out." For Curtis, this is madness: "And freeze to death? What are you, fucking crazy?" He assumes, as everyone assumes—this is the fundamental premise of the train—that no life is possible beyond the train. But as Namgoong explains:

What if we could survive outside? Remember Yekaterina bridge. When your guys were getting chopped up? There's something I look at every New Year. A crashed airplane buried under the snow.

All I saw 10 years ago was the tail. Now the body and the wings are peaking out. Less ice and snow means . . . It's melting. It's the type of snow that's about to melt. A little push and it all falls down. And you know what I saw recently? Outside the window there was . . . Never mind. No need to tell you this.

True to the type of the rough-hewn American action hero—Chris Evans himself played Captain America in the Marvel franchise—Curtis responds: "You gotta take it easy on that Kronole. Snorting that flammable shit is going to fry your brain." But then Namgoong reveals he's not hoarding Kronole for the high but to build a bomb to pierce a hole through the train. Master of the train's interior gates, he wants to create a new gate, a real gate, from what has become a wall: a gate to the outside.

He takes out the Kronole, molds it into a bomb, and demands the matches, yelling "Fire!" Beyond its multiple symbolic functions, the cigarette plays a concrete role in the plot; its accompanying match can alone ignite the explosives.

The Snowflake

Only now does Namgoong's quest, the third quest, come into clear view. This quest cannot be contained within the train's system. Whereas the other quests seek ends that have meaning within the logic of the train, escaping the train transcends the train and its closed horizon of signification. It can mean nothing else for the train than its total negation. It is, in other words, the quest for the event: the rupture of the system and its closure. For within a closed system where everyone should have their place, Namgoong's place is as ambiguous as the prison car where they find him. An employee of the train, he belongs neither to the ragged masses—the absolute proletariat of the tail—or the ticketed passengers. And among the train's employees, he belongs neither to the mere workers, nor to the uniformed military officers and soldiers, nor to the plain-clothes special agents—Franco the Elder, Franco the Younger (Adnan Hasković), Egghead—working outside the ordinary chain of command. As a former security officer, disgraced and imprisoned, his knowledge of the train far exceeds his authority, his vested powers. He thus represents a significant threat to the system's order.

It's also worth noting that Namgoong is not only a rare surname in Korean, containing two syllables rather than one, but that, as Bonnie Tilland and Beth Tsai observe, it appears throughout Bong's *oeuvre*. In *Barking Dogs Never Bite*, it is given to Yun-ju's ill-fated predecessor, and in *Parasite*, it is the name of the Korean-French architect who designed the mansion where the action unfolds.[22]

We have already spoken at some length about the camera apparatus's polarization into a "negative" and "positive" camera. This polarization dovetails with the opposition between the first and second quests, on the one hand, and the third quest, on the other. The plot polarizes into one plot exhausting itself in the quest for purposes inscribed within the system, and another seeking to explode the system, to escape from it. The first and second quests suggest something close to a Hollywood blockbuster with heroic heroes striving to gain what is desired or restore what is lost. The third quest—the second plot— is, in contrast, altogether different and largely incomprehensible; the only horizon within which it can be understood is one that is excluded by, negated through, the train system.

The spectator, in this way, is split into a comprehending and an uncomprehending viewer: the viewer of the action and the viewer of the event. The viewer of the action is the typical viewer of a typical Hollywood "action" film, held in rapt suspense by a series of struggles and obstacles, fights, and oratory. Such viewers, to use Deleuze's language, find themselves in a "sensory-motor situation," a situation articulated through the potential for action.[23] The viewer of the event, confronted as it were with an "optical situation," is in a completely different position; when we witness the event, bear witness to the event, we do not know what we are witnessing; we can't know, since knowledge is always within the existing horizon.[24]

Cinema is an exemplary medium for the event; it has the potential to achieve avant-garde art's struggle to see the world with new eyes. But it also allows for the most extreme negation of this possibility. To a great extent, the dominant tendencies of mainstream Hollywood, and the action film especially, work in this direction, though there are certainly striking exceptions as well. Moreover, just when the stereotypical action film seems to negate the event most thoroughly, reducing it to a taut sequence of comprehensible actions performed by iconic stars, the event returns, though in an inverted form: as the negative image of the event. The event appears only as an absolute threat to the world, absolute danger: the doomsday machine contrived by some madman to "end the world as we know it." The ultimate quest of the hero is reduced to stopping the event and saving the world.[25]

Rather than affirming the world of action, the plot of action, Bong, by negating the action, allows the event to break through the action, appearing positive rather than negative. This sleight of hand—the greatest magic of cinema is nothing else—involves a subtle, extraordinary juggling of signifiers. The negative event is the terror of catastrophe, the devastation of the world. The positive event is the glimpse of another world, be it in something as small as a snowflake.

Oikonomia

"Fire!" Just as Namgoong screams out this ambiguous command, the door opens and Claude enters. She shoots Namgoong, measures the lump of Kronole, pries it off the door, and, addressing Curtis with a pointed gun, extends a "formal invitation" to meet Wilford for dinner. Namgoong's ambiguous, primal Promethean word—it should command the system's death but instead triggers his own—signifies this moment of reversal (*peripeteia*) and recognition (*anagnorisis*). Not only does this last gate open *for* Curtis, as if spontaneously, but he is invited to meet Wilford.

After congratulating Curtis—claiming he's the first human being to walk the total length of the train—and offering him steak, Wilford presents his own vision of the system. Maintaining perpetual balance, he explains, occasionally demands culling the population by fomenting rebellion. Thus, Curtis learns not only that his own revolt had been planned, with the messages sent to him by Wilford himself, but also that Wilford and Gilliam had been in cahoots the whole time. Wilford even considered Gilliam a friend.

This last revelation is especially devastating for Curtis. It destroys not only his whole sense of purpose, based on reverence for Gilliam and hatred for Wilford, but negates the very possibility of a revolutionary politics. In a seminal work of political philosophy, Eric Voegelin argues that radical political movements involve a "secularized" gnostic theology, a revolutionary struggle of the true order against the false, of light against darkness, to create a transfigured world.[26] Crucial to Gnosticism is the opposition of two divinities: the evil demiurge, who created the world to imprison the soul, and the liberator. In Christian Gnosticism, these correspond to the God of the Old Testament and Christ. Gilliam's complicity with

Wilford undermines this gnostic opposition and any revolutionary politics depending on it: the evil demiurge, the creator of the train, sustaining it in its eternal operation, is in league with the Christ-figure, who offers his own flesh to eat. But this is because Gilliam is not a liberator in any sense: the ultimate meaning of his extreme self-sacrifice consists in the recognition that the tail section is necessary to the train and must also be sustained, however wretchedly, as part of the train: as part of humanity.

Wilford's highest principle is sustaining ecological balance, suggesting at once the theological concept of *oikonomia* and the *yinyang* cosmology of East Asian philosophy.[27] Gilliam's religious-philosophical genius consists in recognizing that the static order that Wilford had envisioned, based on eternal class division, must be supplemented by a dynamic principle, just as the official order of the train (Wilford, ticketed passengers of various classes, officers, soldiers, employees) needs a disordered, protean/proletarian, endlessly dynamic part: human stem cells from which the other parts of the train—human and mechanical—can be endlessly regenerated.

One of the most famous examples of early cinematic montage appears in Eisenstein's *Strike* (1925), where a cow's slaughter suggests the butchering of the striking workers. Bong invokes this by accompanying Wilford's speech both with images of Egghead machine-gunning down the insurgents and of Wilford cooking steak and offering one to Curtis. It signals a striking reversal: Curtis now refuses the very steak he had once so coveted. With this refusal, he rejects the entire system of civilization as the distribution of consumption, the system of the train. Meat has become repugnant to him.

But more than just meat, what has become repugnant to him is the entire "culinary" logic of the train: the ecological-economic organization of life as an organization of consumption, of pleasure. Gilliam's autophagic gospel does not belong to the strict ideology of the train, but it *supplements* it in an essential way. The heterophagy of the train needs this autophagic supplement, however spontaneously it may have arisen, since without it, its own survival would become impossible. Maybe the fixed order even needs spontaneity (*ziran*, *to automaton*) as such. Just this makes this fixed order so insidious, and perhaps, more than anything, explains the meaning that Daoism will assume in Bong's films: unlike Christianity, which, precisely in its purest and most exalted form, cannot but serve the existing order, Daoism, in the radical sense suggested here, has made itself useless to power. Daoism does not negate, transcend, repudiate, or preserve the official ideology; it is in no sense an *Aufhebung*, nor an order-preserving spontaneous supplement. It just *strays* from it, loses itself to it—but, with this, it also becomes possible to think of the official ideology (say, Confucianism or Neo-Confucianism) as, in fact, the one that strayed from Daoism.

The Gates

At this point, the action shifts back and forth in quick succession between the antechamber and the engine. *Here* Franco the Elder gets back on his feet, pulls the knife from his chest, as the partiers, zombie-like, march in and begin to fight with Namgoong, who, still living despite his wound, orders Yona to open the gate to the engine and retrieve the Kronole. *There* Wilford continues his speech. *Here* Namgoong guides Yona as she tries to connect the wires to open the gate. *There* Wilford shows Curtis the eternal engine and invites him to walk inside it, to experience its magnificent solitude, before handing him the final capsule. Its red scrap—the plot of the plot— reads "train." The most extreme peripeteia and anagnorisis: Curtis, the outcast rebel, is to inherit the train, taking Wilford's place—to tend the engine, "keep her humming," preserving the eternal order.

The final gate having opened, the total order at last comes into view. Wilford, standing slightly behind Curtis, hand on his shoulder—this evokes Gustave Doré's 1868 illustration of Dante and Virgil before the uppermost heaven—now offers his vision, the kernel of his political philosophy:[28]

> Look, Curtis, beyond the gate. Section after section precisely where they've always been and where they'll always be, all adding up to what? The train. And now the perfectly correct number of human beings, all in their proper places, all adding up to what? Humanity. The train is the world, we the humanity. And now you have the sacred responsibility to lead all of humanity. Without you, Curtis, humanity will cease to exist. You've seen what people do without leadership. They devour one another.

Here, back in the antechamber, as if confirming Wilford's ultraconservative plea for "leadership"—the *Führerprinzip* in the language of MBAs—a shouting mob of drug-addled costumed revelers press forward. Namgoong stabs Claude from behind, then commands his daughter to grab the Kronole. Yona picks up Claude's gun and starts shooting at Franco the Elder, now standing front and center of the mob. And back *there*, in the engine, Wilford, his face looming behind Curtis, as if Curtis's inner voice, continues:

> Look at them. That's how people are. You know. You've seen this. You've been this. Ridiculous. Pathetic, aren't they? You can save them from themselves. This is what Gilliam saved you for. Curtis, this is your destiny.

Here: the Kronole is on the gate, but Curtis has the matches. Yona runs back into the engine.

With its dizzying back and forth between the antechamber and the engine, the scene involves the parallel exposition of an action taking place in two different locations. Such parallel exposition is the most inconspicuous, seemingly natural form of montage, since it follows directly from the quality of the action itself. Yet in this case, the seemingly natural montage follows divisions of a setting—the train itself—that is not only an artificial environment, reconstituting nature only after excluding it, but that is built upon the principle of montage itself. The train's artifice, exemplified by the separation of cars—hence by the gates—consists in nothing else than submitting nature to the principle of montage. But montage is nothing else than the essence of *technē* and could almost be translated as *Gestell*.

As the originary rupture of continuity, montage is pure artifice. But as the originary continuity of what has already been reduced to fragments, it also recuperates nature's continuity. Precisely because the train itself is organized along the principle of montage, the natural montage of concurrent narration converges with dialectical montage. Dialectic discovers the artifice inhabiting nature, the artifice that *is* nature. Because *technē* is at the very origin of *nature*—because nature opposes itself to itself of its own accord—the natural-artificial train repeats artificial-natural nature. With repetition, an undifferentiated unity appears through a system of differences. Hence, the engine and the antechamber are opposed as end and means, exposition and action, stillness and noise, reason and emotion, order and chaos. Separated by a gate—the final gate, it seems—the antechamber and the engine present the dyadic order of Western metaphysics.

But something more is also going on, bringing the most radical gesture of Bong's cinema into view: the dyadic order of metaphysics is not only staged and exhibited through montage but appears, through a consequent visual analogy, as the cinematic apparatus itself. Just as the tubular train resembles a lens, and the sequence of cars a strip of celluloid film, the engine itself, mysteriously opening and closing, suggests an aperture (Figure 8). In his speech to Curtis, Wilford speaks

Figure 8 Snowpiercer *directed by Bong Joon Ho. © Radius-TWC 2013.
All rights reserved.*

of the "need to maintain a proper balance of anxiety and fear, chaos
and horror in order to keep life going."[29] "And if we don't have that,"
he continues, "we need to invent it. In that sense, the Great Curtis
Revolution you invented was truly a masterpiece." While the train's
order is an ordering of life, of ranks and positions, of production and
consumption, this is only possible through the "invention" of affect.
There might seem to be something careless in Wilford's formulation:
anxiety and horror are species of fear, whereas chaos isn't an affect at all.
Yet if chaos is not an affect per se, it suggests the mode of beings in their
totality—how a world discloses itself—that corresponds to an affect,
or indeed, to the entire range of affects comprising fear in the general
sense. For all fear originates in the radical unpredictability of beings;
fear discloses the world as an unpredictability inclining toward chaos,
just as hope, the converse of fear, discloses a seeming unpredictability
overcome through a providential order. Consequently, there can be no
fear without hope, no hope without fear; the Epicurean poet Lucretius
names hope and fear in the same breath. The opposite of fear and hope
alike is boredom, *ennui*: this happens when there's nothing to fear and

nothing to hope for—it involves total submission to the mechanical, routinized, or even perhaps, in Heidegger's formulation, the *Gestell*.

What Wilford is talking about, what needs to be invented, are not simply affects but moods, in the powerful sense developed by Heidegger: fundamental ways in which the world discloses itself as a world.[30] We don't just feel bored: the world shows itself to us as boring, as devoid of possibilities, meanings. We don't just feel fear: the world shows itself as unpredictable, unknowable, with something unexpected, threatening always able to break in.

Whereas music can still claim unrivaled dominance over affect, film, the art of mood, for the most part shows us neither simply the world as it is nor the feelings of the characters but the world as it discloses itself in the situation where the characters find themselves. This is achieved through the application of lighting, camera angle and movement, as well as extradiegetic music, whose complete artifice shows just how far the language of cinema is from pure naturalism.

Wilford's train as cinematic apparatus—allowing for the "invention" of moods—thus assumes the same function as the blockbuster action film, which, soliciting hope together with fear, allows an experience of chaos. The "Great Curtis Revolution"—this film within a film—is, accordingly, the quintessential action film, satisfying its most precious conventions: there is a muscular protagonist and his sidekick, a reluctant morally compromised facilitator, a sage guru, and a villain with his lieutenants, henchmen, and faceless minions. The conventional action film, after all, is anything but innocent entertainment; it sustains the existing order by "inventing" madness. It proves that we need superheroes, Gods, the providential order of the state.

The metaphysical dyad, represented statically through the conjunction of the antechamber and the engine room, comes alive as the cinematic exhibition of the alternating moods sustaining the train's order. But this brings us before an unruly thought. While the train represents the metaphysical dyad as the ordering of chaos, it also reveals that the ordering order needs chaos: that chaos itself is the means of rule. The imposition of order on chaos can only ever take place as the imposition of chaos on order—the disordering of order. What keeps the train eternally on track is the absolute threat of derailment. The eternal order of the train is the eternal ennui of the frozen world: without hope/fear, it would fade off into somnambulant mechanized routine and then go off the rails.

One begins to suspect, in this way, that the exhibition of the cinematic apparatus of philosophy must become the exhibition of its impossibility—of a contradiction that the eternity machine itself cannot manage to control. While this scene allows the dyadic order of metaphysics to unfold before the spectator's eyes, this spectacle comes into immediate conflict with Wilford's words, which grasp the dialectic in the crude form of Platonic political philosophy: the subordination of unruly chaotic life under the leadership of the philosopher-king. Wilford, indeed, is apocalyptic capitalism's philosopher-king: just as Plato's *Republic* elevates the Greek aristocratic way of life, more Spartan than Athenian, into an eternal and absolute order, Wilford eternalizes the values of a world that, under the pressures of capitalism, can grasp the purpose of human life only as the pleasures of "conspicuous consumption" made possible through social distinctions, a system of stations. Yet if Wilford is a philosopher-king cut from the Platonic cloth, he also acknowledges the necessity of spectacle, and hence of violence, war, fervent passions—all the things that the *Republic* sought to keep at bay. Recognizing the power of the negative, he betrays a Hegelianism that, so much in the spirit of the times, has become instinctive. His train, likewise, encompasses both the Platonic beginning of metaphysics and its Hegelian destination, though here the Hegelian tail leads to the Platonic head. Consequently, Wilford and his vision are necessary following the total inclusion of life within the *polis*, yet this total inclusion, turning the *polis* into the universe, is already demanded by Plato's vision of the city. The ideal republic must be self-sufficient while excluding poets and whatever else imperils it. But with this very self-sufficiency, its wall closes in on itself; it contracts into its limits. The outside disappears. And hence it ends up including the very chaos that it had sought to exclude. No longer appearing as Other, as target of a protective violence, chaos contaminates order, which now must solicit chaos to maintain itself.

Simply put: *Snowpiercer* shows us a world without external enemies. But the enemy is always an external enemy; the internal enemy is merely a criminal. A world without enemies is a world without an outside. While Wilford is as crudely Hegelian as he is crudely Platonic, this Hegelian dialectic is also a false totality—a pretense to the absolute that implodes through the pressure of the outside that it has excluded.

Yet we may also interpret his political philosophy in terms of East Asian thought, where the question of whether the original nature of human beings is good or evil assumes no less importance than in the West. When in the second century BCE, Dong Zhongshu fashions Confucianism into the official state ideology of the Han dynasty by synthesizing Confucian ethical ideas with the cosmological frame of Chinese thought, *yinyang* duality assumes the form of a dichotomy between two terms, with *yin* clearly subordinated to *yang*. "Political power," as Wang explains, "is governed by the yang and avoids the yin [. . .] Anything that is identified with yin is bad, problematic, or in need of reshaping."[31] The result of this transformation of *yinyang* from a natural process into a normatively weighted description of social relationships is a state-sanctioned "phallocentric" privilege of the male over the female, with disastrous consequences for gender relations. As Bret Hinsch explains:

> The cosmological turn in elite thought had profound consequences for gender discourse. Most early Chinese discussed the relations of woman and man in terms of gendered social roles. Debates about gender relations tended to be arguments about which social roles are appropriate for each sex, and what sort of ideal behavior ought to append each role. . . . But cosmologists understood gender in an entirely different light. Instead of viewing gender as interlocking sets of dynamic roles, they believed that we should see gender as a static fact . . . Gender became something increasingly simple, clear cut, and unequal.[32]

These tendencies become further consolidated in Korean Neo-Confucianism, which, as suggested earlier, establishes a hierarchical and dichotomous relation between *li/i* and *qi/ki.* This certainly contributes to the marked decline in the status of women within Korean society that took place during the Chosŏn period.[33]

We may see Wilford not only as the heir to Plato but as a caricature of Confucianism codified into a repressive state ideology. He speaks a New Agey jargon of harmony and balance, yet he cannot imagine harmony otherwise than as an order born of violent subjugation.

The Dragon

The train's final gate, the last internal gate, has now been breached. All these gates are so many locks—closures and enclosures—preserving, in a world without exterior, the semblance and spectacle of an outside. What follows, accordingly, is not just the action's climax but also the transformation of action, of the logic of the action film, into something else. The gate breached, Yona rushes into the engine room, shouting to Curtis to give her the matches. Yet she pauses at the threshold of the engine's cylinder, backs away with an expression of horror, and begins scraping at one of the large tiles covering the floor. Curtis joins her and together they lift it up, discovering Timmy toiling away machine-like—his expression blank, his gestures automatic—in the machine box. For as Wilford explains:

> The space only allows for a very small person. Young children under five. The engine lasts forever, but not all of its parts. That piece went extinct recently. We needed a replacement. Thank goodness the tail section manufactures a steady supply of kids. So we can keep going manually.

Taking the place of the dramato-theo-urgical *deux ex machina* is the *puer in machina*, the boy in the machine. Adam Smith describes a boy who, assigned the dreary task of opening and closing the valve of a crude steam engine, rigged the valve to another part of the machine such that it would open and shut unassisted, leaving him "at liberty to divert himself with his play-fellows."[34] Returning to this primal scene of capitalist ingenuity, Bong shows the futility of the liberty envisioned: the boy will always be forced back into the machine, forced to become machine, since the dependence of the machine on human participation, human parts, is not accidental but essential.[35] Understanding this leads to Marx's account of the role of labor in value and profit. While the capitalist system of production is "eternal" just as cancer is eternal—lacking capacity for self-limitation—it still depends on the finitude of human life. Only in light of this finitude could labor time become the metric of value.

But there is more. *The engine lasts forever, but not all of its parts.* This echoes Peter Yarrow's elegiac children's song, "Puff, the Magic Dragon": "a dragon lives forever, but not so little boys." The similarity between the dragon, literally a "serpent," and the train is too glaring for this not to draw our attention, and not simply because the train, the *Zug*, is what can and must *drag on*. Yet if the dragon is a figure belonging to the archaic mythic imagination, the train and its engine claim the eternity of the machine. In an age of mass reproduction, automation, information technologies, the most fundamental task of ideology is to transfigure the machine into poetry, to poeticize the automatic mechanism of everyday life while leaving no space for the originally poetic. Anticipated by the magic lantern, this becomes the primary ideological function of cinema; the strip of celluloid, spooled through the machine, becomes the perfect means by which imagination is fulfilled . . . and exhausted. And it is not just, not primarily, the mechanical machine that needs the boy but the ideological machine: the cinematic machine. The boy is firstly the child, childish imagination, childish innocence—the desire for play. It is, however, not just the inner life, the moral sensibility and imagination, of the child that must be colonized by the machine but the poetic imagination of Western civilization's other. His ebony-golden skin identifies him also with the global South, just as Wilford's train marks the absolute culmination of the European project of colonial domination; the globe, first subsumed under the gaze of the rootless tourist wandering endlessly from city to city, is now negated and preserved in the eternal machine. And this touristic-colonial machine converges with cinema. The traditional etymology of the Greek *drakōn* traces it back to *derkomai*, "to see." The dragon is the one who stares, the sharp-sighted one: the camera.

But if the train-dragon is cinema itself, it is also "global" cinema in all its ambiguity. While the dragon—one of the earliest attempts to "express the dualism of nature and society within a consistent framework"—is common to both East and West, there are striking differences both in how the dragon functions as sign and in what it signifies.[36] Western dragons, while heterogeneous in appearance, tend to symbolize one thing—an "evil or obstacle to be overcome"— implying a Faustian view of nature as an obstacle whose dangerous independence must be conquered and forced to submit—reduced to a mere factor of production—or just destroyed.[37] In this, we find, in Ji-Yeong Yun's words, the "Anthropocene divide" that, underwritten by Cartesian metaphysics, leads to the "dichotomous hierarchization between nature and culture, non-human and human."[38] Eastern dragons, in contrast, are more regular in appearance—there are nine classical representations—but more semantically ambiguous, with a positive meaning prevailing. In the *Book of Changes*, for example, the "dragon is a symbol of the spiritual, dynamic, arousing force that manifests itself in the sublimity of the Creative," and thus akin to the vital energy of nature (*qi/ki*) that, appearing in spring and withdrawing in winter, "causes the germination and sprouting of all living things."[39] And the dragon stands in a special relation to Daoism. A legend tells of an encounter between Confucius and Laozi. Rebuked by the great Daoist sage, told to "renounce his arrogant ways," Confucius goes off shaking his head, and then addresses his disciples:

> I understand how birds can fly, how fishes can swim, and how four-footed beasts can run. Those that run can be snared, those that swim may be caught with hook and line, those that fly may be shot with arrows. But when it comes to the dragon, I am unable to conceive how he can soar into the sky riding upon the wind and clouds. Today I have seen Laozi and can only liken him to a dragon.[40]

Snowpiercer's train-dragon, like the *koemul*, speaks to humankind's relation to the natural world. But whereas the river monster is a symptom of polluted nature, the train is this very relation itself: the total system of earthly life as existing for the sake of human life, ordered to the demands of a human life that is itself submitted—brutally, despotically—to the imperative of its own survival. It is the absolute Western dragon as already slain, nature subordinated once and for all to human will, art, *technē*—a frozen dragon coursing eternally through a frozen world. And at the helm: Wilford—Faustian dragon slayer turned philosopher-king. But if the Western dragon has already been slain—the heroic project of the West was achieved at the outset—it survives, even more potently, as an idea; its destruction is its sublimation, its preservation: in a (German) word, its *Aufhebung*. The Western dragon, slain, becomes the train as the total system in which the oppositional violence of chaotic nature is applied to human life to preserve natural life for eternity in its subordination to human will. And so there remains another dragon to be slain: the idea of the Western dragon.

Slaying the idea of the Western dragon—the technical domination of nature—has preoccupied "continental" Western philosophy since the twentieth century, beginning with György Lukács's *Geschichte und Klassenbewußtsein* (History and Class Consciousness), Heidegger's critique of the *Gestell*, Theodor Adorno and Max Horkheimer's *Dialektik der Aufklärung* (Dialectics of Enlightenment), and Herbert Marcuse's *One-Dimensional Man*. But perhaps the slain *idea* of the dragon, like the slain dragon, will inevitably sublimate itself again, preserving itself in an even more subtle, rarified, insinuating-serpentine form. The sublimation of the idea is, of course, the image, the simulacrum. For late capitalism has increasingly assumed a form in which the violent ordering of the real is thoroughly compatible with the disintegration of the ideals of the West; with the "postmodern" triumph of simulacric virtuality. Perhaps it is not enough to slay the idea of the dragon; another idea of the dragon, another dragon, must take its place. The slain Western dragon, and its idea-soul, must open the way to the resurrection of the Eastern, "Daoist" dragon. Could this be the mad wager of Bong's cinema?

But the dragon, as mentioned, is also the power of vision. Our adventurous interpretation seems to have left us hopelessly confused: how is it that nature—whether taken as the unordered chaos confronting the ordering human will or as the vital power manifesting in all things—can also be the power of vision? If this seems so strange and unsettling, it is precisely because the Western dragon of technological domination has always insisted on an oppositional relation of object and subject. This oppositional relation, realized through the camera, is at play in the cinematic apparatus of philosophy. There is, to be sure, a power of vision that sunders *physis* and *technē*, object and subject, Being and Truth—but there is also a power of vision that joins them and rejoins them ever anew. The vision-dragon, the camera-dragon—the eye of the dragon—is therefore the sole spot where the conquered and pacified Western dragon, gliding eternal on the frozen expanse of a deadened world, nature swallowed in its belly, is vulnerable. And yet let us not, repeating Odysseus's heroic cunning, thrust the burning shaft into its single eye. This deed—repeated on the *koemul*—can only make the monster more monstrous, striking out the last trace of vision. Another heroism is needed: ripping out—and thus creating—another eye, another opening. Only in this way could the Eastern dragon rise from the Western dragon's smoldering wreck.

There is, however, no vision, and no camera, without light. And the dragon breathes fire. For the modern Western dragon, oppositional nature pacified and subordinated to human will, *fire* is energy channeled, stored, distributed; the domesticated explosion. Wilford's engine must appear as the culmination of the trajectory of technical progress begun by the steam engine: the heavenly fire captured by the eternal machine. And yet the eternal machine is not only afflicted with less than eternal parts: it leaves a remnant, a trace . . . Kronole, the "industrial waste"—intoxicant and explosive in one. In this first capacity, Kronole allows Namgoong and Yona to see beyond the walls of the train. Addicts, they are chasing the dragon: for what does every hallucinogenic intoxicant offer, in the end, but a fleeting glimpse of an otherwise. In the second capacity, it unleashes the light—explosive, uncontrolled, spontaneous—through which a new kind of vision becomes possible.

Melodrama

The moment Wilford names Curtis his heir, bequeathing the train and its engine, and indeed the care of humanity, to him, it becomes clear that Curtis's heroic quest was never really his own. Nevertheless, every action hero descends from the archaic heroes, and these—Gilgamesh, Beowulf, Hercules—were all dragon slayers, as is Odysseus, who drove a fiery stake into the Cyclops Polyphemus's eye. What Curtis realizes, thus, is that his quest amounts to one more repetition of a gesture that, far from either founding a new order or revolutionizing the old, merely reinstitutes it. The existing order is the subordination of nature to human will; slaying the dragon merely repeats the submission of nature to the human violence arising within it. And indeed, if Curtis—clever, resourceful—suggests Odysseus, the self-apotheosized Wilford is Virgil's Aeneas, having brought a remnant to the safety of the eternal city, which in turn becomes an asylum for the wretched. Odysseus now finds himself captive in Rome: a gladiator—constitutive, world-creating violence becomes a spectacle of violence to keep the bloodthirsty, restive mob entertained. Rome becomes America, the coliseum becomes Hollywood, Curtis the last action hero, who, having defeated all his opponents, receives the ultimate reward: power over death and life.

Still, couldn't he have become Spartacus? Whether this imperium has been seized or granted makes no difference: the *fasces*, power of death over life, could be restrained, a kinder, gentler empire might be possible. Space may even be granted for something like the rule of law. Yet the power over life, the responsibility for life, demands another cruelty—one that cannot be renounced. It is precisely this that he finds hidden behind the tile. Minister Mason's extravagant cruelty might be superfluous: not so the little boy, whose mechanical motions sustain the system.

This final discovery is tragic. Yet, action hero that he is, he doesn't do tragedy. And so, he has no words for it: only his fist and his curses. He punches Wilford in the face, shouting, "You fucking bastard," before pulling Timmy out from the tiny compartment. As the engine begins to shut down, he calls out to Yona to take the fire; she runs back to Namgoong, who is still fighting with Franco the Elder. The front of the engine opens like an aperture as a recorded warning begins to repeat. Andy now climbs out from a sleeping chamber, walking in a trance as Curtis vainly implores him not to enter the compartment that has opened for him. "Oh, Curtis, don't be so melodramatic," Wilford shouts. "You know everyone has their own preordained position." And following Wilford's strange gestures, suggesting a hypnotist or puppet master or even Dr. Caligari, Andy sets to work.

Melodrama is a characteristic quality not only of Korean soap operas and movies, especially from the fifties, the first golden age of Korean cinema, but even *p'ansori*, an indigenous form of epic storytelling. Melodrama might seem closely tied to the national character of Korea itself. It is as if, just as Curtis falls under the sway of Yona, seeing the world through her eyes, Wilford were to rebuke him: "Don't be so Korean!" Or simply: don't feel so much—and if you must feel, don't express your emotions! And certainly don't act on them! Yona's wailing is the siren song that Curtis, having heard, must heed. As Odysseus-like as he, a man of twists and turns, might be, he failed to strap himself to the mast of sober responsibility. Nor is he a deaf somnambulant machine. He hears the siren's wail, the *melos*, and acts on it. And so he reaches in to grasp Andy's hand.

While Namgoong breaks Franco the Elder's neck, Yona lights the explosive with the last match. She and her father then dress in their stolen furs, and, after Timmy rushes into Yona's arms, Namgoong runs up behind Yona, who, holding Timmy, faces Curtis. The music builds to a crescendo as the fuse burns down. Namgoong and Curtis both embrace to protect Yona and Timmy.

Having found his way back to his dining table and his steak, Wilford, culinary spectator par excellence, offers his final verdict: "Nice!" And then the Kronole explodes. Noise gives way to a faint but growing rumble. The mountains appear panoramically, then from closer to the ground, as an avalanche builds and tears the train in half, flinging the rear wagons down into a ravine while the front grinds to a halt inside the tunnel. An aerial shot shows the cars of the train scattered across the snow. If the train is humanity, the human world, then this is the end of the world as anyone has ever known it. The white of the snow fades to black; the last faint rumbles die off into silence.

But suddenly, Timmy and Yona appear, engulfed in their furs; he opens his eyes, which dart to both sides, and then she too awakens. She cries out several times for her dad ("appa"), once for Curtis, then tells Timmy to stay put as she walks through the ruined, still-burning train car. Then the screen turns white: a fur-covered boot steps down. With the overturned train car in the background, Yona walks out into the snow field, Timmy behind her. A look of total desperation passes over her face, but then she returns to Timmy, holds his hand, and continues further. Looking out into the snow with different eyes, she spots a polar bear in the distance. Gentle, hopeful music begins to play as the camera pans down and right to reveal Timmy's face, his eyes turned toward the distance. In the final shot, the polar bear seems to return their gaze.

This is hardly a happy ending. Reduced to a mad girl and a young boy left alone in a snowy wilderness, the human race's chances for survival are grim—even without throwing an apex predator into the mix. It might be too soon to celebrate the bomb as "transformative violence" precipitating a "decolonizing exodus" that will clear the way for "human emancipation."[41] It is only the sentimental gaze of Anthropocene humanity, for whom nature is not threat but threatened, that could imagine anything else than a cold, bloody end for the new Eve and Adam. Yet if not happy, it is still hopeful. Even if it might well be a hope that not only has nothing to do with providential order, and is not the opposite of fear, but that, like Kafka's, is not for us. For we too, after all, are passengers in the train, and, like Wilford with his last word—is he talking about the steak, or the bear hug, or the bomb?—spectators of its spectacle. But another dragon rises from the ruins of the dragon of the West; another nature appears outside the train—and perhaps even another humanity, one in which those who have been at the helm for so long—whether as engineers, leaders, revolutionaries, saints, technicians, or executioners—have gone extinct.

6
Okja

Hope

Snowpiercer has led us into the abyss. A consummately entertaining film, mutant bastard child of a global film industry endlessly churning out marketable blockbusters, it also gives us to think and what it gives us to think is bleak: there is hope, but not for us, not for our world. It envisions a future of capitalism where the total concrete subsumption of human and natural productivity alike under the capitalist mode of production leads to an absolute monopoly on all functions needed for human survival—the ultimate matrix of political life. Capitalism leads not to the abolition of private property but its consolidation in a single hand, combining absolute economic/ecological planning with a strict, immobile division of social classes. Embossed throughout the train, Wilford's emblem seems to have replaced currency: only barter remains to supplement scheduled distributions. The fluid outcomes of capitalism as a dynamic system have gotten frozen for eternity as a total ordering of all life. Yet the dynamism of capitalism and history more generally—class conflict in all its forms—is mobilized from the top down to preserve the system *ad perpetuum.* Thus, the great hope of the radical left—revolutionary politics—has been neutralized. What remains of revolution in the age of "total capitalism" is only the spectacle of revolution—class conflict as spectacle. Nor is the blockbuster action film a neutral player in this: all the various forms of spectacular violence keep the system on track.

This system is so totalizing, so absolute that no transformation from within is possible. Revolutionary politics appears as quixotic as progressivism. Escape is only possible with the destruction of the system. Worse yet, its claims are not false: the total system is real, and our survival as human beings depends on it. Were survival possible outside the system, it must be under conditions so austere as to require abandoning everything we have been up to this point. If Timmy and Yona survive, they'll have left everything behind—human civilization's last sad vestiges. Neither speaks in more than single words; a new language will be born from their mingled, mangled tongues.

Yet *Snowpiercer*, like *The Host*, also ends with a moment of genuine, radical hope: the formation of a new family, no longer defined by consanguinity. In *The Host*, this happens when the older brother, his own daughter killed, adopts the orphan who, already without parents, has now been bereaved of his elder brother. And in *Snowpiercer*, it assumes an even more radical form—the creation of a new primal family—though we can only wonder what role the polar bear will play. We might hope that, as apex predator, it signals the existence of other life-forms, but perhaps it has just been feasting on frozen corpses, having unlearned the taste of living flesh. Will it devour the new family, run away in fear, or start dancing for them? Or is this the beginning of a new relationship between human beings and the other inhabitants of the earth? Tan'gun, the legendary founder of the Korean people and king of Kojosŏn, is said to have been born from Ungnyŏ (熊女, "bear woman"), a bear who, in answer to her prayers, was made human and then impregnated by the divine king Hwanung.

This faint spot of hope, with its accompanying terror, is at the center of Bong's *Okja*, released in 2017 by Netflix with a screenplay co-written by Jon Ronson. Bong's sixth feature-length film—the third with a substantial CGI component—is first and foremost a film about adoption. A girl has adopted a hippo-sized mutant super pig. Adoption per se might seem like the least interesting thing about this film, which combines a scathing critique of industrial agriculture, genetic engineering, and "visionary" capitalism with a satirical but ultimately sympathetic look at animal rights activists. Yet child-animal relations (we recall *A Dog of Flanders*, from which Bong's first feature film took its name), and even girl-pig relations (*Charlotte's Web*), are a common theme in modern children's literature and film, and such relations are fundamentally relations of adoption; nonhuman nature, indeed, can only be adopted by, not born to, human beings. It is the adoption of fellow creatures that discovers our relation to "Mother Earth."

Global and Local Spaces/The Finite Positive and Infinite Negative

While *The Host*, *Snowpiercer*, and *Okja* embrace a Hollywood blockbuster style, they are no less expressions of a coherent artistic vision than those of Bong's films with a more obvious art-house feel. For globalization involves the emergence of a new sensorium, a new field of vision turned toward itself; globalization is itself a cinematic apparatus—with all the ambiguity this entails. By exploiting rather than despairing at the changing economic conditions under which Korean directors were compelled to operate, Bong's "Hollywood" films achieve ever more commanding, more sovereign views on the new planetary order. Despite the absence of a shared fictional world, common characters, and contiguous elements, they form a de facto unity. Just as critics have come to speak of Park Chan-wook's vengeance trilogy, one might also speak of Bong's globalization trilogy.

The deep connection between these three films can be seen from the subtle system of distributed oppositions they unfold. Consider, for example, the relation between the local/Korean and the global/American. In *The Host*, the global/American is a seemingly marginal—but insidious, contaminating—presence within a film that, set in Seoul, is filmed almost entirely in Korean, with English appearing only at the periphery as the language of the neocolonial American elite. In *Snowpiercer*, however, we are entirely submerged in the global/American order, which, through the train, has become absolute. The two Korean characters don't make their entrance until a quarter into the film, and while they first appear merely as reluctant assistants, their own quest, radically different from the others, gradually comes into view. Korean, when spoken, is almost always in dialogue with English speakers and thus mediated through a universal translator. Thus, the English subtitles not only translate for the audience but indicate a moment of comprehension occurring within the film, as if transcribing the unheard but implicit output of the intradiegetic translation device.

Okja, in contrast, is set in both a local Korea and a global America. Much dialogue is either purely in Korean or in English, but there is also dialogue across languages, often facilitated through interpreters. Moreover, the opposition between the local and global reproduces itself within both domains. Korea is divided into Mija (Ahn Seo-hyun) and her grandfather Hee Bong's (Byun Hee-Bong) mountaintop farm—a pristine world barely touched by modernity, it evokes not so much the Judeo-Christian Eden as Laozi's vision of isolated communities where "people reach old age without meeting each other"[1]—and a Seoul that, bursting with people and commodities, houses a Mirando branch office. The United States, likewise, is divided into New York City, the absolute global city, and the New Jersey suburb Paramus, home to Mirando's industrial-scale meat production and packing facility.

Not only does the main action of the film unfold in sequence across these four spaces, moving from the remote Korean mountain (the local-local) to Seoul (the local-global) to New York City (the global-global) and then to Paramus (the global-local), but the distinction between local and global spaces forms a chiasmic relation with the "topological" opposition between the vertical and horizontal. In Korea, we descend from the mountain farm with its vertical topography to Seoul, where much of the action takes place in horizontal spaces. In New York City, amid the towering skyscrapers, height again prevails, being identified with the sovereign view of capitalists upon the world beneath them. Yet the Paramus factory is a vast horizontal expanse. Global capitalism, this suggests, reverses the valences of vertical and horizontal. In a Korea still not totally subsumed under the global capitalist order, the vertical signifies the original, pristine productivity of nature; the horizontal, its domination under the capitalist law of exchange. But with capitalism's absolute triumph, capital commands the heights: it is no longer that which flattens, liquefies, undermines—the tunneling power destroying the earth's local contours while erasing the distance between localities. Now it creates ranks, endless distinctions of superior and inferior.

Okja, all this suggests, not only belongs together with *The Host* and *Snowpiercer* as part of a "globalization trilogy," but assumes a mediating function, resolving the dilemma that came to light through the earlier films. For indeed, the two earlier films have led us not only into an abyss but an *aporia*. This impasse is characterized by having to choose between "theatrical" actions unfolding within the given order and an "absolute event" destroying a system upon which, as odious as it is, life depends. Comically appropriating and subverting the conventions of the "monster movie," *The Host* shows a quixotic battle against an enemy whose very visibility owes to the contaminating influence of globalization. In contrast, *Snowpiercer* envisions a genuine event—a radical break with the existing order— but one so extreme as to threaten everything, leaving unclear whether it represents the existing order's destruction or rather its culmination. The choice between Wilford (and Gilliam) and Namgoong is, perhaps, merely between the holding back (*katechon*) of the end of times *(eschaton)* and the rushing toward it.

The impasse comes down to this: action is either so limited, so finite that it can change nothing, only functioning "aesthetically"—a kind of expressive politics—or it is so infinite, so absolute that it must destroy everything. Action is divided between the *finite positive* and the *infinite negative.*

What the *finite positive* and the *infinite negative* share—the common horizon of their legibility—is that both are aesthetic in opposed, though ultimately convergent, senses. With the finite positive, its aesthetic character lies on the surface; it involves political actions and forms of activism aimed against an enemy that is imaginary, not because it doesn't exist—there is little reason to regard the *koemul* as itself fictive relative to the movie's fictional world—but because the concrete visible form it assumes belies its fundamentally structural nature. Following the typical logic of a paranoid, "conspiratorial" political imagination, the truly uncanny, alienating power of industrialization, modernity, history, society, and global capitalism manifest as visible monsters that can be defeated. The aesthetic character of the infinite negative, on the other hand, is harder to grasp, though we've already treated it at length: so far as the entire system is determined by the cinematic apparatus of philosophy—the spectacular order anticipated in Plato's cave—the system is aesthetic through and through. Consequently, the infinite negative action takes form as the total aesthetic negation of the aesthetic order.

We are not, of course, talking about the finite positive or infinite negative action as such but about both as they are represented cinematically. This introduces its own set of paradoxes since cinematic representation is essentially a mode of aesthetic representation. The opposition is between a cinematic/aesthetic representation of an action aimed against a finite representation and a cinematic/aesthetic representation of the negation of the entire system of representation. This suggests the extraordinary significance of CGI, understood not simply as a "special" effect but as representing, together with photography and animation, a third primary cinematic technology, indeed the synthesis of the other two. Whereas photography remains in a subtractive relation to a "superabundant" given reality, and whereas conventional animation presents an impoverished, schematic synthetic representation in place of reality, CGI offers a synthetic appearance that is as richly detailed as reality itself. In the case of Bong's films, where the CGI augments conventional photography and *mise-en-scène*, this allows for a literal representation of the power of fantasy. The CGI monster, appearing real in the context of the film, reveals the power of fantasy constituting an integral part of the real. But *Snowpiercer*'s train, viewed from the outside and in its totality, is also a CGI monster, as is the haunted frozen landscape that it passes through. Just as CGI allows the representation of a battle against a fantastic monster, it can also show the destruction of the entire monstrous system: the entire system of fantastic representation wherein life is captured. And yet these two representations ultimately converge: the *koemul* symbolizes not just one single monster but the entire logic of monstrous appearances and pseudo-battles. Together with the train, the entire system of representation explodes. Yet ultimately, *koemul* and train are still just one more cinematic monster.

Thus, the finite positive and infinite negative come to coincide, revealing, in their convergence, the outer limits of the cinematic anesthetization of politics that achieves its accomplished form with CGI.

It will seem as though CGI subverts the last vestige of cinema's revolutionary potential as conceived by Walter Benjamin. While cinema breaks with the aura, and hence with the cult of creative "genius," CGI marks the culmination of the process that, beginning with the Hollywood star system, sought to re-establish the traditional aesthetic values rooted in cult and ritual.[2] This makes it even more necessary to engage with CGI just as thoughtfully as with the charismatic presence of the movie stars—especially since CGI offers the aesthetic correlate to emergent technologies of genetic manipulation and engineering, with both allowing for the synthesis of the real, the total submission of the real to the power of imagination. Today's monsters are no longer montage-monsters—montagesters, as it were—stitched together, like Frankenstein's, from *disjecta membra*.

What the forced choice between the finite positive and the infinite negative excludes is infinite positive action—creating a new world. But the infinite positive coincides with, and becomes possible through, the finite negative action. The finite negative action is the real event. An event, since it transforms the existing order, breaking through the relentless determinism of what is given. And real, since it assumes the form of a concrete determinate action irrupting the new into the given. But how is this real event possible for cinema? And indeed for CGI-cinema, which seems to force the choice between the finite positive and the infinite negative? Not otherwise than through a cinematic gesture allowing a relation to emerge, within cinema, to CGI. The CGI monster appears—an ethical decision becomes necessary. One can adopt the monster or one can reject it. The CGI monster allows the question of adoption to appear in the most radical light: as the radical ethical openness to a new species, a new form of life.

Adoption

With adoption, the most natural relation—childbirth, natality—is repeated, duplicated as an artificial relation. That adoption is possible reveals the radical excess of the artificial over the natural. It follows from this excess that the artificial (culture in the broadest sense), far from being reducible to nature, is itself constitutive of the natural order. This is rather obvious in the case of paternity, where the natural relation, lacking immediate and natural signs, can only ever be established through symbolic, ritual, or juridical acts. But it is also true, in a more interesting way, of the maternal relation. Maternity has two quite different components: birthing, which might amount to nothing more than spewing fertilized eggs out into the world, and nurturing. Whereas birthing happens and is done with, thoroughly determined by a natural process, nurturing is habitual, repetitive, and, with humans, forever unfinished. Thus, nurture marks the emergence of culture within the natural order. A continual adoption, readopting what is already adopted, the essence of nurture is *care*. Even granting Heidegger's deep insight into care as the Being of *Dasein* (the entity that we ourselves are) as Being-in-the-world, we need not attribute care only to humans.[3] For even granting that other animals can never relate to their existence in its radical singularity, and thus that their care lacks the ultimate orientation toward meaning, nurture nevertheless discloses a horizon of care that crosses over the "natural" boundaries of species. It becomes possible for a human to adopt an animal by nurturing it, caring for it, or even for one animal to adopt another. And the adoption of humans by animals is a recurrent trope in mythology, as most famously in Rome's founding myth. For in essence, adoption is always reciprocal; the adopted child should eventually care for the parents. All creaturely dependence is codependence.

Moreover, the double excess of culture over nature, signaled through adoption, cuts in two opposite directions. While, following the paternal logic of adoption, it may speak to the ultimate impossibility of grasping nature outside the artifice of significance, maternal adoption suggests that nature itself, in its seemingly immediate materiality, is constituted through an originary excess; neither a blind dead mechanism nor a homogenous field of immanence, nature is not only adaptive but adoptive: "choosing toward" possibilities that open up within itself as the fractures wrought by the incursion of transcendence.

Adopting the monster thus involves an adaptive relationship to the adaptive power of nature. The artificial-natural adapts to—at once artificially and naturally grows toward, opens to, affirms—the artificial-natural. What is ultimately affirmed is a new form of life, a new political community—not through the blind negation of the existing order but through the concrete, finite affirmation of concrete possibilities already manifest within the real. Adoption opens the way toward a new political order, a new community, but it remains always a concrete ethical relation between one living being and another.

Playing together in the mountaintop terrain, with its steep crags and waterfalls, Mija and Okja offer the most beautiful and poignant illustration of the ethical. This reveals not only Mija and Okja's deep bond but the mental, emotional, and physical capacities of this strange and new creature. In a scene recalling the Aesopian fable of the lion and the mouse, Okja approaches Mija, showing a thorny mass embedded in her humongous paw, which Mija then removes. Clearly, Okja regards Mija as her caregiver, her benefactor. While Okja communicates through a range of grunts, she also understands human words. When Mija says she wants fish for dinner, Okja tosses herself into a pond; the explosive impact of her body ejects their quarry onto the mud. Mija then falls asleep atop Okja. The perfect joy of this idyll, however, is interrupted when the grandfather, returning home with a wood bundle lashed to his back, summons Mija back home with his public address system, comically recalling the speakers embedded in the walls of Korean apartments broadcasting periodic announcements. But it also suggests a deeper tension: Mija is literally "named" and "addressed," indeed in absurdly formal language ("Mija Joo of 37–1, Sanyang Town! Promptly return home for dinner"); Okja is not. While Okja and Mija are partners within the order of nature, only Mija belongs to the political order that has established itself even here—*et in Arcadia.*

Abruptly summoned by her grandfather, Mija must return quickly, and so, after tying a rope around Okja, she tries to lead her along a precarious shortcut. But then Mija slips, slides down a rock face, and plunges off a high cliff, saved from certain death only by the rope binding her to her charge. Attempting to pull Mija up by the rope, Okja loses her footing, sliding to the very edge of the precipice. But then something extraordinary happens. After surveying the surroundings, Okja runs toward a stump jutting out from the rocks and, guiding the rope over it, jumps down. Mija is pulled up to the branch while Okja, releasing the rope from her jaw in the nick of time, plunges down into the forest canopy.

Cartoonish as it may seem, this action sequence develops a rich texture of meanings. No mere childish reverie, it paints the primal scene of a "natural" political community, opposed to the formal political community instituted through "public address." This natural community, already anticipated by Okja and Mija gathering and hunting together, solidifies in the face of the danger posed by the natural world. The rope Mija ties around Okja's neck offers an allegorical representation of the original form of political community: the yoking of nature—unspeaking, brutish—to a guiding human will and intelligence. Yet once Mija begins slipping, the nature of the rope changes: the rope of servitude, of subjugation—gentle as it may be—transforms into the rope of interdependence, codependence. Mija planned to guide Okja, against her inclinations, with this rope. But now it supports Mija, keeping her tethered to the unspeaking creature that she was to lead. Moreover, having already shown herself capable of understanding human language, Okja now not only demonstrates an intuitive grasp of physics—cartoonishly distorted, admittedly, as the physics of this fictive world is—but also a capacity for ethical action, risking her own life to save the other.[4]

For Aristotle, the human slave possesses a deficient form of reason: capable of obeying orders but lacking the capacity to posit the ultimate ends orienting human life.[5] This allows Aristotle to uphold his belief in natural slavery, despite the seeming universality of language among human beings, despite all humans being political animals in virtue of possessing *logos*.[6] Thus, Okja first appears as a natural slave. For Aristotle, indeed, the beast of burden is the poor man's slave.[7] Yet this changes the moment Okja risks her own life to save Mija's. Her action evinces a freedom standing in a negative relation to, and thus surpassing, mere life by assigning a meaning to it, a purpose beyond mere life. The moment Okja risks her own life she can no longer simply be a "natural slave." She has given a sign of her membership in a community of free rational beings, the Kantian "kingdom of ends." Yet this sign remains ambiguous. Perhaps Okja is merely acting on instinct. Perhaps she values Mija's life more than her own because of her servility. Every good Kantian knows, of course, that nothing in the phenomenal world can unambiguously demonstrate freedom.[8] Yet the problematic nature of such evidence changes nothing. Even the barest hint of freedom is enough to beckon toward a new community.

And indeed, the sublimity of Kant's ethics consists, above all, in the demand that we must treat the Other as an end and not just a means despite the absence of an unambiguous physical sign—despite the fact that we can only ever hear our own inner voice.[9] It is significant, moreover, that whereas the modern novel allows us to assume the inner voice of the Other, cinematic media, which can only convey thought through artificial contrivances, exaggerates the ethical ambiguity of physical appearance. We see the tears of the Other, the most nuanced expressions of the face, the visceral signs of affect that elicit sympathy and compassion. But the Other always appears as if through a target finder. Nor is there any guarantee tears are sincere; no omniscient narrator can speak for a truth *beyond* the phenomena.

Inhuman Potentials/The Freak

Adoption's deepest ethical significance consists not merely in caring for and providing for some given creature, whose possibilities have already been grasped and understood, but in caring for the unrevealed, ungiven, unknown. In extremis, adoption is adoption of what is alien to our world, our horizon of significations, even our planet. One might object, however, that whereas the radical potential of adoption is already realized in nurturing the human child—the newborn, as Arendt remarks, represents a radical new beginning in the world— the nonhuman animal, not to speak of the true alien, overshoots the mark.[10] Standing outside the human world—the human horizon of meaning—their potential can never come into existence for us except by being reduced to our terms.

Indeed, for Arendt, following Aristotle in attaching an absolute privilege to the human, nonhuman animal life must lack a biographical dimension. The individual life of the nonhuman animal can only exemplify the universal type, the species.[11] Yet there's a contradiction between, on the one hand, conceiving of potential as biographical—as the possibility of having an individual "life-story"—and, on the other, in understanding the biographical as the privilege of this special genus, namely us, human beings—animals who are not mere animals. For if the human being is automatically recognized from birth as beginning a life story, it is precisely because the potential to be realized through a life story has already been grasped in advance as unfolding within the general limits of human potential or, rather, within the range of human potential belonging to this historical world, this social context. This historical world thus appears as a "second nature"; it presents itself as natural. Even though all these social positions are historical, they come to be understood as natural, eternal; the "real world" that the child must fit into to become something at all.

Consequently, the nonhuman animal's nonbiographical life possesses a deeper, more radical potential than human biography. For animal life remains alien to human potential. Nonhuman, otherwise-than-human animals surely have a given place within our human world, but this place is so narrow—cute pet, delicious food, pest, threat—that any real expression of animal life collides against its walls. Adopting an animal thus means becoming open to an alien potential that, as such, is more radical, more profound than merely human potential. Hitting up against the limits of the naturalized historical life of the human world, animal life, seemingly merely natural, in fact reveals that the natural is itself always historical. No mere fixed eternal order, nature is also evolving. Only the historicity of nature can undo the naturalization of history. Or put another way, the ultimate horizon of human history is the metabolic relation between human beings and the natural world, or indeed the metabolic relation of all beings (human and otherwise-than-human, living and otherwise-than-living) to one another. To speak of human history is already to render its own truth incomprehensible.

The naturalization of history consists in its normalization: its reduction to an order of hierarchically nested general categories and the things subsumed under them. The privilege of human beings within such an order is the potential to be many things and not just to become what one already is. But this *many* still only consists in different generic types. Because theoretical knowledge presupposes this normalization—we can experience particulars, but knowledge is always about something general, about this sort of thing—one cannot raise any purely theoretical objections against this. Every real objection, even if eventually expressed in theoretical terms—through philosophical arguments—begins with some *this*: an experience that is not merely real but superreal, surreal, since it surpasses the horizon of our world. Such an evental experience, which we have designated as *mythic*, can assume many forms: the beautiful object, which seems comprehensible without being comprehended; the inner voice that calls us to recognize the singular ethical significance of our life; and not least, unworldly life—mutant life, artificial life, alien life.

Hence there can be no more radical form of adoption than adopting and nurturing such unworldly, unclassifiable life; a life whose potential—irreducible to existing forms of realization—is out of this world. This explains the tremendous importance that such freak adoptions assume in the cultural imagination of modernity, beginning with Victor Frankenstein's refusal to adopt the monster he created. While this motif originates in literature, it nevertheless stands in a special relation to film with its "special effects," culminating in CGI. This is because the language of words can never escape the generic. This is the melancholy message of Kafka's "Ein Bericht für eine Akademie [Report to The Academy]": the monkey, abducted and adopted into European civilization, has adapted itself to this new milieu in the most extraordinary way.[12] Yet far from fulfilling his *own* potential, he has merely reached "the cultural level of an average European."[13] The thought of another potential, utterly incommensurable with the human world, haunts him. And even if he might have known it as an ape, he cannot even speak this word to his human audience save through apophasis: "I deliberately do not use the word 'freedom.' I do not mean the spacious feeling of freedom on all sides. As an ape, perhaps, I knew that, and I have met men who yearn for it."[14] For not only can humans know nothing of this freedom, but they too often deceive themselves with this word: they think of something like a trapeze act.[15] They imagine, as it were, a freedom that can be reached only through artistic virtuosity, extreme discipline.

What literature can speak of, positively, is only a way out. But perhaps film is not bound by this same limitation. Perhaps it can show the *freak*.[16] One possible etymology of freak, originally meaning a sudden and seemingly causeless change of mind, derives it from the Middle English *friken*, "to move nimbly or briskly" and from Old English *frician*, "to dance."[17] Film can show us movements without reducing them to concepts and also without the need for the special technique of acrobats, dancers, or stage-fighters, where technique is first and foremost what allows the consistent repetition of the same movement by the same body. And film can also show the aberrant, anonymous, singular, unique.

Each of the three primary technological apparatuses of cinema—photography, drawn animation, and CGI—corresponds not only to a different epistemic regime but to the different problems it is suited to explore. With the photographic apparatus, these problems revolve around the relation between the generic and singular, the *studium* and *punctum* (the weakly mythic), the body and the soul, exteriority and interiority, as well as the *Doppelgänger* and the entire pathos of the crime and its discovery (which of these faces hides a guilty soul?).

Animation, in contrast, understands the physical world only as an expression of inner life; the toon's body is not a tawdry image of a real body but desire, yearning, suffering translated into movement and plasticity. The absolute toon is the ghost, even the soul. With CGI, an altogether new problematic comes into view: it is no longer a question of the Cartesian dualism and of the luminous symbolic representation of inner reality through a beautiful surface, nor of the immediate plastic expression of inner drives, but of the emergence of the radically new. Identifying the innermost tendency of all three apparatuses, we might refer to three different kinds of freakishness. Photography documents the penetrating singularity of the world's surface—the objective freak; drawn animation shows us the inner life of the soul, left to freak out— the subjective freak; but CGI gives us the absolute freak.

Just as the photographic apparatus demands of the audience the attentive gaze of the detective, and just as the cartoon solicits an oneiric trance, CGI places the viewer face-to-face with the new that one must either adopt—becoming open to its potential—or kill. Or one can consume, eat the Other. Adoption realizes alterity by becoming open to it; killing destroys concrete alterity but, since the Other is never assimilated, preserves it even more purely as an ideal. But eating assimilates the Other: it adopts by killing, kills by adopting. The nonethical relation par excellence, eating is the total eradication of alterity, the absolute reduction of the potential of the Other to the impotence, the impotentiality, of the Same.

Visionary Capitalism

Speaking before a packed crowd in her grandfather's old factory in New York City, Lucy Mirando (Tilda Swinton), the newly inaugurated CEO of her family's company, introduces herself to the world:

Now, I know, we all know, that Grandpa Mirando was a terrible
man.
We know of the atrocities he committed in this space.
We know these walls are stained with the blood of fine working
men.
But today, I reclaim this space . . . to tell you a beautiful story.
Now the rotten CEOs are gone.
It's Mirando's new era with me, and with new core values,
environment and life.

The beautiful story of this new era begins with a miracle: the
super pig. This "beautiful and special little creature," "miraculously
discovered on one Chilean farm," was brought to the Mirando Ranch
in Arizona, where, under the care and observation of scientists, it was
no less miraculously transformed "by non-forced, natural mating"
into twenty-six super piglets—one little piggy for each of the twenty-
six countries with Mirando branch offices. Each will be given to an
"esteemed local farmer," asked to raise their "special guest" "honoring
traditional techniques unique to their respective cultures," while
benefiting from the support of the corporation's scientists.

These little piggies will be the ancestors of a whole new species.
Mama Nature's gift.
A revolution in the livestock industry.

"And now we have a competition." The twenty-six farmers will
compete against each other, and when the competition reaches its
climax, after ten years of lip-smacking anticipation, the "ultimate
super pig" will be unveiled during a live telecast of *Magical Animals*,
the TV show hosted by the beloved veterinarian-zoologist Dr. Johnny
Wilcox (Jake Gyllenhaal), judge of the competition and the "new
face" of Mirando Corporation.

Lucy's speech is, of course, a virtuoso display of corporate greenwashing, mobilizing a crunchy, New Age idiom, familiar to anyone who has ever shopped at Whole Foods, now a subsidiary of Amazon. The space she reclaims with a performative utterance ("But today, I reclaim this space") has always belonged to her family. Only its surface will be reclaimed; the reclamation only changes the surface ideology of capitalism, which has now learned to speak a new idiom, invoking new values, without any change in the actual relations of production. Capitalist property remains as before. The Mirando CEO, the "face" of capitalism, divides herself, as if in an act of asexual reproduction, into two "faces": Nancy Mirando (also Tilda Swinton), who represents instrumental rationality, the calculation of the shareholder's report and the balance sheet, and Lucy, who is vision, purpose, ethics, the authenticity of the local: the beatific vision of a global capitalism transformed from a malicious octopus, stretching out its poisonous tentacles, to humanity's savior.

Her speech, moreover, invokes a strongly religious language. Many, from Marx to Max Weber, Walter Benjamin, and Louis Althusser, have tried to understand capitalism as involving a secularized theology, whether at the level of ideology or practice. But if capitalism secularizes the lived experience of the Christian believer, who escapes the absolute debt of original sin through the absolute credit of faith, the various revolutionary movements mobilize in secularized form both the historical potency of the messianic event, which severs history into before and after, and the gnostic juxtaposition of the evil creator, who fashioned this world as a prison, and the son-liberator freeing souls from their captivity. It is even more striking, then, that Lucy's speech mobilizes both messianic and gnostic imagery in the service of reinventing the language that capitalism speaks. It is no longer enough for capitalism to identify its survival with the continuation of the existing order, whether achieved through the brutal repression of organized labor or by staving off crisis through a Welfare State and Keynesian interventions. Capitalism must appropriate the rhetoric, if not the reality, of revolution. Hence, the primary ideological forms no longer involve the lived praxis of the believer but reach deep into a gnostic version of the messianic event. Grandpa Mirando becomes the evil demiurge, granddaughter Lucy the liberator. Though, of course, the true "miracle baby," the real savior, is the original super pig herself: a gift not of God but of "Mamma Nature." Giving birth to a new species, the miraculously conceived super pig will feed humanity with blood and flesh not transubstantiated or symbolic but sizzlingly, scrumptiously real.

Watching this five-minute opening scene, we can hardly help getting caught up in the excitement of Lucy's words. We too begin to feel the rapturous hope of a new beginning. The camera sweeps through the old factory's baroque ruins, narrowing in on Lucy's body from various angles, exaggerating her already exaggerated gestures. It is as if her body were being drawn apart into fragments; at one point, only her hand appears before the projection screen as she points to the countries where "esteemed local farmers"—and Mirando branch offices—are found. This fragmentation of the kinetic body and its gestures, however, is countered not only by the intradiegetic soundtrack accompanying her presentation but also by the presentation itself, which unfolds as a montage of animated sequences in a style suggestive of the video played in *Snowpiercer*'s schoolroom. And just as her body is fragmented, so too is our gaze as viewers of the film. Now we see just her speaking, now the audience en masse, now close-ups of individual members with their occasional interjections and questions, now only the screen, and now she is in front of her screen, an awkward shadow cast against it.

The language of Lucy's speech stands out: it is not the language of the Hollywood blockbuster but of Brecht and especially his *Die heilige*

Johanna der Schlachthöfe (*Saint Joan of the Stockyards*), which resonates in so many ways with *Okja*. No less remarkable, or Brechtian, is Tilda Swinton's performance. Eschewing the insidious psychological naturalism of method acting for exaggerated vocal and physical gesture, she's not only acting the role but simultaneously commenting on it through her acting.[18]

What this commentary might tell us, should we watch and listen carefully, is that her exaggerated, awkward confidence—posturing as the CEO—is born of the primal scene of childhood rivalries, and especially her resentment of her domineering twin sister Nancy. Precisely this sibling rivalry—siblings, after all, only appear after the fall—will infect and ultimately thwart the new capitalist paradise. The "harvest for the world" heralded by the miracle pig, healing the rift between haves and have-nots, will only be allowed following a competition. Competition thus appears no longer just as the mechanism of capitalist efficiency, the miracle of the market and its invisible hand, or even, as for Marx, the force driving capitalism to ultimate crisis and self-destruction. Competition is not the hidden reality of human nature or economic law, but the appearance that must be given to all things by organizing the world as a "reality show" from the top down.

If the idea of competition is so seductive, it's precisely because the trauma of sibling rivalry remains with us, as it certainly does for Lucy and Nancy. Yet the most original sibling rivalry, almost entirely suppressed in the anthropocentric myths of the Ancient Greeks and Hebrews, is the rivalry between the animals, and above all between human beings, clever but otherwise ill-equipped for survival, and all the others. The "good news" of the "harvest for the word"—lyrics from the gospel-inflected song by the Isley Brothers cued up at the close of her speech—will leave this last rivalry not only unhealed but even more incapable of appearing in its true form.

It is not only the words of Lucy's speech or Swinton's performance that suggest a Brechtian impulse: the entire scene implements the alienation effect—not as a static imitation of a long-established theatrical practice but in a manner recognizing the problem presented by the mainstream Hollywood culture industry. For even as we are thoroughly absorbed in Lucy's *Spiel* and her video presentation, mobilizing cinema's dark manipulative powers in the name of propaganda—advertising, by another name—we are jarringly reminded of the staged fakeness of it all. *Now* we see Frank Dawson (Giancarlo Esposito), the Machiavellian Mirando executive, standing in the back of the stage with a spotlight visible behind him, silently voicing along with Lucy as, lifting her eyes toward the sky as if dreaming of sugarplum fairies, she describes the twenty-six super piglets as "like nothing on Earth" (Figure 9). *Now* her words appear in front of her on teleprompters. Seemingly improvised and inspired—a voice of spontaneous authenticity—her speech is scripted, as also, we suspect, the audience's comical interventions. If such scripted performances are so manipulative, it is due to the simple naturalistic immediacy of the performance. They need not explicitly claim *not* to be scripted. By incorporating evidence of its "scriptedness" into Lucy's presentation—a movie within a movie carrying us away in a kinetic rush of enthusiasm—Bong allows the cinematic apparatus to appear in an estranging defamiliarization.[19] The magic of cinema,

Figure 9 Okja *directed by Bong Joon Ho.* © *Netflix 2017. All rights reserved.*

mobilized for the out-of-this-world super pig, is contaminated with the scriptural trace—at the very moment we are ready, like Lucy staring girlish-naïvely into the sky, to believe in miracles again.

The entire scene, moreover, presents a résumé of cinema and its techniques: natural and artificial sets combining natural, artificial, and diegetic lighting; the complex *mise-en-scène* of the factory with its sinister staircase; an astounding variety of shots from intense close-ups to panoramic landscapes, fixed and moving, taking in the body and face from above, below, behind, and the side; deep and shallow focus; montages of newspaper headlines; drawings of silly cute animals; color and black and white; and finally—a vestige of the silent film—intercalated credit captions. But above all, it plays out the tension between the two principal technical apparatuses of cinema prior to the digital revolution: photography and animation. The photographic stays centered on the human body and in particular the human visage, with the opening shot giving a teasing glimpse of high heels stepping onto a podium before revealing Lucy's face. Her eyes—blue, piercing—stare straight into the camera in medium close-up while makeup artists tussle her platinum hair and dab powder at her face.

This contributes to the estrangement mentioned earlier. But it also reveals the human face and especially the mouth—made more prominent by Lucy's braces—as the abiding focus of cinematography, recalling, in its deformation, the time when "capturing the human face still plunged audiences into the deepest ecstasy [. . .], when the face represented a kind of absolute state of the flesh, which could be neither reached nor renounced."[20] If the human face is the center around which the meaning of photographic cinema eddies and swirls, it is because the face exposes the drama of human morality. It is the surface that hides and reveals intentions, thoughts, and character. The human face doubles into two faces: not just good and evil, human and monster, but the face that reveals and the face that hides: Nancy and Lucy.

Animation, in contrast, has always had a special connection to animals. And so too, the animals in Lucy's presentation appear as cute cartoons. The animal cartoon expresses a soul that, like a child's, has yet to learn to hide behind the face: an immediacy that has not yet mastered dissemblance and that is at most capable of crude comical ruses. The conjunction of the photographed, photogenic human face and the cartoon animal thus brings into view the theologically inflected "anthropocentric machine" *in nuce*: the total submission of natural life, animal life, to a humanity whose highest purpose shines through in the very capacity to choose between good and evil, light and darkness, life and death, love and hate. There is no contradiction, therefore, in saying that the animal cartoon represents at once the animal subjected to human moral decision and the natural immediacy of the human soul; the nature of animals is also nature within us, simple childish-childlike desire. The violence of our relation to nonhuman animals is also the violence of our relation to ourselves, as when we find in our natural desires only an occasion for their overcoming and sublimation.

The conjunction of moving photographic images and drawn animation thus marks the outermost tendencies of the ideological apparatus that brought us to the end of the twentieth century, but which, on the eve of Lucy's inauguration, has already exhausted itself. Responding to this exhaustion, capitalism reinvents itself, transforms. It becomes visionary. Visionary capitalism claims to envision the highest good, the ultimate harmonious relation to life. This is no longer the limited economy formed by the interactions of human actors with each other and with mere nature as raw material, but the absolute economy, the *oikonomia*—household—uniting all the living beings of the earth. Yet, in taking its departure from the dyadic opposition of the human face and the cartoon animal—transcendent, unworldly moral sublimity versus merely natural desire—it cannot but repeat the oppressive logic that it seeks to overcome. Rather than becoming open to the life of nonhuman animals and the animal life of human beings, the visionary offers a manufactured, engineered harmony while concealing it under the appearance of the natural and spontaneous. The miraculous super pig that the visionary Lucy proclaims upon the world, we discover, is not an immaculately conceived mutant but genetically engineered. And of course, the cinematic correlate of visionary genetic engineering is CGI. In Lucy's presentation, indeed, the use of CGI comes into play in what seems like the purest photographic image: the black-and-white picture of the indigenous Chilean farmer lovingly embracing the world's very first super pig.

Lucy's inauguration ends with her standing before goofy toon animals and a cartoon Dr. Wilcox sitting on a tree, waving placidly to the audience, to us, as "Harvest for the World" begins to play: "All babies together . . . " Cinematography and animation unite in beckoning the new order of CGI and GMOs as Lucy brings her inaugural speech to a close:

> Our super pigs will not only be big and beautiful, they will also leave a minimal footprint on the environment, consume less feed and produce less excretions. And most importantly, they need to taste fucking good.

The grammatical incoherence of this passage, an anacoluthon switching from the future indicative to an implicit third-person jussive, is telling. It betrays the constitutive incoherence of visionary capitalism, whose beautiful, bountiful dreams collapse in the last instance into a crude market-driven calculation. The miracle birth, the new life, is dead on arrival. It's just food.

Commodity Exchange

Whether manufactured or spontaneous, the GMO is an event. Two very different relations to this event are possible: one can adopt it, becoming open to its truth, discovering the new truth of this new life, or one can turn it into a commodity, fit only for exchange and consumption. *Okja* unfolds within the contours of this choice, represented through the opposition of Mija and Mirando. But the Mirando corporation itself has two sides: Lucy and Nancy; entrepreneurial and visionary capitalism; exchange and use value. Visionary capitalism seeks to advance beyond exchange value; it offers a vision of the highest utility, the very purpose of life. And yet this vision remains the vision of consumption, allowing no other truth to manifest.

In the penultimate scene of the movie, Nancy has replaced her sister: the façade of visionary capitalism has fallen away to reveal brazen entrepreneurial calculation. In the gruesome meat factory located in Paramus, Mija, accompanied by ALF's leader and translator, finds Okja just as she's about to be slaughtered. Nancy walks in with her entourage. "Why do you want to kill Okja," Mija asks, in English. "Well, we can only sell the dead ones," Nancy answers. "I want to go home with Okja." "No, it's my property."

When Jay and K (Steven Yeun) excoriate Nancy ("You're a fucking psychopath" … "You ought to be ashamed of yourself"), she responds:

Fuck off! We're extremely proud of our achievements.

We're very hardworking businesspeople.

We do deals, and these are the deals we do.

This is the tenderloin for the sophisticated restaurants.

The Mexicans love the feet. I know. Go figure!

We all love the face and the anus, as American as apple pie! Hot dogs.

It's all edible. All edible, except the squeal. [Okja squeals]

For old-fashioned entrepreneurial capitalism, taste, a concrete experience, disappears into the abstraction of the edible, just as the super pig's miraculous body is shattered into fragments. Everything is edible, all these fragments: everything except the squeal. Yet this exception is telling: the squeal is the primal expression of life force, of the animal's vital essence, its soul, its *qi /ki*. For Aristotle, as for Herder, the language of nonhuman animals is a language of expressive noises.[21] These reveal pleasure and pain, desire, fear. Here we might begin to discover the truth of animals. And it is precisely this truth that commodification occludes. Nevertheless, the occlusion by exchange value is not as absolute as that which visionary capitalism will bring about. Just as Okja is about to be executed with an air gun, Mija pulls out the solid gold pig her grandfather had given her before Okja was led away. "I want to buy Okja . . . alive." Nancy's green eyes pop open at the sight of gold, and after checking it with a bite, she happily agrees and walks off: "Our first ever Mirando super pig sale. Pleasure doing business with you." Commodification hangs thick over the world, yet the individual can still occasionally wiggle through its net. Moreover, the gold, which Mija's grandfather gave her and which she in turn gives to Nancy, represents a genuinely global medium of exchange. The glib, fluent English of visionary capitalism, in contrast, not only allows no exceptions but makes it impossible for the non-Anglophone Other even to come to word.

Hooliganism

If *Snowpiercer* leads to an impasse where escape is only possible through the absolute destruction of the system, this is precisely because visionary capitalism, represented in its purest form by Wilford, has realized itself so perfectly that the entire system of capitalist production, the anarchy of the market, has been superseded. Throughout *Snowpiercer* we see signs of the emancipatory potential of commodity exchange, which, relegated to the margins of the system, can only take the form of informal barter. It is not that Bong wishes to defend a "purified" anarcho-capitalism against what Friedrich Pollock had felicitously called the totalitarian form of state capitalism.[22] Nancy's worship of exchange value and "deal making" appears sufficiently odious to dispel any such illusions. The point, rather, is that we must reject the visions that capitalism concocts and, indeed, its entire tendency, facing absolute crisis, to refashion its surface ideology around a utopian vision of social/ecological harmony. Most suggestive, in this regard, is the similarity in meaning of *Mija* and *Mirando*: Mija in *hanja* could be 美子 ("beautiful child"), whereas Mirando suggests the Latin gerundive: one who ought to be looked at. The vision of visionary capitalism is offered to us only to be demanded from us. Forced upon us, it ought to be looked at. Against this is a beauty resonant with possibilities of new life.

Hope only exists for us when capitalism's net hasn't yet been woven so tight as to keep everything from escaping—when it isn't yet necessary to destroy the net. Paradoxically, however, the freedom of global commodity exchange, even while constituting the substance of capitalism, also marks its limit. Defined in terms of commodity exchange, capitalism remains formal. This formal web can be spun to the most gossamer refinement. Yet it remains form; something can always pass through—if only a squeal. But this something, this squeal, this grunt of life, is everything. Animals squeal, chirp, wail, grunt, yip before even opening their eyes: it is not the human face that summons us to the ethical encounter but the animal noise, the cry. Or maybe even the screams that the wind draws from the hollows of the earth.[23]

A more positive message about the possibility of concrete resistance, however, complements this negative message. Even though there is something comical about ALF and its activists with their aliases (K, Red, Blond, Silver), and even though Jay, with his studied calm voice and affect, gives off the somewhat creepy vibe of a cult leader, their depiction is ultimately more sympathetic than satirical. Through a brilliantly executed plan, always one step ahead of Mirando's goons and stooges, Jay and his followers sabotage its elaborate PR campaign, exposing its horrific abuse of the super pig. While it is Mija who heeds the squeal, it is they who allow it to be heard. Their activism, moreover, is not aimed at systematic revolution but only at local, seemingly anarchic forms of resistance.

Telling are Nancy's words to her entourage upon encountering Mija, Jay (Paul Dano), and K on the factory floor: "I'm flummoxed that security is so lax as to allow a bunch of hooligans to delay the production line, even for a second." The word *hooligan* might seem out of place in the mouth of the quintessential American capitalist. Strongly associated with the juridical and political vocabulary of the Soviet Union, hooliganism (*khuliganstvo*) came to be used for a wide range of petty crimes involving some form of antisocial behavior. Its emphatic use thus suggests nothing less than the ultimate convergence of statist socialism and capitalism in their shared obsessions with maintaining order, state authority, and the appearance of social cohesion. The absurd spectacle of a corporate rally held in a blocked-off avenue of Midtown New York drives this home: in its visionary reinvention, American capitalism, having created a cult of personality around business leaders who exemplify a leadership freed from democratic mediation and due process, seeks to mobilize the desires of the multitude through a spectacle of unity, gathering them around the commodity. Appearing before the smiling, ethnically and racially diverse crowd, some dressed in pink with pig-ear hair bands or pompoms, "Stars and Stripes" flapping beside the Mirando corporate logo, Dr. Wilcox, after rallying it to a frenzy, introduces Lucy. Making a heart sign—low-rent *aegyo*— she walks out in garish pink *hanbok*. Mija, in a matching outfit and with a pained expression, joins the stage through an elevator. Mija pulls out a persimmon, Okja's favorite fruit, as together they wait for her to arrive on a float, escorted by gigantic pig balloons. Okja grunts and squeals aggressively as she emerges from her tent, and Mija struggles to calm her down.

ALF now puts its plan into action. Replacing the Mirando promotional video with gruesome footage of the drunken, deranged Wilcox torturing and taunting Okja, they then pierce the pig balloons, drenching the crowd with flyers exhibiting Mirando's atrocities. The crowd now turns on Lucy and Wilcox, and chaos ensues, with the traumatized Okja charging at the crowd. It is only after Mija saves Okja from Jay, who attacks her fearing that the girl's life is threatened, that a touchingly emotional, if brief, reunion takes place between her and her giant friend. Meanwhile, Nancy, dining with Frank in a fancy restaurant far above the fray, has called in "Black Chalk," private security, with the blessings of the NYPD. ("We have an arrangement," Frank assures.) Armored military vehicles drive up, and mercenaries run at the crowd and the activists, chasing them down and beating them with batons as they try to escape with Okja.

In an age of visionary capitalism, genuine activism cannot be separated from "hooliganism." The most radical activism is organized tactical hooliganism; its most fundamental aim is to disrupt the consolidation of corporate interests, the police state, paramilitary forces, and the culture industry into a united front. This united front is even more insidious for the very reason that, having rejected the clumsier gestures of authoritarianism, having dispensed with explicit totalitarian control, it presents itself as the very fulfillment of individual desire. And what the individual desires, above all, is that *it* taste fucking good. The work of the activist-hooligan is, in a word, to disrupt the spectacle.

The rally reprises the inauguration from ten years before, with both featuring a similar video backdrop. Yet with the inauguration, the inner space of the decommissioned factory was transformed into a theater's cavernous interior, suggesting a material and ideological production that, disjoint yet correlated, remains confined to the private sphere, to civil society. But with the rally, this inner cave-theater is brought back into the open; the city street, the public space par excellence, now becomes the site of spectacle. The private spectacle of capitalist modernity is thus returned to a classical political form. And simultaneously, the material (at least as consumption—tasty pork is being handed out) and the ideological are returned to unity even as the actual site of production is hidden away in darkness. The rally is not only the spectacle but the coming-real of the spectacle, which occupies the public space in such a way as to become identified, seamlessly, with a total social order that in turn appears as the fulfillment of individual desire. Yet, just as with the Classical Greek *polis*, the realization of an imminent political community is only possible through the most absolute exclusion and Othering.

The activists' hooliganism revolves around freak acts, carefully choreographed against the mass choreography. Disrupting the nascent order, these acts cause the assembled crowd to freak out. In this, we might discover Bong's most radical cinematic gesture: a freakish disruption of the Hollywood mass spectacle that, if briefly, holds open a space for the event of the moral recognition of the suffering subalterns upon which the happy spectacle of our world has been built. Or in a word: against the fraud of the "ethical corporation," he launches ethical hooliganism. Granted, this is only the spectacle of hooliganism, the spectacle of anarchy—and ultimately it too sells tickets. But perhaps, twisting the biblical proverb, we could say that the needle-hole of commodity exchange is precisely what can still sometimes let the disruptive ethical event through into capitalism's paradise—an event that might announce itself in the most camel-like way possible: by grunting and spitting us in the face.

The ethical event is the grunt, the squeal, the howl: the music, the *melos*, of nature. Just as Bong's vision of activism can't be separated from exuberant hooliganism, his conception of drama, for all its subtlety and irony, remains rooted in melodrama. *Okja* would hardly work as a film if we did not identify with Mija and Okja and their suffering; if it didn't make us laugh and cry, sometimes at once. We are reminded of Wilford's reprimand to Curtis: *don't be so melodramatic*. Melodrama is what holds us open to an ethical experience not contained within the limits of ethical calculation. Not to be melodramatic is, like Wilford or Nancy, to be a psychopath. Yet ethical hooliganism is, nevertheless, not without its rigor. Jay follows severe ethical principles in his activism, based on a forty-year credo. Before going ahead with his plan—to release Okja to Mirando with a hidden camera broadcasting her tortures—he asks for Mija's consent. This she refuses. But not speaking Korean, he must ask through his translator K, who deliberately misrepresents her answer. When he later discovers this double betrayal, his calm façade shatters; he savagely beats K before expelling him. *Never mistranslate. Translation is sacred.* At once disturbing and comical, this points to the vital ethical significance of translation. Translation is sacred because it's the site of the most radical ethical openness: to human Others, even to nonhuman animals, who communicate only through gestures and sounds and movements. Translation is sacred because it is at once necessary and impossible; because translating means transferring, "handing it over" from one language to another is also always a betrayal. Crossing over from one order of meaning to another, translation belongs to neither; it is the disruptive, anarchic movement par excellence.

Epilogue
Parasite

The Burrow

"I have completed the construction of my burrow and it seems to be successful." Uttered by Kafka's creature at the start of "The Burrow," these words might rather have come from Namgoong, the French-Korean architect and erstwhile owner of the house in *Parasite* (2019). His seventh feature film, *Parasite* earned Bong international fame when, after winning the *Palme d'Or* at Cannes, it swept the Academy Awards, receiving Oscars for Best Picture, Best Director, Best International Feature Film, and, with Han Jin-won, Best Original Screenplay. For amid the wild luxuriant ugly-beautiful-sublime chaos of Korea's built environments, the *Parasite* house realizes a dream driving Korean capitalist modernity: the transfiguration of mere living, mere surviving into a lifestyle, marked not only by the abundance of things but by their calm, elegant façade. The endless refrain of appliance and detergent ads, this dream already animates such postwar Korean films as Kim Ki-young's *The Housemaid* (1960). But what distinguishes the *Parasite* house most of all is how it balances and harmonizes contradictory imperatives: the giant glass windows—Western, modern, open—combine with the fortress-like walls of the Korean courtyard house, hiding it from view to the outside; smooth grey concrete contrasts with the luxuriant green of the yard, closing in on all sides to form a private little paradise.

And the *Parasite* house, it seems, also represents the culmination of Bong's search for the perfect set. An abiding preoccupation throughout this book, indeed, has been the close connection between architectural space, political space, and cinematic space. Compressing the spatial contradictions of his previous films into a single locale, Namgoong's house is the perfect set and indeed a cinematic space like no other. There is an esoteric audio system but no visible TV; instead, the couch faces a vast window framing the lush green yard— as if it had been projected onto a movie screen through the abundant natural light pouring in.

Parasitic Order

The perfect set is, however, the perfect setup; the movie director is the alter ego, the *Doppelgänger* even, of the architect, who—think Ayn Rand's *Fountainhead* or Orson Welles's *Citizen Kane*—is the archetype/ego ideal of the visionary capitalist. The movie director raises the set only to destroy it; only to have it destroy itself, exposing its vulnerabilities. The deepest vulnerability of the *Parasite* house surfaces only when its architect no longer resides there: the abstraction of capitalist ownership sunders building from dwelling and, with this, renders dwelling problematic. The new owners—the wealthy Park family: father Dong-ik (Lee Sun-kyun), mother Yeon-gyo (Cho Yeo-jeong), daughter Da-hye (Jung Ji-so), and son Da-song (Jung Hyeon-jun)—have never really begun to fully dwell in the space that they call their own; they depend on their housekeeper, Gook Moon-gwang (Lee Jung-eun), who was inherited from Namgoong. She, in turn, conceals from them the secret of the house; the labyrinthine bunker hidden behind a shelf in the pantry—a typical feature, we learn, of such upper-class homes. Namgoong, it seems, was no stranger to the worries that plagued Kafka's burrower: he created just the kind of ruse of which the mole-creature had dreamt but lacked the strength to carry through.[1]

Parasite hinges on the presence of this hidden, repressed yet sheltering space. This is the space of the unconscious, of memory and trauma, of a brutal and tragic history hidden behind the shiny, immaculate faces of K-pop idols; of Japanese colonialism, comfort women, and painful national division; of the Korean War and the uncanny presence of that other Korea North of the 38th parallel; of the continuing presence of the US military. But it is also the space of the economically subaltern and socially marginalized. And not least, it is the space of a darkness opposed to the sun's light—and hence the "dark room," the secret site of cinematic production, hidden behind set, stage, screen, and theater.

As Kafka's burrower tries to suss out his enemy, it becomes ever clearer that it could only be a creature just like him: another burrower, another builder. And so too, the Kim family—the father Ki-taek (Song Kang-ho), the mother Chung-sook (Jang Hye-jin), the daughter Ki-jung (Park So-dam), and son Ki-woo (Choi Woo-shik)—might appear, were they not half a generation older, as *Doppelgänger* of the Park family. Dwelling in a semibasement apartment (*banjiha*), eking out a wretched existence doing odd jobs, they represent the underclass whose existence is already implied by the bunker. Occupied, we later learn, by the housekeeper's indebted husband Oh Geun-sae (Park Myung-hoon), what the hidden bunker means, above all, is that the utopian space, the envisioned dream of Korea's ultra-capitalist postmodernity, cannot be without parasites (*kisaengch'ung*) and cannot cease to hide them from view, deny their presence.

Speaking about the film's title, Bong draws attention to the central ambiguity: while the poor family, infiltrating the rich, obviously appear as parasites, the rich might also be seen as "parasites in terms of labor," who can't even wash dishes or drive themselves.[2] Perhaps even more important, though, is the paradoxical logic of the parasite—the structural function it plays in capitalism itself and indeed within any modern rationalized economic regime, which is to say, whenever the polemical order of politics has been subordinated to the rational, quantitative domain of economics. This logic is as follows: the parasite is that which must exist outside a rational order demanding absolute transparency precisely for this very rational order to maintain itself. Hence, the parasite is an originary surplus; the rational order is itself parasitic on the parasite.

This can be understood, at a deeper level, in terms of spatiality. The parasite signifies that the rational ordering of space depends on a relation to the irrational, anomic surplus. The parasite, in other words, is that *intensive* dimension of space that the rational order depends on but that it cannot represent on its own terms, and hence rationally. So far as the parasite appears within the rational order, it is always as a specific relation of parasitism, a specific kind of parasite: the servant, the housewife, the capitalist, the stockbroker, the indigent, the immigrant—or even the human itself in relation to nature. Entering the para-logic of the parasite means discovering the parasite not as specific threat to the operation of the system but as the system's essence: the fundamental structure of the economic, political, social, natural order. It is to realize that, from a certain point of view, all life is parasitism, and that there could be no rational order, no civilization, without this parasitic dependence on the parasitic excess. For indeed: the normalized logical order—within which the parasite can appear as threat—is merely a special case of the para-logical order of parasitism. This originary, constitutive parasitism is also the original wound, the original trauma. The tragedy of *Parasite* unfolds when Ki-jung, posing as an art therapist, discovers Da-song's trauma, which we later learn was caused when, on his birthday—having snuck into the kitchen to finish off his cake—he saw a ghost: the revenant Oh Geun-sae, briefly emerging, like Kafka's burrower, from his subterranean lair.

By around halfway into the film, the Kim family seems to have succeeded in their grift. First, Ki-woo gets hired as the Park daughter's English tutor. Shortly after, Ki-jung, given the English name Jessica, is taken on as the Park son's art tutor. Then, through increasingly daring ruses, the chauffeur and housekeeper are fired, and the father and mother take their place. When the Parks suddenly leave on a family camping trip, the Kims install themselves in their place, getting drunk in the living room from their store of fine spirits.

It is at this moment that the film turns from a dark comedy to a comic tragedy: the former housekeeper shows up and is forced to reveal her secret: that her husband is hidden away in the secret bunker. When she, in turn, discovers *their* secret, a fight ensues. The Kims manage to subdue the housekeeper and her husband, locking them in the subterranean shelter, but then the heavy rain causes the Parks to call off their trip, returning home. The Kim father escapes with his daughter and son back to their apartment only to find it flooded with sewage water. But the next day, the Park mother Yeon-gyo calls Ki-jung, announcing a special improvised gathering to celebrate Da-song's birthday, which, since his encounter with the ghost, they have always celebrated away from home. The chairs and tables are arranged in a semicircle around Da-song's teepee—just like Admiral Yi's turtle boats around a Japanese ship, the mother ludicrously suggests. A barbecue is set up, and there's even a cellist accompanying a soprano singing Italian opera. But the highlight of the celebration is a special performance to heal the boy's trauma. With both dressed up as Indian braves, father Park explains his wife's plan to father Kim:

> There'll be a parade with Jessica [Ki-jung] carrying a birthday cake.
> Then we jump out and attack Jessica.
> Swinging our tomahawks!
> And then, Da-song the good Indian will jump out and we'll do battle.
> Finally he'll save Jessica the cake princess, and they'll all cheer.

The idea, it seems, is to heal the trauma through its repetition; if Da-song had been traumatized by the original event, which combined his own gluttonous transgression with the threat of a punishment that never materialized, he is to heal by assuming agency, by becoming the warrior. It is, moreover, a reenactment of an Oedipal trauma: as if the feral, arrow-shooting Da-song, having glimpsed the threat of the father's castrating law as he laid his hands on forbidden sweets, must symbolically do battle with the father, destroying him to become savior and protector of his sister.

This bizarre little piece of theater, also suggesting the play-within-a-play in *Hamlet*, turns out as catastrophically as one would suspect. Ki-woo had entered the bunker carrying a rock to finish off Geun-sae, but instead, Geun-sae takes him by surprise, hits him on the head, and escapes the bunker. Rushing out into the midst of the party, he stabs Jessica the cake princess, and is in turn skewered by Chung-sook. When the retraumatized Da-song starts to suffer a seizure, the Park father orders the Kim father, tending to his own dying daughter, to drive the boy to the hospital. At this, his accumulated *han* explodes. He snaps and stabs Nathan, father killing father.[3] The real trauma of Korea's history and contemporary society, it seems, is too much for a cheap theatrical trick, which ends up summoning the very ghosts and terrors it seeks to expel. The symbolic becomes real.

Given the hallucinogenic intensity of this scene, one might well have to watch it several times to notice a minuscule but significant detail: when Guen-sae emerges from his cave into the backyard, a white butterfly flutters screen-right. And when, after stabbing the cake princess, the camera rests on him as he screams out for Chung-sook, a white butterfly again appears next to him. While the butterfly might be taken as an omen of death, it also recalls one of the most famous passages from the *Zhuangzi*, which seeks to explain the concept of the transformation of all things.

> Once Zhuang Zhou dreamt he was a butterfly, fluttering about joyfully just as a butterfly would. . . . Suddenly, he awoke and there he was, the startled Zhuang Zhou in the flesh. He did not know if Zhou had been dreaming he was a butterfly, or if a butterfly was now dreaming it was Zhou.[4]

This scene represents not only the dramatic climax, the point of *peripeteia* ("reversal of fortune"), but also the moment when the entire world, with all its petrified differences in status, dissolves as if it were but a dream. What brings about this dissolution is the sudden irruption of death, the hidden monster stalking us throughout our lives and always triumphing in the end. When the father, having hidden in the cave, recounts to his son what happened—the birthday party scene resumes but as if narrated from memory—he begins: "Even now, what happened that day doesn't seem real. It feels like a dream." The shelter-cave, the most hidden place, is also the place from which the manifest world is revealed in its oneiric unreality.

The Birthday

The savage-crazy-child-genius Da-song with his theatrical eccentricities—of the three older Parks, only the daughter sees through him—plays a crucial role in the symbolic economy of the film: he turns the yard into an endless frontier. It is only by including the infinity of the frontier, only through this pretension to the absolute, that the *Parasite* house can constitute itself as a totality. If *Snowpiercer* offered a vision of American-style globalization, folding nature back into an endless loop, *Parasite* suggests nothing so much as a Korea that, without ever really opening itself up—still walled off to the outside—has created within itself a virtualized simulacrum of globalization. Walking into the Park home for the first time, looking at framed articles that pass by too quickly for the film's audience to read, Ki-woo would have discovered the source of their wealth: the father is CEO of a company, absurdly named "Central Park," that provides a "Hybrid Module Map" of New York City, allowing "you to 'walk around' the streets of New York and browse real-time information wherever in the world you connect from." This suggests that when, midway through the birthday performance, the actual ghost runs into the party and stabs the Kim daughter, this represents nothing less than a catastrophic inversion of "Central Park"'s virtualized globalization. The virtual is now augmented by the repressed real; actual violence laid over simulated violence. It is as if, amid a virtualized globalization, the *real* itself were the ultimate point of parasitic dependence; suddenly the real gushes back into the rationally ordered representational space. Moreover, though, the mother's carefully choreographed theater, performed in the garden stage to which the living room looks out, offers a reduced synopsis of the endlessly repeated good-over-evil triumphs of the typical

Hollywood blockbuster. These have their roots in the Western, a cinematic imagination trained on the broad open frontier. If the mother's attempt at therapeutic catharsis went so horrifically awry, it is not least because, in taking recourse to the Hollywood formula, it failed to grasp the deeper nature of Korean trauma.

Because Korea has no frontier, it cannot allow itself even the delusion of escaping its past. The birthday of the youngest child holds such special significance because it is the celebration of the new world, the new order; ensconced in their new virtual Eden, the Parks are already almost as if born again. Only the son's trauma, real or imagined as it may be, separates them from their paradise. To the time of the past, of a rootedness born of trauma, belongs the logic of the parasite, of radical codependence. This codependence exists in and through melodrama.

What the Park family, and the mother above all, have forgotten is a melodramatic way of being-with-others born of both the harsh struggle for survival and the forced intimacies of domestic life. They are "nice"—smooth, soft, gentle—even though they are rich, or rather: nice because they are rich. Melodrama is, as it were, the entire palette of affects belonging to a radically parasitic existence; an existence where individuals have not yet carved out a solitary space for themselves, have not yet escaped codependence. What has taken the place of melodrama is hysteria and an allergic sensitivity to foreign contaminations: smells that "cross the line," peach fuzz, the planted panties (which then become a means of arousal), the very thought of illegal drugs in a house with a well-stocked liquor cabinet. The deeper root of this hysteria, though, is the extreme passivity of the Park family, the mother and daughter most of all. When the mother first appears, she is slumped over a table in the garden; the housekeeper calls out to her several times and then rushes at her in a burst and claps right above her head. The mother rises as if being pulled from the top of her head; now sitting up with perfect posture, her arms resting limply on her lap, she appears in a state of total alertness, reminiscent of the ballerina-doll Coppélia, as she awaits the next command from her servant. And likewise, when Ki-woo is tutoring Da-hye for the first time—a trial run in his mother's presence—he picks up her arm, which seems to lie weightless and enervated, by the wrist.

Da-song, on the other hand, seems quite unlike the rest of his family. He is ostentatiously wild, a prodigy at that game of posturing that the Western "cult of genius" sometimes seems to have devolved into; in his genius-cosplay, he suddenly stops, stares off into the sky. His trauma nevertheless binds him to their passivity, showing that he and they are of a piece; that they all belong to the same regime of affect, the same form or style of life. This, at least, suggests the ambiguous significance of this last little bit of theater. Even while subordinating the last little piece of pure, wild, errant movement to rational enframing, it also submits the passivity of the rational frame—the material, receptive matrix—to chaos as leading principle. As cute as Da-song may be, we can hardly help but discover in him the budding traits of a baby Hitler, devoid of every talent but the absolute belief in his genius—just as the mother's puppet-like movement evokes the somnambulant horror of Robert Wiene's *The Cabinet of Dr. Caligari* (1920), and, in turn, Siegfried Kracauer's thesis on the origins of fascism.

In this ambiguity, we find the ultimate denouement of the cinematic apparatus of philosophy. The rationalization of errant movement assumes its most insidious and dangerous form precisely when appearing in fetishistic opposition to the rational order itself. This is the moment of greatest danger; chaos rationalized through the submission of reason to chaos as its ruling principle. At this point, moreover, the cinematic apparatus of philosophy (subordinating chaos to reason) becomes indistinguishable from the philosophical apparatus of cinema (freeing and discovering chaos, bringing pure movement to representation). Da-song's birthday celebration, repeating a trauma that occurred with the repetition of the natal event, unleashes original chaos even while turning it into a mere representation, another piece of theater, making the event into a fetish of the event. But so long as the event is understood historically, as an event within history—so long as history's proper names, such as "Korea," mediate the experience of trauma—such fetishization may well prove ineluctable. Perhaps just by mentioning Admiral Yi, the mother courted disaster. The very opposition between constituting event and constituted order, between "event" and "eventuated," saying and said, or even between pure movement and enframing, repeats the logic of parasitic representation; the constituted order appears as parasite to the event, and vice versa. This logic can only be overcome, or at least eluded, by entering so deeply into the logic of the parasite as to see only parasites; only life yielding to and consuming itself. At the limit of the philosophical apparatus of cinema, beyond this limit even, is a cinema of the parasite, a parasite-cinema.

Waterstones

Parasite is the comic—we could even say, "hysterical"—tragedy of the Park family, but it is also something else: an episode from the melodramatic life of Ki-woo, an aspiring scholar from a poor family, who, in his struggles to pass the exams opening the path to upward mobility, confronts the fraudulent promise of Korean meritocracy. This episode begins when his friend, a college student at an elite university, gifts him a scholar's rock from his grandfather's collection. The stone in question, the friend explains, is said to bring material wealth to families. Gazing at it, Ki-woo explains: "This is so metaphorical." The entire film, indeed, unfolds under the talismanic presence of this stone, which he eventually rescues from his flooded basement apartment and brings with him to the shelter, hugging it as he sleeps—"It keeps following me"—even bringing it to the Park house to kill Geun-seo. At a certain point, it even assumes a magical lightness: as the house is flooded—here we might recall the significance of water for Daoism—it floats up to the surface, suggesting a special affinity with the watery element. It seems to teach, in the words of Jean Louis Schefer's brilliant schizo-poetics of cinema, that "a universe of acts transitions through objects and that for characters, what motivates the plot may be the unconsciousness of this force of action latent in things."[5]

While the scholar's rock (*susŏk* 水石 in Korean, *suiseki* in Japanese, *gongshi* 供石 in Chinese) is eminently metaphorical, its metaphorical sense remains ambiguous. It certainly stands for the conventional Neo-Confucian ideal of the scholar and for the promise of education as a path to wealth. And it also has a concrete historico-sociological significance: the eighties witnessed a sudden surge of interest among businessmen in collecting *susŏk* as a more affordable, if less prestigious, alternative to painting and calligraphy.[6] The friend's grandfather's collection of hundreds of *susŏk* identifies him as belonging to a certain class of parvenu businessmen with pretensions to status but cut off from the genteel cultivation of the *yangban* elite.

But it also has a more esoteric sense. *Susŏk*—literally, water stones—are natural rocks, carved out by nature's erosive flows into shapes pregnant with latent energy. When the Kim father, looking at it, wonders whether it is a "landscape" or abstract, he is alluding to two very different criteria by which *susŏk* have traditionally been appraised: for their resemblance to mountains, caves, animals, birds or mythical creatures, but also for nonrepresentational qualities of form and material. What manifests here is nothing less than the "dynamic transformational processes of nature"; in its rigid immobility, the rock is heavy with the latent dynamic power of nature, "solidified *qi* [*ki*]."[7] Within the Chinese classical tradition, their appreciation is closely connected to Daoist currents of thought.[8] Most important is that the aesthetics at play here is deeply opposed to the guiding tendencies of Western aesthetics. This is true, indeed, even if we consider only the more representational side of *susŏk* aesthetics: shaped by the flowing forces of nature into a resemblance to natural forms, the representational value of *susŏk* has nothing to do with the talent, let alone genius, of a human artist. The meaning of such resemblances, it would seem, rests rather on revealing a common formative power, even if, to be sure, there is also the pleasure of recognition, and of the miniature, the microcosmic. But it is even clearer with the abstract side of *susŏk*. This leads to a subtle classification of qualities; besides the four major criteria of *thinness*, *wrinkles*, *channels*, and *holes*, stones are also spoken of, inter alia, as *handsome, stubborn, clumsy, simplistic,* and *ugly*.[9]

Just as a melodramatic affective palette, rooted in *han*, stands opposed to the Parks' hysterical passivity, an analogous opposition can be drawn between the aesthetics of *susŏk* and the wild expressive posturing of Da-song's ostentatious cult of genius. *Susŏk* points toward an aesthetics of radical parasitism; literally a water-rock, the water is as parasitic on the rock, at which it eats away, as the rock is parasitic on the water to which it owes its existence.

But why does the *susŏk* assume such malicious power, leading the Kims first to luxury, then to disaster, and becoming the weapon with which Ki-woo, having wielded it against the housekeeper's burrowed husband, is almost bludgeoned to death? Is this punishment for "crossing the line," as Nathan Park puts it? Perhaps the *susŏk* assumes its fateful potency precisely because it has been wrested from the whole, turned into a collectible, a commodity, a fetish. If it signifies wealth, metaphorically, it is because money is itself metaphoric in its operation; gold, a synecdoche, torn out from the earth's hidden shelters, comes to signify the productive powers of nature, in its totality, as the generative, yielding source of all things. Perhaps, in this way, *Parasite* is also the story of the *susŏk* seeking to return to chthonic depths.

Nothing Doing

The similarities between the first and the last of Bong's films to date—between the least successful, least celebrated, least profitable and the most—are striking. Both are set entirely in Seoul; both explore the tragicomic contradictions of one of the new lived spaces defining postwar Korea; both feature basements, and, in both, the most subaltern is a basement dweller, later identified by the police as a homeless person; both involve ghost stories ultimately given a non-supernatural explanation; both feature a canine trinity, even though, admittedly, the dogs play little role in *Parasite*. And perhaps most curiously, both have an epilogue in which a character whose quest is at the center of the narration returns to the forest.

With *Parasite*, this epilogue, a montage held together through voice-over narration, is quite long—around fifteen minutes—and crucial to the interpretation of the film. It begins with Ki-woo waking up in the hospital, laughing uncontrollably from brain surgery—a hysterical laughter that continues for a long time afterward. He and his mother, he explains, were put on trial, ending in probation, but long afterward detectives continue to tail him, suspecting he knows his father's whereabouts. It is on a rare snowy winter day that things have cooled down enough for Ki-woo to ascend the mountain, looking down with binoculars at the house far below. He sees that a new family has moved in. But he also sees a light flashing in an odd rhythm; he realizes that it is his own father communicating—as the housekeeper's husband had once tried to communicate—in Morse Code, a binary language suggesting the *yinyang* hexagrams of the *Book of Changes*, themselves featured on the *T'aegŭkki*, the national flag of the Republic of Korea. Stuttering as he struggles to decipher the message while riding in the subway, Ki-woo reads, "son," *adŭra*. His voice passes over, seamlessly, into his father's, who goes on to tell what happened to him and the house after the fateful day: how instead of fleeing into the wind, as everyone had supposed, he doubled back and entombed himself in the shelter; how he buried the housekeeper, whose name he struggles to remember; how the house eventually was sold to foreigners, a German family, ignorant of the grisly murders that took place. Rushing home, the son writes back to the father, reading his letter in his own voice: "Dad, today I made a plan. A fundamental plan. I'm going to earn money." As he says this, we see him—another example of Bong's exquisite use of montage—placing the stone into a riverbed where, returned to its element, it now appears perfectly unexceptional as the waters crease over it. Abandoning his more conventional dreams—university, career, marriage—he will earn enough money to buy the house where his father dwells parasitically.

> On the day we move in,
> Mom and I will be in the yard,
> Because the sunshine is so nice there.
> All you'll need to do is walk up the stairs.

The last image of the film—the father walking up into a living room littered with boxes and then embracing the son while the mother stands outside—is so stunning, so haunting, and these last haiku-like lines so beautiful that one could almost forget that here too, just as at

Figure 10 *Parasite directed by Bong Joon Ho. © CJ Entertainment 2019. All rights reserved.*

the end of *Snowpiercer*, there is an unsettling ambiguity (Figure 10). For the son's plan to save the father is also the deepest betrayal of the father who, asked by his son, as the family lay on the shelter floor, about the plan he boasted to have, answers with a laconic Koan-like riddle: "Ki-woo, you know what kind of plan never fails? No plan." This is foolishness, and the father is the most foolish of the clan, but there is also a deeper wisdom to it; a touch of the Daoist *wu wei*. The son returns the stone to a natural setting, but he then dedicates his life to the pursuit of extravagant wealth, as deluded and impossible as this might be. Rejecting parasitic life, ignoring the binary, yet cyclic and fluid, logic of the medium for an imagined message summoning him to renewed responsibility, he is forced by the claim of filial loyalty to abandon not only this Daoist wisdom, but all wisdom, all tradition—just to regain the house which he never owned, where his sister died, where his father is imprisoned; the house of his trauma, his crimes, but also the house of dreams, of paradisiac tranquility, beauty, harmony, resplendent in the light of the sun.

Notes

Introduction

1 Karen Han, *Bong Joon Ho: Dissident Cinema* (New York: Abrams, 2022), 26.

2 Regarding the out-of-field, see Gilles Deleuze, *Cinema 2: The Time-Image* (Minneapolis: University of Minnesota Press, 1989), 235.

3 Martin Heidegger, *Basic Writings* (New York: HaperCollins, 2008), 152.

4 See James Monaco, *How to Read a Film* (New York: Oxford University Press, 2009), 83–7.

5 Regarding this resistance, and the complex relation between speech and visual image, see Christian Metz, *Film Language* (Chicago: University of Chicago Press, 1991), 49–56.

6 Bela Balazs, *Theory of the Film* (London: Dennis Dobson LTD, 1952), 45.

7 See Deleuze, *Cinema 2*, 226.

8 Metz, *Film Language*, 54.

9 Monaco, *How to Read a Film*, 174.

10 Ibid., 505.

11 Siegfried Kracauer, *Theory of Film* (Princeton: Princeton University Press, 1960), identifies movement as one of the natural objects of cinematic representation. Deleuze's *Cinema 1: The Movement-Image* (Minneapolis: University of Minnesota Press, 1986), applies Bergson's philosophy to cinema while rejecting his criticism of cinema as giving a "false movement."

12 Leo Tolstoy, *Anna Karenina* (New York: Penguin Books, 2002), 279.

13 Regarding the sociological dimension, see Nam Lee, *The Films of Bong Joon Ho* (New Brunswick: Rutgers University Press, 2020), 10.

14 Joseph Jonghyun Jeon, *Vicious Circuits* (Stanford: Stanford University Press, 2019), 4.

15 Martin Heidegger, *Erläuterungen zu Hölderlins Dichtung* (Frankfurt am Main: Vittorio Klostermann, 1981), 34.

16 Ibid., 193.

17 "Bong Joon-ho—Mother: Scene by Scene, Shot By Shot," *Sight & Sound*, September 2010: 26–28, 28.

18 Robin R. Wang, *Yinyang* (Cambridge: Cambridge University Press, 2012), 59.

19 Jana S. Rošker, "Classical Chinese Philosophy and the Concept of Qi," *NEARCO: Revista Eletrônica de Antiguidade e Medievo* 12, no. 2 (2020): 116–34, 131.

20 Norbert Wiener, *Cybernetics or Control and Communication in the Animal and the Machine* (Cambridge, MA: MIT Press, 2019), 53–4.

21 Cf. Jean-Louis Baudry, "Ideological Effects of the Basic Cinematographic Apparatus," in *Narrative, Apparatus, Ideology*, ed. Philip Rosen (New York: Columbia University Press, 1986), 286–98.

22 Plato, *Republic* 473 c-d.

23 Ibid., 484 b.

24 Ibid., 484 c.

25 Ibid., 485 b; trans. Bloom, 164.

26 Ibid., 515 c; trans. Bloom, 194.

27 Roger T. Ames and David L. Hall, *Dao De Jing: A Philosophical Translation* (New York: Ballantine Books, 2002), 76.

28 Heraclitus *Fragment Diels B123*.

29 Joseph Needham, *Science and Civilization in China*, 7 vols. (Cambridge: Cambridge University Press, 1956), 2: 232, cited in Wang, *Yinyang*, 3.

30 Wang, *Yinyang*, 7–8.

31 Ibid., 8–12.

32 Heidegger, *Basic Writings*, 184, 317.

33 Aristotle, *Nicomachean Ethics* 1094a 1–5.

34 Harold D. Roth, "*Daoist Inner Cultivation Thought and the Textual Structure of Huainanzi* 淮南子," in *The Contemplative Foundations of Classical Daoism* (Albany: SUNY Press, 2021), 235–76, 241.

35 A. Charles Muller, "Translator's Introduction," in *Korea's Great Buddhist-Confucian Debate* (Honolulu: University of Hawai'i Press, 2015), 1–42, 33.

36 Isang Yun and Luise Rinser, *Der verwundete Drache* (Frankfurt am Main: S. Fischer, 1977), 96.

37 Roger T. Ames and Henry Rosemont Jr, *The Analects of Confucius: A Philosophical Translation* (New York: Ballantine Books, 1998), 20.

38 Zhuangzi, *The Complete Writings* (Indianapolis: Hackett, 2020), 285; See also Hans-Georg Moeller, *Daoism Explained* (Chicago: Open Court, 2004), 105.

39 Michael Nylan, *The Chinese Pleasure Book* (Brooklyn: Zone Books, 2018), 48.

40 Ibid.

41 Ibid., 46.

42 Zhuangzi, *The Complete Writings*, 3.

43 For an introductory overview of Daoism, see Holmes Welch, *Taoism* (Boston: Beacon Press, 1957); Recent scholars, such as James Robson, reject the distinction between pure philosophical Daoism and debased religious practices. [See James Robson, ed., *Norton Anthology of World Religions: Daoism* (New York: W.W. Norton, 2015)].

44 Eugene Y. Park, *Korea: A History* (Stanford: Stanford University Press, 2022), 56, 108, 184–91.

45 Ibid.

46 Moeller, *Daoism Explained*, 149.

47 Ibid., 150.

48 Anonymous, *The Story of Hong Gildong* (New York: Penguin, 2016), 5, 21.

49 Michael C. Kalton, et al., eds., *The Four-Seven Debate* (Albany: SUNY Press, 1994), xxiii.

50 Ibid., xxiv–xxv; for a nuanced account of the intricacies of the Four-Seven Debate, Bongrae Seok, "Toegye's and Gobong's Li-Qi Metaphysics and the

Four-Seven Debate," in *The Idea of Qi/Gi* (New York: Lexington Books, 2019), 75–94.

51 Ibid.

52 Harold D. Roth, "The Classical Daoist Concept of Li 理 (Pattern) *and Early Chinese Cosmology*," in *The Contemplative Foundations of Classical Daoism* (Albany: SUNY Press, 2021), 349–75, 375.

53 Regarding the intertwinement of aesthetics and politics in Chinese thought, see Zehou Li, *The Chinese Aesthetic Tradition* (Honolulu: University of Press, 2010).

54 Moeller, *Daoism Explained*, 6.

55 Han, *Bong Joon Ho*, 18.

56 Jean-Luc Godard, *Godard on Godard* (Boston: Da Capo, 1972), 19.

57 Friedrich Schlegel, *Philosophical Fragments* (Minneapolis: University of Minnesota Press, 1991), 2, 7, 11, 16, 47.

Chapter 1

1 Writing to Benjamin in 1934, Adorno speaks of Kafka's novels as "the last, disappearing textual links to silent film" [Theodor W. Adorno and Walter Benjamin, *Briefwechsel: 1928–1940* (Frankfurt am Main: Suhrkamp, 1994), 95]. For a recent study of Kafka, cinema, and noise, see Kata Gellen, *Kafka and Noise* (Evanston: Northwestern University Press, 2019).

2 Franz Kafka, "The Burrow," in *The Complete Stories* (New York: Schocken Books, 1971), 325–359, 325.

3 Ibid., 343.

4 Walter Benjamin, "The Work of Art in the Age of Mechanical Reproduction," in *Illuminations* (New York: Schocken Books, 2007), 217–51, 239–40; Regarding the close relation of cinema and space, see Mark Shiel, "Cinema and the City in History and Theory," in *Cinema and the City*, ed. Mark Shiel and Tony Fitzmaurice (Oxford: Blackwell, 2001) 1–18.

5 Gustave Flaubert, *Madame Bovary* (New York: Random House, 1992), 37.

6 The panopticon-like quality of the apartment complex is increased by two features that identify it as on the lower end of the scale of prestige—

probably "lower middle-class": the exterior walkway and the ninety-degree angle between buildings; regarding the history of the Korean housing complex, see Valérie Gelézeau, "Changing Socio-Economic Environments, Housing Culture and New Urban Segregation in Seoul, " *European Journal of East Asian Studies* 7, no. 2 (2008): 295–321. Korean apartment complexes, Gelézeau argues, are primarily oriented toward the middle and upper-middle classes, excluding lower income groups.

7 Deleuze, *Cinema 2*, 203.

8 Lady Hyegyŏng, *The Memoirs of Lady Hyegyŏng* (Berkeley: University of California Press, 2013). I first learned of this incident through a wonderful thesis written by my undergraduate student, Yongkyung Chung.

9 Hae-rin Lee, "Korea Bans Age-old Tradition of Dog Mean Consumption," *Korea Times*, January 9, 2024 (updated January 10). https://www.koreatimes.co.kr/www/nation/2024/01/113_366614.html (accessed July 7, 2024).

10 Monaco, *How to Read a Film*, 59.

11 Most suggestive in this regard is the connection Deleuze draws between the political act of storytelling, wherein speech withdraws from the image to become "founding act," and the surging forth of the "*archeological, stratigraphic, tectonic*" potency of the image [*Cinema 2*, 243].

12 For an alternative reading of spatiality in *Barking Dogs Never Bite*, focusing more immediately on social class, see Bonnie Tilland and Beth Tsai, "Of fleas and Parasite," *New Review of Film and Television Studies* 21, no. 4 (2023): 668–85.

13 Deleuze, *Cinema 1*, 49.

14 Wang, *Yinyang*, 24.

15 Regarding the significance of *cropping* in photography and cinema, see Stanley Cavell, *The World Viewed* (Cambridge, MA: Harvard University Press, 1979), 24.

16 Jean Epstein, *The Intelligence of a Machine* (Minneapolis: Univocal, 2014), 2–3.

17 Plato, *Republic* 473 c–d.

18 Deleuze, *Cinema 1*, 109.

19 Kyounghoon Lee, *A Cultural History of Modern Korean Literature* (London: Lexington, 2022), 83.

20 Ibid., 39.

21 Ibid., 1.

22 Following the closing credits.

23 For a concise account of the Tonghak movement, see Park, *Korea*, 221–2.

24 Regarding Bong's political activities as a student at Yonsei University, see Han, *Bong Joon Ho*, 13–14.

25 Han, *Bong Joon Ho*, 28.

26 My wife, who grew up in Korea at the same time as Bong, vividly remembers the cartoon series.

27 "'p'ŭllandasŭŭi kae' pongjunho kamdok," *Maeil kyŏngje*, February 23, 2000.

28 Sergei Eisenstein, *On Disney* (Calcutta: Seagull Books, 2017), 7.

29 Ibid., 8.

30 Ibid., 9.

31 Regarding *aegyo* culture in Korea, see Aljoša Pužar and Yewon Hong, "Korean Cuties," *The Asian Pacific Journal of Anthropology* 19, no. 4 (2018): 333–49.

32 Exemplifying this genre of comedy, typically connected to the office place, is NBC's *30 Rock*.

33 Eisenstein, *On Disney*, 54.

34 Regarding the influence of Tarantino's *Pulp Fiction* (1994), see Han, *Bong Joon Ho*, 48.

35 Shin-Dong Kim, "The Creation of Pansori Cinema: *Sopyonje* and *Chunhyangdyun* in Creative Hybridity," in *East Asian Cinema and Cultural Heritage*, ed. Yau Shuk-ting Kinnia (New York: Palgrave Macmillan, 2011), 151–71.

36 Ho-Keun Song, *The Birth of the Citizen in Modern Korea* (Paju: NANAM Publishing House, 2016), 147–8.

37 Ibid., 376.

38 Ronald Bergan, *Sergei Eisenstein* (New York: Arcade Publishing, 2016), 91–2.

39 Sergei Eisenstein, *Film Form* (San Diego: Harcourt, Inc., 1977), 28.

40 Ibid., 35.

41 Regarding the emergence of a *han'gŭl* discourse, see Song, *The Birth of the Citizen in Modern Korea*, 59–72.

42 On the "phonetic" bottleneck, see Hana Jee, Monica Tamariz, and Richard Shillcock, "Exploring Meaning-sound Systematicity in Korean," *Journal of East Asian Linguistics* 31 (2022): 45–71, 48. They give the example of "sago," corresponding to twenty-one different Sino-Korean words.

43 Plato, *Republic* 440e–441a.

44 Aristotle, *Politics* 1253a.

45 Nam-Joo Cho's *Kim Jiyoung, Born 1982* (London: Simon & Schuster, 2020), though concerned with a slightly younger generation, offers a powerful account of the travails faced by Korean women at the workplace.

46 Aristotle, *Nicomachean Ethics* 1099b–1100a.

47 Ibid., 1176a.

48 Dante, *Inferno* Canto I, 1–3. My translation.

49 Nietzsche, *Kristische Studienausgabe*, 5: 12.

50 Zhuangzi, *The Complete Works of Zhuangzi*, trans. Burton Watson (New York: Columbia University Press, 2013), 31.

51 The Korean equivalent *yu* appears in the common words *mongyubyŏng* ("sleepwalking") and *yusŏng* ("planet").

52 Thorsten Botz-Bornstein, *Daoism, Dandyism, and Political Correctness* (Albany: SUNY Press, 2023), 14; see also Li, *The Chinese Aesthetic Tradition*, 79.

Chapter 2

1 Tony Rayns, "Suspicious Minds," *Sight & Sound*, September 2004, 18–20.

2 Lee, *The Films of Bong Joon Ho*, 72–3.

3 For an illuminating account of the aporetic dimension of singularity, see Samuel Weber, *Singularity* (Minneapolis: University of Minnesota Press, 2021), 1.

4 Immanuel Kant, *Critique of the Power of Judgment* (Cambridge: Cambridge University Press, 2000), 120.

5   Ibid., 100.

6   Whereas both the merely typical (the generic, the abstract) and the purely
    singular (the idea) exist outside of time, it is precisely this coincidence of
    the typical and the singular, the concretization of the typical in *this* matter,
    that allows the photo to appear, thus Bazin argues in "The Ontology of the
    Photographic Image," as the *trace* of a past life, *embalming time*, rescuing
    it from corruption. [André Bazin, *What is Cinema?* 2 vols. (Berkeley:
    University of California Press, 2005), 1: 14] For while the photograph
    proliferates copies, each copy is a concrete copy of the concrete, depending
    neither on a prior moment of abstraction or idealization.

7   Edgar Morin, *The Cinema: or the Imaginary Man* (Minneapolis: Minnesota
    University Press, 2005), 15; Cavell, *The World Viewed*, 19.

8   This absence is of special significance for Cavell, *The World Viewed*, 23.

9   Zhuangzi, *Complete Writings*, 12.

10 Akim Volynsky, *Ballet's Magic Kingdom* (New Haven: Yale University Press,
    2008), 131.

11 Chang Kyung-sup, "Compressed Modernity and Its Discontents," *Economy
    and Society* 28, no. 1 (1999): 30–55; Lee, *A Cultural History of Modern
    Korean Literature*, offers a compelling account of the cultural symptoms of
    Korea's traumatic modernity; see also Lee, *The Films of Bong Joon Ho*, 90.

12 Walter Benjamin, "The Paris of the Second Empire in Baudelaire," in
    Selected Writings—Volume 4: 1938–1940 (Cambridge, MA: Harvard
    University Press, 2003), 3–92, 27.

13 Hannah Arendt, *The Human Condition* (Chicago: University of Chicago
    Press, 1998), 19.

14 For Deleuze, the *time-image*, the subject of the second volume of his
    treatise, is juxtaposed to the *movement-image*, representing a more radical
    development of cinema as a language of signs and images, as reflected
    by the fact that, following the intrinsic relation between movement and
    time, the movement-image is already an *indirect* time-image (See *Cinema
    2*, 98–125). The direct time-image, however, emerges only when classical
    American cinema reaches its limit with the accomplished action-image,
    and thus appears primarily either outside Hollywood or among American
    auteur directors, like Orson Welles, with a contentious relation to the
    industry. One of the basic claims of the present book is that, in the films
    of Bong Joon Ho, Hollywood classicism (the action-image reconfigured in

hyperbolic terms through the "blockbuster") and avant-gardism come into a productive conflict with each other; this is reflected in the intercalation of movement (already a tension between capture and liberation) and temporality.

15 As Metz writes: "Because still photography is in a way the *trace* of a past spectacle [. . .] one would expect animated photography [. . .] to be experienced similarly as the trace of a past motion. This, in fact, is not so; the spectator always sees movement as being present (even if it duplicates a past movement)" [8].

16 For a compelling analysis of the historiographic dimension of *Memories of Murder*, see Jeon, *Vicious Circuits*, 27–48.

17 Tzvetan Todorov, "The Typology of Detective Fiction," in *Crime and Media*, ed. Chris Greer (London: Routledge, 2010), 293–301, 295.

18 Ibid.

19 Ibid., 295.

20 Ibid.

21 Ibid.

22 François Jullien, *From Being to Living* (Los Angeles: Sage, 2020), 3–6; See also *The Propensity of Things* (New York: Zone Books, 1995).

23 Christiana Klein, "Bong Joon-ho's *Parasite* as a Remake of Kim Ki-young's *The Housemaid*," in *The Routledge Companion to Asian Cinemas*, ed. Zhen Zhang, Sangjoon Lee, Debashree Mukherjee, and Intan Paramaditha (London: Routledge, 2024), 291–300.

24 Deleuze, *Cinema 1*, 87.

25 Žižek, Slavoj, *For they Know Not What they Do*, 2nd ed. (London: Verso, 2002), xvi.

26 François Jullien, *In Praise of Blandness* (New York: Zone Books, 2004), 41.

27 For Aristotle, a *polis* naturally consists in a multitude; if unified beyond a certain point, it becomes a household. [*Politics* 1261a-b].

28 Deleuze, *Cinema 1*, 172.

29 Han, *Bong Joon Ho*, 59.

30 Alan Moore, *From Hell* (San Diego: Top Shelf Publications, 2020), Chapter 5, 1–3.

31 See Park, *Korea*, 315–20.

32 As Bazin notes, sound film, while preserving the essence of montage as a technique, tended to reject "metaphor and symbol in exchange for the illusion of objective presentation" [1: 39].

33 Han, *Bong Joon Ho*, 69.

34 Jeon, *Vicious Circuits*, 29; See also Han, *Bong Joon Ho*, 55; Lee, *The Films of Bong Joon Ho*, 72.

35 Regarding the "evolving landscape of Korean [. . .] mauled by the hurried pace of industrialization and modernization," see Kyung Hyun Kim, *Virtual Hallyu* (Durham: Duke University Press, 2011), 38; For a brilliant analysis of the significance of concrete, see Jeon, *Vicious Circuits*, 27–48.

36 Michel Foucault, *Wrong-Doing Truth-Telling* (Chicago: University of Chicago Press, 2014), 93.

37 Friedrich Nietzsche, *Beyond Good and Evil* (Cambridge: Cambridge University Press, 2002), 20.

38 Lee Chang-dong's *Peppermint Candy* (1999) suggests this ingeniously, with the backward-moving train connecting a series of episodes from the life of the protagonist, presented in reverse chronology.

39 Immanuel Kant, "Ideal for a Universal History with a Cosmopolitan Purpose," in *Political Writings*, trans. H.B. Nisbe (Cambridge: Cambridge University Press, 1970), 43.

40 Immanuel Kant, *Groundwork of the Metaphysics of Morals* (Cambridge: Cambridge University Press, 2012), 41.

41 Walter Benjamin, *Gesammelte Schriften* (Frankfurt am Main: Suhrkamp, 1972–1989), 1: 646. My translation.

42 Benjamin, "The Work of Art in the Age of Mechanical Reproduction," 231.

43 See Friedrich Hegel, *Elements of the Philosophy of Right* (Cambridge: Cambridge University Press, 1991), 198.

44 Li, *The Chinese Aesthetic Tradition*, 18.

45 Song, *The Birth of the Citizen in Modern Korea*, 29.

46 Ibid., 44–58.

47 A seminal figure in Korean rock, Shin was also a political dissident, tortured and imprisoned under Park Chung Hee, with his music banned until the 1980s.

Chapter 3

1 For a contextualizing account of the mother figure in Korean cinema, see Ji-yoon An, "The Korean Mother in Contemporary Thriller Films?" *Journal of Japanese and Korean Cinema* 11, no. 2 (2019): 154–69.

2 By stressing the abstract, universal significance of the *mother*—a concept itself tied to universality—I in no way wish to deny the cultural specificity of the Korean mother, of which Sue Huen K. Asokan offers a brilliant deconstructive analysis ["The 'Good' Mother's Self(ish)-Sacrifice," *Korea Journal* 61, no. 3 (2011): 223–50].

3 Li, *The Chinese Aesthetic Tradition*, 6.

4 Lee, *The Films of Bong Joon Ho*, 36.

5 See Marshal McLuhan, *Understanding Media* (Cambridge, MA: MIT Press, 1994), 317–18.

6 Lee, *The Films of Bong Joon Ho*, 36.

7 For an analogous account of this paradox, see Asokan, "The 'Good' Mother's Self(ish)-Sacrifice."

8 Balazs, *Theory of the Film*, 28.

9 Welch, *Taosim*, 93.

10 This recalls Lee Doo-yong's "village erotica" film *Mulberry* (1986), where the one man in the village rejected by the gorgeous village jezebel is Sam-dol, the superhumanly strong village servant.

11 Bazin, *What Is Cinema?* 1: 92.

12 Wang, *Yinyang*, 55–9.

13 Ibid., 174.

14 Ibid., 56–7.

15   Trichet, in his Lacanian reading of *Mother*, draws attention to the son's psychological and physical transformation [Yohan Trichet, "Une figure de l'idiot criminal," *Cliniques Méditerranées* 91, no.1 (2015): 243–56, 243].

16   As for this function of the buses, I must rely on my wife's testimony. But as Nam Lee notes, "The idea for *Mother* also sprang from a memory from his high school days. He saw a group of middle-aged women enthusiastically dancing in a tour bus when it arrived at its destination," [36–7].

17   Bertolt Brecht, "Mutter Courage und ihre Kinder," in *Gesammelte Werke* (Frankfurt am Main: Suhrkamp Verlag, 1967), 4:1347–443.

18   Sang-Mu Lee, "Korean Agricultural Policy," *Journal of Rural Development* 16 (1993): 307–19.

Chapter 4

1   Plato, *Meno* 89c–d.

2   "In the Name of Love," *Sight & Sound* 20, no. 9 (2010): 24–5.

3   Regarding the monster in *The Host*, see Meera Lee, "Monstrosity and Humanity in Bong Joon-ho's *The Host*," *Positions* 26, no. 4 (2018): 719–47.

4   Here I am paraphrasing Heidegger's formulation regarding *Being* in *Sein und Zeit* (Tübingen: Max Niemeyer Verlag, 1986), 35.

5   For a concise account of the transformation of the economic conditions of the Korean film industry brought in the wake of the IMF-crisis, see Jeon, *Vicious Circuits*, 15–19; for a somewhat broader view, pitched to a more general readership, see Darcy Parquet, *New Korean Cinema* (London: Wallflower, 2009), 44–60.

6   See Hye Seung Chung, "Monster and Empire," *Oakland Journal* 20 (Winter 2011): 59–69.

7   Regarding the significance of fluidity in the Fascist imagination, see Klaus Theweleit, *Male Fantasies* (Minneapolis: University of Minnesota Press, 1987), 229–90.

8   Deleuze, *Cinema 2*, 77.

9   Schlegel, *Philosophical Fragments*, 33.

10 Kohei Saito, *Marx in the Anthropocene* (Cambridge: Cambridge University Press, 2023) has brought attention to the importance of the human-nature metabolic exchange in Marx's writings.

11 Regarding the biopolitical dimension of *The Host*, see Lee, *The Films of Bong Joon Ho*; Sang-Keun Yoo identifies a transition from the biopolitical to the necropolitical ["Necropolitical Metamorphoses," *Science Fiction Film and Television* 14, no. 1 (2021): 45–69].

12 Friedrich Hölderlin, *Sämtliche Werke* (Stuttgart: W. Kohlhammer, 1951), 2.1:190.

13 This logic is given the most powerful formulation in Hölderlin's brief fragment, "Die Bedeutung der Tragödien." [4.1: 274].

14 Ames and Hall, *Dao De Jing*, 76. What is only tendentially true of most philosophical texts is literally true of the *Daodejing*: all translation is commentary.

15 Quoted in Adam Nayman, "A Relay Race of the Weak. Bong Joon-ho's *The Host*," *Cinema Scope* 30 (Spring 2007): 26–9.

16 Heidegger, *Basic Writings*, 175, 182.

17 See Kim, *Virtual Hallyu*, 43.

18 Regarding the absent mother, see Terence McSweeney, "Nobody Helps the Family," *Cross-Cultural Studies* 20 (2010): 277–94, 284.

19 Lee, "Monstrosity and Humanity in Bong Joon-ho's *The Host*," 728.

20 Barbara Creed, *The Monstrous-Feminine* (London: Routledge, 1993); see also Hsuan Hsu, "The Dangers of Biosecurity: *The Host* and the Geopolitics of Outbreak," in *Eco-Trauma Cinema*, ed. Anil Narine (New York: Routledge, 2014), 113–33.

21 Hölderlin, *Sämtliche Werke*, 2.1: 165. My translation.

22 Regarding water as symbol of the *dao*, see Welch, *Taosim*, 21.

23 Heidegger, *Basic Writings*, 325–6.

24 Deleuze, *Cinema 2*, 216.

25 Schlegel, *Philosophical Fragments*, 21.

26 Karl Marx and Friedrich Engels, *The Marx-Engels Reader* (New York: Norton, 1978), 594.

Chapter 5

1 For a cultural history of the *Minjung* movement, see Namhee Lee, *The Making of Minjung* (Ithaca: Cornell University Press, 2007). For Lee, the Minjung movement sought to identify with the "common people (*minjung*)" rather than elites as the embodiment of the Korean nation, achieving this through the constitution of various "counterpublic spheres" (10). Regarding the connection between *minjok* and *minjung*, see also Luc Walhain's dissertation, *From Minjok to Minjung: The Student Movements' Democratizing of the National Discourse in South Korea*. Dissertation (Bowling Green State University, May 2005), 81–114.

2 Most relevant for comparison with the film is the first volume. For a rather thorough account of the considerable differences between the graphic novel and the film, see Stephen Weninger, "The Sacred Engine," *Journal of Narrative Theory* 51, no. 1 (2021): 104–25; see also Gerry Canavan, "'If the Engine Ever Stops, We'd All Die," *Paradoxa* 26 (2014): 1–26.

3 For a penetrating account of the importance of translation in *Snowpiercer*, see Claire Gullander-Drolet, "Bong Joon-ho's Eternal Engine: Translation, Memory, and Ecological Collapse in *Snowpiercer* (2013)," *Resilience* 7, no. 1 (2019): 6–21.

4 Han, *Bong Joon Ho*, 142.

5 Regarding the significance of geo-engineering, see Ji-Yeong Yun, "The Human-Nonhuman Connected Body in the Era of Climate Change," *The Journal of Popular Culture* 55, no. 5 (2022): 973–91: 976–7.

6 Deleuze, *Cinema 1*, 148.

7 On the significance of the train, see Weninger, "The Sacred Engine," 105–7.

8 So Heidegger writes: "Enframing means the gathering together of the setting-upon that sets upon man, i.e. challenges him forth, to reveal the actual, in the mode of ordering, as standing-reserve" [*Basic Writings*, 325].

9 The graphic novel features a somewhat analogous figure: an "archivist and historian" of the train sympathetic to the plight of those in the rear of the train [Jacques Lob and Jean-Marc Rochette, *Snowpiercer 1: The Escape* (London: Titan Comics, 2013), 63].

10 Cavell writes, suggestively: "The possibilities of moving pictures speak of a comprehensibility of the body under conditions which destroy the

comprehensibility of speech. It is the talkie itself that is now exploring the silence of movies" [149].

11 Ludwig Wittgenstein, *Tractatus Logico-Philosophicus* (New York: Harcourt, Brace & Company, 1922), 74.

12 Plato, *Laws*, 722e–723b.

13 For Giorgio Agamben, the "state of exception tends increasingly to appear as the dominant paradigm of government in contemporary politics" [*State of Exception* (Chicago: University of Chicago Press, 2005), 2].

14 Roland Barthes, *Mythologies* (New York: Farrar, Straus & Giroux, 1972), 52–5.

15 Lob and Rochette, *Snowpiercer 1*, 91.

16 Yun [975] draws a parallel with the blue and red pills from the *Matrix*. But significantly, in *Snowpiercer*, one and the same "pill" performs both functions.

17 Georges Bataille, *The Accursed Share* (New York: Zone Books, 1988), 60–1.

18 Eisenstein, *Film Form*, 45–63.

19 Barthes, *Mythologies*, 142.

20 Metz, *Film Language*, 34; The curious phenomenon that is "Barbenheimer" consists not least of all in the striking juxtaposition of two very different boxes of cinematic toys.

21 Regarding the centrality of these two characters, see Mansu Kim, "Global Contents but Nationalistic Themes," *International Journal of Korean Humanities and Social Sciences* 8 (2022): 7–23.

22 Tilland and Tsai, "Of fleas and Parasite," 681.

23 Deleuze, *Cinema 2*, 2–3.

24 Ibid.

25 See Anthony Curtis Adler, *The Afterlife of Genre* (Brooklyn: Punctum, 2014).

26 Eric Voegelin, *The New Science of Politics* (Chicago: University of Chicago Press, 1952).

27 Regarding *oikonomia*, see Agamben, *The Kingdom and the Glory* (Stanford: Stanford University Press, 2011).

28 Weninger, "The Sacred Engine," 115.

29 In his insightful reading, Weninger stresses the biopolitical dimension of Wilford's theocratic ideology [111].

30 Heidegger, *Sein und Zeit*, 134–40.

31 Wang, *Yinyang*, 107.

32 Bret Hinsch, *Women in Early Imperial China* (New York: Rowman & Littlefield Publishers, 2002), 13, cited in Wang, *Yinyang*, 108–9.

33 Regarding women's changing status from Koryŏ to Chosŏn, see Park, *Korea*, 104, 156.

34 Adam Smith, *An Inquiry into the Nature and Causes of the Wealth of Nations* (Indianapolis: Liberty Classics, 1981), 20.

35 Gullander-Drolet, "Translation, Memory, and Ecological Collapse in Snowpiercer (2013)," stressing the importance of race in this scene, notes that Alex Haley's *Roots* is the only book vaguely visible in Wilford's bookshelf [16].

36 Qiguang Zhao, *A Study of Dragons East and West* (New York: Peter Lang, 1992), 2.

37 Ibid., 4.

38 Yun, "The Human-Nonhuman Connected Body in the Era of Climate Change," 975; Regarding the "Anthropocene," see also Rob Wilson, "*Snowpiercer* as Anthropoetics," *Boundary 2* 46, no. 3 (2019): 199–218.

39 *Zhao, A Study of Dragons East and West*, 79.

40 Quoted in Welch, *Taosim*, 1–2, with slight modifications for orthographic consistency.

41 Fred Lee and Steven Manicastri, "Not All Are Aboard," *New Political Science* 40, no. 2 (2018): 211–26.

Chapter 6

1 Laozi, *Daodejing* (Oxford: Oxford World University Press, 2008), 165.

2 For Benjamin, the "cult of the movie star, fostered by the money of the film industry, preserves not the unique aura of the person but the 'spell of the personality,' the phony spell of a commodity" [231]. It is this "phony spell," it would seem, that CGI brings to its conclusion.

3 Heidegger, *Sein und Zeit*, 180–4.

4 Regarding the significance of anthropomorphism for cinema, see Bazin, "The Virtues and Limitations of Montage," in *What Is Cinema?* 1: 41–52.

5 Aristotle, *Politics* 1254b.

6 Ibid.

7 Ibid., 1252b. Literally: "for the poor, the ox takes the place of the household slave (*oiketos*)."

8 Kant, *Groundwork of the Metaphysics of Morals*, 59–60.

9 Ibid., 37–8.

10 Arendt, *The Human Condition*, 9.

11 See Arendt, *The Human Condition*, 19; Aristotle, *Economics* 1343 b24.

12 Franz Kafka, "Report to an Academy," in *The Complete Stories* (New York: Schocken Books, 1971), 250–59.

13 Ibid., 258.

14 Ibid., 253.

15 Ibid.

16 Of course, one thinks of Tod Browning's untimely masterpiece *Freaks* (1932).

17 Robert K. Barnhart, ed., *The Barnhart Dictionary of Etymology* (Bronx, New York: H.W. Wilson Compony, 1988), 407.

18 Brecht's epic theater requires that the actor appear in a "doubled form" on the stage, as himself and as the character ["Kleines Organon für das Theater," in *Gesammelte Werke* (Frankfurt am Main: Suhrkamp Verlag, 1967), 16: 661–707, 683.]

19 Regarding Bong's technique of defamiliarization, see Lee, *The Films of Bong Joon Ho*, 58–60.

20 Barthes, *Mythologies*, 56.

21 Aristotle, *Politics* 1253a 7–18; Herder, "Treatise on the Origin of Language," in *Philosophical Writings* (Cambridge: Cambridge University Press, 2002), 65–164, 65.

22 Friedrich Pollock, "State Capitalism: Its Possibilities and Limitations," in *The Essential Frankfurt School Reader,* ed. Andrew Arato and Eike Gebhardt (New York: Continuum, 1990), 71–94.

23 Zhuangzi, *Complete Writings*, 11.

Epilogue

1 Kafka, "The Burrow," 330.

2 Adele Ankers-Range, "Parasite: Bong Joon-ho Reveals the Meaning Behind the Title of the Oscar-Nominated Film," *IGN*, January 31, 2020 (updated April 21, 2021). https://www.ign.com/articles/parasite-bong-joon-ho-reveals-the-meaning-behind-the-title-of-the-oscar-nominated-film (accessed July 2, 2024).

3 For a philosophical treatment of *han*, see Iljoon Park, "Korean Social Emotions: *Han, Heung*, and *Jeong*," in *Emotions in Korean Philosophy and Religion*, ed. Edward Y.J. Chung and Jea Sophia Oh (New York: Palgrave Macmillan, 2022), 235–56. Especially significant is the dynamic and intertwined relation between *han* and *heung* (興), the exhilarating, joyful feeling that accompanies the release of *han*. Thus, "street demonstrations burst forth into singing and shouting our rallying words together" [248].

4 Zhuangzi, *Complete Writings*, 21.

5 Jean Louis Schefer, *The Ordinary Man of Cinema* (Pasadena: Semiotext(e), 2016), 29.

6 Karen Chernick, "A Highly Collectible Rock Plays a Key Role in the Oscar-Nominated Film 'Parasite.' Here's the Actual Meaning Behind it," *Artnet*, February 7, 2020. https://news.artnet.com/art-world/guide-suseok-stone-parasite-1768059 (accessed July 3, 2024).

7 Ian Wilson, "Spirit Stones," in *The Spirit of Gongshi*, ed. Kemin Hu (Newton: L.H. Inc., 1998), 10–11, 10.

8 Ibid.

9 Kemin Hu, "The Spirit of *Gongshi*," in *The Spirit of Gongshi*, ed. Kemin Hu (Newton: L.H. Inc., 1998), 21–31, 27.

Filmography

12 Angry Men directed by Sidney Lumet. © United Artists 1957.

8 ½ directed by Federico Fellini. © Cineriz 1963.

A City of Sadness directed by Hou Hsiao-hsien. © Era Communications 1989.

Avatar directed by James Cameron. © 20th Century Fox 2009.

Barking Dogs Never Bite directed by Bong Joon Ho. © Cinema Service 2000.

Battleship Potemkin directed by Sergei Eisenstein. © Goskino 1925.

Burning directed by Lee Chang-dong. © CGV Arthouse 2018.

Citizen Kane directed by Orson Welles. © RKO Radio Pictures 1941.

Fight Club directed by David Fincher. © 20th Century Fox 1999.

Incoherence directed by Bong Joon Ho. © Korean Academy of Film 1994.

Lolita directed by Stanley Kubrick. © Metro-Goldwyn-Mayer 1962.

Memories of Murder directed by Bong Joon Ho. © CJ Entertainment 2003.

Merbabies directed by Rudolf Ising and Vernon Stallings. © RKO Radio Pictures 1938.

Mirror directed by Andrei Tarkovsky. © Mosfilm 1975.

Mother directed by Bong Joon Ho. © CJ Entertainment 2009.

Mulberry directed by Lee Doo-yong. © TaeHeung Pictures 1986.

Okja directed by Bong Joon Ho. © Netflix 2017.

Parasite directed by Bong Joon Ho. © CJ Entertainment 2019.

Peppermint Candy directed by Lee Chang-dong. © Shindo Films 1999.

Pulp Fiction directed by Quentin Tarantino. © Miramax Films 1994.

Roshomon directed by Akira Kurosawa. © Daiei 1950.

Snowpiercer directed by Bong Joon Ho. © Radius-TWC 2013.

Spring, Summer, Fall, Winter . . . and Spring directed by Kim Ki-duk. © Sony Pictures Classics 2003.

Stalker directed by Andrei Tarkovsky. © Goskino 1979.

Strike directed by Sergei Eisenstein. © Goskino 1925.

Sunset Boulevard directed by Billy Wilder. © Paramount Pictures 1950.

The 400 Blows directed by François Truffaut. © Cocinor 1959.

The Cabinet of Dr. Caligari directed by Robert Wiene. © Decla-Film 1920.

The Host directed by Bong Joon Ho. © Showbox 2006.

The Housemaid directed by Kim Ki-young. © Kuk Dong Seki Trading Co. 1960.

The Lady Vanishes directed by Alfred Hitchcock. © Metro-Goldwyn-Mayer 1938.

The Last Picture Show directed by Peter Bogdanovich. © Columbia Pictures 1971.

The Truman Show directed by Peter Weir. © Paramount Pictures 1998.

The Wizard of Oz directed by Victor Flemming. © Loew's Incorporated 1939.

Tokyo Story directed by Ozu Yasujirō. © Shochiku 1953.

Yellow Door: '90s Lo-fi Hilm Club directed by Lee Hyuk-rae. © Netflix 2023.

Bibliography

Adler, Anthony Curtis. *The Afterlife of Genre: Remnants of the Trauerspiel in Buffy the Vampire Slayer.* Brooklyn: Punctum, 2014.

Adorno, Theodor W. and Walter Benjamin. *Briefwechsel: 1928-1940.* Edited by Henri Lonitz. Frankfurt am Main: Suhrkamp, 1994.

Agamben, Giorgio. *The Kingdom and the Glory: for a Theological Genealogy of Economy and Government.* Translated by Lorenzo Chiesa. Stanford: Stanford University Press, 2011.

Agamben, Giorgio. *State of Exception.* Translated by Kevin Attell. Chicago: University of Chicago Press, 2005.

Ames, Roger T. and David L. Hall. *Dao De Jing: A Philosophical Translation.* New York: Ballantine Books, 2002.

Ankers-Range, Adele. "Parasite: Bong Joon-ho Reveals the Meaning Behind the Title of the Oscar-Nominated Film." *IGN*, Jan 31, 2020 (Updated Apr 21, 2021) (https://www.ign.com/articles/parasite-bong-joon-ho-reveals-the -meaning-behind-the-title-of-the-oscar-nominated-film, accessed July 2, 2024).

Ames, Roger T. and Henry Rosemont Jr. *The Analects of Confucius: A Philosophical Translation.* New York: Ballantine Books, 1998.

An, Ji-yoon. "The Korean Mother in Contemporary Thriller Films: A Monster or Just Modern?" *Journal of Japanese and Korean Cinema* 11, no. 2 (2019): 154–69.

Anonymous. "In the name of love." *Sight & Sound* 20.9 (2010): 24-25.

Anonymous. "'p'ŭllandasŭŭi kae' pongjunho kamdok" *Maeil kyŏngje.* February 23, 2000.

Anonymous. *The Story of Hong Gildong.* Translated by Minsoo Kang. New York: Penguin, 2016.

Arendt, Hannah. *The Human Condition.* 2nd ed. Chicago: University of Chicago Press, 1998.

Asokan, Sue Huen K. "The 'Good' Mother's Self(ish)-Sacrifice: Violence, Redemption, and Deconstructed Ethics in Bong Joon-ho's *Mother*." *Korea Journal* 61, no. 3 (2011): 223–50.

Balazs, Bela. *Theory of the Film: Character and Growth of a New Art*. Translated by Edith Bone. London: Dennis Dobson LTD, 1952.

Barnhart, Robert K., ed. *The Barnhart Dictionary of Etymology*. Bronx, New York: H.W. Wilson Compony, 1988.

Barthes, Roland. *Mythologies*. Translated by Annette Lavers. New York: Farrar, Straus & Giroux, 1972.

Bataille, Georges. *The Accursed Share: An Essay on General Economy: Volume I—Consumption*. Translated by Robert Hurley. New York: Zone Books, 1988.

Baudry, Jean-Louis. "Ideological Effects of the Basic Cinematographic Apparatus." In *Narrative, Apparatus, Ideology: A Film Theory Reader*. Edited by Philip Rosen. New York: Columbia University Press, 1986.

Bazin, André. *What is Cinema?* Translated by Hugh Gray. 2 vols. Berkeley: University of California Press, 2005.

Benjamin, Walter. *Gesammelte Schriften*. Edited by Rolf Tiedemann und Hermann Schweppenhäuser. 7 vols. Frankfurt am Main: Suhrkamp, 1972–1989.

Benjamin, Walter. "The Paris of the Second Empire in Baudelaire." In *Selected Writings—Volume 4: 1938-1940*. Translated by Edmund Jephcott et al. Edited by Howard Eiland and Michael W. Jennings. Cambridge, MA: Harvard, 2003: 3–92.

Benjamin, Walter. "The Work of Art in the Age of Mechanical Reproduction." In *Illuminations*. Edited by Hannah Arendt. Translated by Harry Zohn. New York: Schocken Books, 2007: 217–51.

Bergan, Ronald. *Sergei Eisenstein: A Life in Conflict*. New York: Arcade Publishing, 2016.

Bloom, Allan. *The Republic of Plato*. 2nd ed. New York: Basic Books, 1991.

Botz-Bornstein, Thorsten. *Daoism, Dandyism, and Political Correctness*. Albany: SUNY Press, 2023.

Brecht, Bertolt. "Kleines Organon für das Theater." In *Gesammelte Werke*. vol. 16. Edited by Elisabeth Hauptmann. Frankfurt am Main: Suhrkamp Verlag, 1967: 661–707.

Brecht, Bertolt. "Mutter Courage und ihre Kinder." In *Gesammelte Werke*. vol. 4. Edited by Elisabeth Hauptmann. Frankfurt am Main: Suhrkamp Verlag, 1967: 1347–443.

Canavan, Gerry. "'If the Engine Ever Stops, We'd All Die': *Snowpiercer* and Necrofuturism." *Paradoxa* 26 (2014): 1–26.

Cavell, Stanley. *The World Viewed: Reflections on the Ontology of Film*. Enlarged ed. Cambridge, MA: Harvard University Press, 1979.

Cho, Nam-Joo. *Kim Jiyoung, Born 1982*. Translated by Jamie Chang. London: Simon & Schuster, 2020.

Chung, Hye Seung. "Monster and Empire: Bong Joon-ho's *The Host* (2006) and the Question of Anti-Americanism." *Oakland Journal* 20 (Winter 2011): 59–69.

Creed, Barbara. *The Monstrous-Feminine: Film, Feminism, Psychoanalysis*. London: Routledge, 1993.

Deleuze, Gilles. *Cinema 1: The Movement-Image*. Translated by Hugh Tomlinson and Barbara Habberjam. Minneapolis: University of Minnesota Press, 1986.

Deleuze, Gilles. *Cinema 2: The Time-Image*. Translated by Hugh Tomlinson and Robert Galeta. Minneapolis: University of Minnesota Press, 1989.

Eisenstein, Sergei. *Film Form: Essays in Film Theory*. Edited and translated by Jay Leyda. San Diego: Harcourt, 1977.

Eisenstein, Sergei. *On Disney*. Translated by Alan Upchurch. Calcutta: Seagull Books, 2017.

Epstein, Jean. *The Intelligence of a Machine*. Translated by Christophe Wall-Romana. Minneapolis: Univocal, 2014.

Flaubert, Gustave. *Madame Bovary*. Translated by Francis Steegmuller. New York: Random House, 1992.

Foucault, Michel. *Wrong-Doing Truth-Telling: The Function of Avowal in Justice*. Edited by Fabienne Brion and Bernard E. Harcourt. Translated by Stephen W. Sawyer. Chicago: University of Chicago Press, 2014.

Gelézeau, Valérie. "Changing Socio-Economic Environments, Housing Culture and New Urban Segregation in Seoul." *European Journal of East Asian Studies* 7, no. 2 (2008): 295–321.

Gellen, Kata. *Kafka and Noise: The Discovery of Cinematic Sound in Literary Modernism*. Evanston: Northwestern University Press, 2019.

Godard, Jean-Luc. *Godard on Godard*. Translated and edited by Tom Milne. Boston: Da Capo, 1972.

Gullander-Drolet, Claire. "Bong Joon-ho's Eternal Engine: Translation, Memory, and Ecological Collapse in *Snowpiercer* (2013)." *Resilience: A Journal of the Environmental Humanities* 7, no. 1 (2019): 6–21.

Han, Karen. *Bong Joon Ho: Dissident Cinema*. New York: Abrams, 2022.

Hegel, Friedrich. *Elements of the Philosophy of Right*. Edited by Allen W. Wood. Translated by H.B. Nisbet. Cambridge: Cambridge University Press, 1991.

Heidegger, Martin. *Basic Writings*. Edited by David Farrell Krell. New York: HaperCollins, 2008.

Heidegger, Martin. *Erläuterungen zu Hölderlins Dichtung*. Frankfurt am Main: Vittorio Klostermann, 1981.

Heidegger, Martin. *Sein und Zeit*. 16th ed. Tübingen: Max Niemeyer Verlag, 1986.

Herder, Johann Gottfried von. "Treatise on the Origin of Language (1772)." In *Philosophical Writings*. Edited by Michael N. Forster. Cambridge: Cambridge University Press, 2002: 65–164.

Hinsch, Bret. *Women in Early Imperial China*. New York: Rowman & Littlefield Publishers, 2002.

Hölderlin, Friedrich. *Sämtliche Werke*. Edited by Friedrich Beissner and Adolf Beck. 15 vols. Stuttgart: W. Kohlhammer, 1951.

Hsu, Hsuan. "The Dangers of Biosecurity: *The Host* and the Geopolitics of Outbreak." In *Eco-Trauma Cinema*. Edited by Anil Narine. New York: Routledge, 2014: 113–33.

Hu, Kemin. "The Spirit of *Gongshi*." In *The Spirit of Gongshi: Chinese Scholar's Rocks*. Edited by Kemin Hu. Newton, MA: L.H. Inc., 1998: 21–31.

Jee, Hana, Monica Tamariz, and Richard Shillcock. "Exploring Meaning-sound Systematicity in Korean." *Journal of East Asian Linguistics* 31 (2022): 45–71.

Jeon, Joseph Jonghyun. *Vicious Circuits: Korea's IMF Cinema and the End of the American Century*. Stanford: Stanford University Press, 2019.

Jullien, François. *From Being to Living: a Euro-Chinese Lexicon of Thought*. Translated by Michael Richardson and Krzysztof Fijalkowski. Los Angeles: Sage, 2020.

Jullien, François. *In Praise of Blandness: Proceeding from Chinese Thought and Aesthetics*. Translated by Paula M. Varsano. New York: Zone Books, 2004.

Jullien, François. *The Propensity of Things: Toward a History of Efficacy in China*. Translated by Janey Lloyd. New York: Zone Books, 1995.

Kafka, Franz. "The Burrow." In *The Complete Stories*. Edited by Nahum N. Glatzer. New York: Schocken Books, 1971: 325–359.

Kafka, Franz, "Report to an Academy." In *The Complete Stories*. Edited by Nahum N. Glatzer. New York: Schocken Books, 1971: 250–59.

Kalton, Michael C., et al., eds. *The Four-Seven Debate: An Annotated Translation of the Most Famous Controversy in Korean Neo-Confucian Thought*. Albany: SUNY Press, 1994.

Kant, Immanuel. *Critique of the Power of Judgment*. Translated by Paul Guyer. Cambridge: Cambridge University Press, 2000.

Kant, Immanuel. *Groundwork of the Metaphysics of Morals*. Translated by Mary Gregor and Jens Timmermann. Rev. ed. Cambridge: Cambridge University Press, 2012.

Kant, Immanuel. "Idea for a Universal History with a Cosmopolitan Purpose." In *Political Writings*. Translated by H.B. Nisbet. Cambridge: Cambridge University Press, 1970.

Kim, Kyung Hyun. *Virtual Hallyu: Korean Cinema of the Global Era*. Durham: Duke University Press, 2011.

Kim, Mansu. "Global Contents but Nationalistic Themes: Bong Joon-ho's *Snowpiercer*." *International Journal of Korean Humanities and Social Sciences* 8 (2022): 7–23.

Kim, Shin-Dong. "The Creation of *Pansori* Cinema: *Sopyonje* and *Chunhyangdyun* in Creative Hybridity." In *East Asian Cinema and Cultural Heritage: From China, Hong Kong, Taiwan to Japan and South Korea*. Edited by Yau Shuk-ting Kinnia. New York: Palgrave Macmillan, 2011: 151–71.

Klein, Christiana. "Bong Joon-ho's *Parasite* as a Remake of Kim Ki-young's *The Housemaid*." In *The Routledge Companion to Asian Cinemas*. Edited by Zhen Zhang, Sangjoon Lee, Debashree Mukherjee, and Intan Paramaditha. London: Routledge, 2024. 291–300.

Kracauer, Siegfried. *Theory of Film: The Redemption of Physical Reality*. Princeton: Princeton University Press, 1960.

Kyung-sup, Chang. "Compressed Modernity and Its Discontents: South Korean Society in Transition." *Economy and Society* 28, no. 1 (1999): 30–55.

Lady Hyegyŏng, *The Memoirs of Lady Hyegyŏng*. Translated by JaHyun Kim Haboush. Berkeley: University of California Press, 2013.

Laozi, *Daodejing*. Translated by Edmund Ryden. Oxford: Oxford World University Press, 2008.

Lee, Fred and Steven Manicastri. "Not all are Aboard: Decolonizing Exodus in Joon-ho Bong's *Snowpiercer*." *New Political Science* 40, no. 2 (2018): 211–16.

Lee, Kyounghoon. *A Cultural History of Modern Korean Literature: The Birth of Oppa*. Translated by John M. Frankl. London: Lexington, 2022.

Lee, Meera. "Monstrosity and Humanity in Bong Joon-ho's *The Host*." *Positions* 26, no. 4 (2018): 719–47.

Lee, Nam. *The Films of Bong Joon Ho*. New Brunswick: Rutgers University Press, 2020.

Lee, Namhee. *The Making of Minjung: Democracy and the Politics of Representation in South Korea*. Ithaca: Cornell University Press, 2007.

Lee, Sang-Mu. "Korean Agricultural Policy: Past, Present and Future." *Journal of Rural Development* 16 (1993): 307–19.

Li, Zehou. *The Chinese Aesthetic Tradition*. Translated by Maija Bell Samei. Honolulu: University of Hawai'i Press, 2010.

Lob, Jacques and Jean-Marc Rochette. *Snowpiercer 1: The Escape*. Translated by Virginie Selavy. London: Titan Comics, 2013.

Marx, Karl and Friedrich Engels. *The Marx-Engels Reader*. Edited by Robert C. Tucker. 2nd ed. New York: Norton, 1978.

McLuhan, Marshal. *Understanding Media: The Extensions of Man*. Cambridge, MA: MIT Press, 1994.

McSweeney, Terence. "'Nobody helps the family.' South Korean Cultural Identity in Bong Joon-ho's *The Host* (2006)." *Cross-Cultural Studies* 20 (2010): 277–94.

Metz, Christian. *Film Language: A Semiotics of the Cinema*. Translated by Michael Taylor. Chicago: University of Chicago Press, 1991.

Moeller, Hans-Georg. *Daoism Explained: From the Dream of the Butterfly to the Fishnet Allegory*. Chicago: Open Court, 2004.

Monaco, James. *How to Read a Film: Movies, Media, and Beyond*. 4th ed. New York: Oxford University Press, 2009.

Moore, Alan. *From Hell: The Master Edition*. San Diego: Top Shelf Publications, 2020.

Morin, Edgar. *The Cinema: or the Imaginary Man*. Translated by Lorraine Mortimer. Minneapolis: Minnesota University Press, 2005.

Muller, A. Charles. "Translator's Introduction." In *Korea's Great Buddhist-Confucian Debate: The Treatises of Chŏng Tojŏn (Sambong) and Hamhŏ Tŭkt'ong (Kihwa)*. Translated by A. Charles Muller. Honolulu: University of Hawai'i Press, 2015.

Nail, Thomas. *Theory of the Image*. New York: Oxford, 2019.

Nayman, Adam. "A Relay Race of the Weak. Bong Joon-ho's *The Host*." *Cinema Scope* 30 (Spring 2007): 26–29.

Needham, Joseph. *Science and Civilization in China*. 7 vols. Cambridge: Cambridge University Press, 1956.

Nietzsche, Friedrich. *Beyond Good and Evil: Prelude to a Philosophy of the Future*. Translated by Judith Norman. Cambridge: Cambridge University Press, 2002.

Nietzsche, Friedrich. *Kristische Studienausgabe*. Edited by Giorgio Colli and Mazzino Montinari. Berlin: de Gruyter, 1988.

Nylan, Michael. *The Chinese Pleasure Book*. Brooklyn: Zone Books, 2018.

Park, Eugene Y. *Korea: A History*. Stanford: Stanford University Press, 2022.

Park, Iljoon. "Korean Social Emotions: *Han, Heung*, and *Jeong*." In *Emotions in Korean Philosophy and Religion: Confucian, Comparative, and Contemporary Perspectives*. Edited by Edward Y.J. Chung and Jea Sophia Oh. New York: Palgrave Macmillan, 2022: 235–56.

Parquet, Darcy. *New Korean Cinema: Breaking the Waves*. London: Wallflower, 2009.

Pollock, Friedrich. "State Capitalism: Its Possibilities and Limitations." In *The Essential Frankfurt School Reader*. Edited by Andrew Arato and Eike Gebhardt. New York: Continuum, 1990: 71–94.

Pužar, Aljoša and Yewon Hong. "Korean Cuties: Understanding Performed Winsomeness (Aegyo) in South Korea." *The Asian Pacific Journal of Anthropology* 19, no. 4 (2018): 333–49.

Tony Rayns. "Suspicious Minds." *Sight & Sound*. September 2004: 18–20

Robson, James, ed. *Norton Anthology of World Religions: Daoism*. New York: W.W. Norton, 2015.

Rošker, Jana S. "Classical Chinese Philosophy and the Concept of Qi." *NEARCO: Revista Eletrônica de Antiguidade e Medievo* 12, no. 2 (2020): 116–34.

Roth, Harold D. "*The Classical Daoist Concept of Li* 理 *(Pattern) and Early Chinese Cosmology*." In *The Contemplative Foundations of Classical Daoism*. Albany: SUNY Press, 2021: 349–75.

Roth, Harold D. "*Daoist Inner Cultivation Thought and the Textual Structure of Huainanzi* 淮南子." In *The Contemplative Foundations of Classical Daoism*. Albany: SUNY Press, 2021: 235–76.

Saito, Kohei. *Marx in the Anthropocene: Towards the Idea of Degrowth Communism*. Cambridge: Cambridge University Press, 2023.

Schefer, Jean Louis. *The Ordinary Man of Cinema*. Translated by Max Cavitch, Paul Grant, and Noura Wedell. Pasadena: Semiotext(e), 2016.

Schlegel, Friedrich. *Philosophical Fragments*. Translated by Peter Firchow. Minneapolis: University of Minnesota Press, 1991.

Seok, Bongrae. "Toegye's and Gobong's *Li-Qi* Metaphysics and the Four-Seven Debate." In *The Idea of Qi/Gi: East Asian and Comparative Philosophical Perspectives*. Edited by Suk Gabriel Choi and Jung-Yeup Kim. New York: Lexington Books, 2019: 75–94.

Shiel, Mark. "Cinema and the City in History and Theory." In *Cinema and the City: Film and Urban Societies in a Global Context*. Edited by Mark Shiel and Tony Fitzmaurice. Oxford: Blackwell, 2001: 1–18.

Smith, Adam. *An Inquiry into the Nature and Causes of the Wealth of Nations*. Edited by R.H. Campbell and A.S. Skinner. Indianapolis: Liberty Classics, 1981.

Song, Ho-Keun. *The Birth of the Citizen in Modern Korea*. Paju: NANAM Publishing House, 2016.

Theweleit, Klaus. *Male Fantasies: Women, Floods, Bodies, History*. Translated by Stephen Conway. Minneapolis: University of Minnesota Press, 1987.

Tilland, Bonnie and Beth Tsai, "Of Fleas and *Parasite*: Unpacking Class and Space in Bong Joon-ho's *Barking Dogs Never Bite*." *New Review of Film and Television Studies* 21, no. 4 (2023): 668–85.

Todorov, Tzvetan. "The Typology of Detective Fiction." In *Crime and Media: A Reader*. Edited by Chris Greer. London: Routledge, 2010: 293–301.

Tolstoy, Leo. *Anna Karenina*. Translated by Richard Pevear and Larissa Volokhonsky. New York: Penguin Books, 2002.

Trichet, Yohan. "Une figure de l'idiot criminel. Crimes sans châtiment dans *Mother* de Joon-ho Bong." *Cliniques Méditerranées* 91, no. 1 (2015): 243–56.

Voegelin, Eric. *The New Science of Politics: An Introduction*. Chicago: University of Chicago Press, 1952.

Volynsky, Akim. *Ballet's Magic Kingdom: Selected Writings on Dance in Russia (1911-1925)*. Translated by Stanley J. Rabinowitz. New Haven: Yale University Press, 2008.

Walhain, Luc. *From Minjok to Minjung: The Student Movements' Democratizing of the National Discourse in South Korea*. Dissertation. Bowling Green State University, May 2005.

Wang, Robin R. *Yinyang: The Way of Heaven and Earth in Chinese Thought and Culture*. Cambridge: Cambridge University Press, 2012.

Weber, Samuel. *Singularity: Politics and Poetics*. Minneapolis: University of Minnesota Press, 2021.

Welch, Holmes. *Taosim: The Parting of the Way*. Boston: Beacon Press, 1957.

Weninger, Stephen. "The Sacred Engine: Myth and Fiction in *Snowpiercer*." *Journal of Narrative Theory* 51, no. 1 (2021): 104–25.

Wiener, Norbert. *Cybernetics or Control and Communication in the Animal and the Machine*. Reissue ed. Cambridge, MA: MIT Press, 2019.

Wilson, Ian. "Spirit Stones." In *The Spirit of Gongshi: Chinese Scholars' Rocks*. Edited by Kemin Hu. Newton: L.H. Inc., 1998: 10–11.

Wilson, Rob. "*Snowpiercer* as Anthropoetics: Killer Capitalism, the Anthropocene, Korean-Global Film." *Boundary 2* 46, no. 3 (2019): 199–218.

Wittgenstein, Ludwig. *Tractatus Logico-Philosophicus*. Translated by C.K. Ogden. New York: Harcourt, Brace & Company, 1922.

Yi, Mun-yol. *Son of Man*. Translated by Brother Anthony. London: Dalkey Archive Press, 2015.

Yoo, Sang-Keun. "Necropolitical metamorphoses: Bong Joon-ho's The Host and Parasite." *Science Fiction Film and Television* 14, no. 1 (2021): 45–69.

Yun, Isang and Luise Rinser. *Der verwundete Drache: Dialog über Leben und Werk des Komponisten*. Frankfurt am Main: S. Fischer, 1977.

Yun, Ji-Yeong. "The Human-Nonhuman Connected Body in the Era of Climate Change: Interpreting Bong Joon-ho's Film *Snowpiercer* from the Perspective of Actor-Network Theory." *The Journal of Popular Culture* 55, no. 5 (2022): 973–91.

Zhao, Qiguang. *A Study of Dragons East and West*. New York: Peter Lang, 1992.

Zhuangzi. *The Complete Works of Zhuangzi*. Translated by Burton Watson. New York: Columbia University Press, 2013.

Zhuangzi. *The Complete Writings*. Translated by Brook Ziporyn. Indianapolis: Hackett, 2020.

Žižek, Slovoj. *For they Know Not what they Do: Enjoyment as a Political Factor*. 2nd ed. London: Verso, 2002.

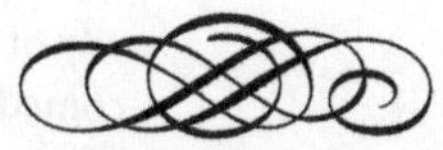

Index

Note: Page numbers followed by 'n' indicate note number(s).